John K. Downey, Jürgen Manemann, Steven T. Ostovich (Eds.)

Missing God?

RELIGION – GESCHICHTE – GESELLSCHAFT

Fundamentaltheologische Studien

herausgegeben von

Johann Baptist Metz (Münster / Wien)
Johann Reikerstorfer (Wien)
Jürgen Werbick (Münster)

Band 30

LIT

John K. Downey, Jürgen Manemann,
Steven T. Ostovich (Eds.)

MISSING GOD?

Cultural Amnesia and Political Theology

LIT

Gedruckt auf alterungsbeständigem Werkdruckpapier entsprechend
ANSI Z3948 DIN ISO 9706

Bibliographic information published by the Deutsche Nationalbibliothek
The Deutsche Nationalbibliothek lists this publication in the Deutsche Nationalbibliografie; detailed bibliographic data are available in the Internet at http://dnb.d-nb.de.

ISBN 3-8258-7651-9

A catalogue record for this book is available from the British Library

Auslieferung/Verlagskontakt:
Fresnostr. 2 48159 Münster
Tel. +49 (0)251–62 03 20 Fax +49 (0)251–23 19 72
e-Mail: lit@lit-verlag.de http://www.lit-verlag.de

Distributed in the UK by: Global Book Marketing, 99B Wallis Rd, London, E9 5LN
Phone: +44 (0) 20 8533 5800 – Fax: +44 (0) 1600 775 663
http://www.centralbooks.co.uk/acatalog/search.html

Distributed in North America by:

Transaction Publishers
New Brunswick (U.S.A.) and London (U.K.)

Transaction Publishers
Rutgers University
35 Berrue Circle
Piscataway, NJ 08854

Phone: +1 (732) 445 - 2280
Fax: + 1 (732) 445 - 3138
for orders (U. S. only):
toll free (888) 999 - 6778
e-mail:
orders@transactionspub.com

CONTENTS

Part III. Second Courage

Appendix

INTRODUCTION
MISSING GOD? DOING POLITICAL THEOLOGY

John K. Downey and Steven T. Ostovich

It seems as if the heart of our contemporary world has been hardened: domination, objectification, and control are the new virtues. The human voice is but a whisper drowned out in the cacophony of consumerism under blind economic laws, a voice crying out its political and social fears and silenced by the reduction of human concerns to insignificance in an indifferent universe. Under these conditions it makes sense to ask: are we missing God?

Both the question and its answers are ambiguous. God may be missed in different ways. "Missing God" may be a matter of our missing the signs of God's presence in a world where talk about God and theology have become marginalized relics of the past. "Missing God" also may name our often hidden and sometimes misdirected longing for God - and for our humanity. God may be both missed and missing.

The new political theology, derived from the work of Johann Baptist Metz, raises this question in a radical way. It does this through critical and transformative theological reflection focused on praxis and defined by attention to memory, narrative, and solidarity. It practices an anamnestic and eschatological resistance to forgetting arising from the *memoria passionis, mortis et resurrectionis Jesu Christi* responding to others' suffering. Metz's praxis of critical understanding sublates the modern variations on the dichotomy of reason and faith and provides an antidote to our cultural amnesia in the "mystical-political double-structure of faith."

A political theology takes its shape only when it engages the issues of its time. Thus Johann Baptist Metz opens the discourse with an essay about the danger of cultural amnesia. The following essays in this volume are by political theologians, too, and others influenced by Metz. They set forth a program for responding to the condition of missing God. This program begins by raising the question: *Wo bleibt Gott?* The German form of this question is given here, because it points to an important aspect of the question that may be misunderstood in the English, "Where is God?" The question of the missing God is not the question of an Enlightenment skeptic but the faithful question of an outraged and disappointed Job. It is not grounded in an Enlightenment search for empirical proof but arises from our assumption that our connection to God gives us the right to expect God here and now and to question God about God's tardiness. The issue is not, "Does God exist?" The problem of the missing God is much better expressed by questions like,

"Where is God hiding?" or "When is God coming?" or perhaps most radically, "Have we been abandoned by God?" Peters and Manemann raise these questions in the first section of the book.

Expressed this way, the question of missing God is the form theodicy takes in political theology. "Theodicy" here is not the project of justifying God or belief in God but the question of Job: asking God to be God. For Metz, traditional theodicy may actually lead to the denial of human suffering by repeating it in God resulting in a "ghastly abstraction" and "the ontologization of human torment." Instead he offers a "suffering unto God" that attempts to respond to human suffering in all its concreteness. No explanations, just questions and expectations. No less is demanded by the specific memory of suffering that is at the heart of Christianity, the *memoria passionis Jesu Christi*.

The essays in the second section of this book take this concrete memory as the starting point for responding to what might be described as the "cultural amnesia" that is another form of missing God - God as absent from contemporary thinking about human existence in history. We need to remember who we are, where we are going, for what we may hope. But there is an amnesia in our culture, a climate of forgetting our humanity, forgetting that being human is being in relation to others. Forgetting that using the word "God" as Jesus did means reaching out to others, feeling the natural claim of others on us - even our enemies. Metz reminds us that for Augustine sin was turning the heart inward.

The way to recover our memory is to follow the thread of suffering: seeing the face of the other. Our mysticism, our turn to God, must also be political. History is the history of suffering that calls for "solidarity backwards" or anamnestic solidarity with the victims of oppression whose voices continue to cry out for justice from the grave. But how does one render the dead justice? Neither theoretical responses nor notions of future progress are capable of rendering them justice. This is why these essays turn to narrative as a key category in thinking about history. Stories keep alive memories of suffering. The stories of suffering in these essays come from the experience of African-American slaves (Copeland), Central American victims of oppression (Morrill), victims of domestic abuse (Vento), and Auschwitz (Ostovich). They all testify to the way in which memory is "dangerous" in its power to disrupt theoretical attempts to ignore, explain, or deny the history of suffering. And they call for what might be called anamnestic reason, a way of thinking that constructs a culture of "remembrancing" (*Eingedenken*) rather than amnesia.

The work of memory demands courage, what might be called the "second courage" required by the "eschatological proviso" - the realization in hope that this work is never done, that one must always begin again, that (paraphrasing Walter Benjamin) each moment might be the narrow gate through which the Messiah might enter. We must interrupt business as usual with the authority of others' suffering. This takes the courage to question our community, our culture, and our God - to imagine and risk a more human future in face of the divine. Our grief in *memoria passionis* is also a hope in *resurrectionis*. Our mystical-political hope brings recognition of our concrete social responsibilities to live in practical compassion and to set in motion a new world. Each of the four essays in the final section gives shape to this courage in particular contexts: human rights (Downey), ecology (Ashley), authority (Lamb), and God-talk (Reikerstorfer). We are called to resist hopelessness and resignation and instead to take courage to pray: "Come, Lord Jesus."

The new political theology is always underway and never there yet. Metz retells the old German folktale of the hedgehog and the hare.

> The hedgehog was rather vain and proud of his legs. One day the hare happened to make fun of him, so the hedgehog challenged the hare to a race. The race course was two furrows that kept the runners from seeing each other. Before the race started, the hedgehog begged leave to go home and eat. He returned with his wife, who looked much the same, and hid her at the far end of his furrow. When the hare said, "Go!" the hedgehog just ducked down in place while his wife popped up at the finish line with a cry of "I'm already here!

Traditionally this story is read as praise for the cunning of the weak to overcome the strong. But Metz reads it "against the grain" (or "against the quills," as he says). He wants us to model our theology on the hare rather than the hedgehog. Too often theology has been nothing but a hedgehog trick, talking about history and the world but never mentioning the suffering, a theology whose time is always already there. Metz wants us to have the courage to remember and to hope, to ask the question of the missing God.

Political theology is not so much a school of thought as a project, not a system but a way of thinking and living. It moves the criteria for theology towards the question of what difference one makes in the world. If we ask the question of the missing God, if our praxis is marked by the remembrancing demanded by the *memoria passionis*, and if we have courage, what difference does it make? Does it make any difference at all if one does theology as a political theologian? We shall see.

UNDER THE SPELL OF CULTURAL AMNESIA?

An Example from Europe and Its Consequences

Johann Baptist Metz

I.

Europe, the Europe of the EU, is having trouble with itself these days. Which "Europe" is intended, and what kind of Europe is wanted? In the discussions about adopting the EU-Constitution (or more precisely, the contract for an EU-Constitution) in the past few years, one could hear over and again: "Europe is a secular project - Christianity therefore has no place in a European constitution." We need to pay closer attention here - especially with regard to the meaning of "secular" as well as with regard to the religious neutrality of the constitution that follows from "Europe as a secular project." There are two directly opposed versions of this neutrality. One may be designated the non-religious version (laïcité), the other the pluralist version; correspondingly, the spiritual-moral climate of the new Europe would be characterized as either a-religious or religiously plural.

The pluralist version of the constitutional contract would not ban religion from the public sphere but would locate its value in a constitutional pluralism of world views and religions. It would do this by constitutionally guaranteeing religious freedom, a religious freedom that would be positive as well as negative, providing protection "for" religion as well as protection "from" religion.

Against this, the a-religious version (something that can really be understood only in a historically French constellation) comes down to a strict privatization of religion. This version is not really neutral regarding religion, because its concept of neutrality inevitably privileges negative religious freedom (freedom from religion). It is anti-pluralist to the core. The secular ethos of a European constitution would overwhelm in a fundamentalist manner all those national constitutions in Europe which deal with religion in public life in a different way (than in France).[1]

It might well be that these days there is more than a little to be suspicious about in this secular version of the developing European constitutional ethos.

---

[1] See J. H. H. Weiler, *Ein christliches Europa* (Regensburg 2004) and the Foreword by E. W. Böckenförde that also contains important and stimulating ideas regarding the difference between a secular and a pluralistic Europe. On the whole first part of my reflections, see also J. Casanova, "Der Ort der Religion in säkularen Europa", in *Transit* 27 (2004).

I myself can recognize in it only a kind of "patina-vision" for Europe, a vision that ignores the growing insight today into how the dialectical processes of a one-dimensional Enlightenment and a leveling secularization are full of contradictions. The a-religious version seeks to subject the developing European public sphere (quasi-fundamentalistically) to an undialectical secularization paradigm.

In this connection I would like to at least briefly mention a current discussion in philosophy of religion in Germany. I have always wondered why the Frankfurt School has never really moved beyond its early "dialectic of Enlightenment" to speak of a "dialectic of secularization." For example, it seems to me that the later work of Jürgen Habermas opens up the possibility of a new philosophical "translation" of the substance of religion. In this "translation," philosophy (of religion) doesn't simply replace the authentic language of religion in order to make religion superfluous to the public discourse of modernity and to its normative integration of constitutional pluralism.[2] As Habermas says: "The guarantee of equal ethical freedoms demands the secularization of state authority, but it forbids the political overextension of the secular worldview. Secularized citizens, in so far as they remain in their roles as citizens, may neither fundamentally deny the potential for truth in religious worldviews nor restrict the right of their believing fellow citizens to make contributions to public discussions using religious language. A liberal political culture might even expect its secularized members to make efforts to translate relevant contributions from religious language into publicly accessible speech."[3]

Critical questions admittedly also appear over against this quasi-operational definition of a "dialectic of secularization" within the framework of a liberal discourse community. Doesn't the discourse-theoretical approach of Habermas undervalue the intelligible and critical power of the anamnestic basis for public discourse, a power that, through the Jewish-Christian tradition, has penetrated not only the ethos of faith but the ethos of human rationality as well? And wasn't this reflected, for example, within the Frankfurt School itself in the negative metaphysics of Walter Benjamin and Theodor W. Adorno?[4]

---

[2] See J. Reikerstorfer, "Jüdisch-christliches Erbe in vernunfttheoretischer Bedeutung bei J. Habermas und J. B. Metz", in: *Orientierung*, 70 (2006), Nr. 3.

[3] J. Habermas, *Zwischen Naturalismus und Religion* (Frankfurt 2005), 322. Habermas speaks expressly in this connection of the "path to a dialectical understanding of cultural secularization."

[4] In addition see J. B. Metz, "Vernunft mit Leidensapriori," in *Vernunftfähiger - vernunftbedürftiger Glaube* (Frankfurt 2005), 25-31.

II.

Indeed, I have never missed the anamnestic basis of public discourse more than in the discussions of the contract for the EU-Constitution. Understandably such an appeal to this anamnestic base would have to be justified in terms of whether and how a remembrance-oriented public sphere - especially in the face of European history - actually can be the foundation for understanding and peace. Wouldn't this instead radically damage or even revoke one of the most important achievements of the political Enlightenment? Isn't it precisely historically and culturally rooted collective memories that always hinder mutual understanding, that continually have led to painful conflicts and dramatic quarrels (between and within nations) and therefore have nourished all open or latent civil wars into the present day? I have tried to meet this danger by formulating *memoria passionis* as a basic category for doing theology in a pluralistic public sphere. This offers a way of dealing with the pluralistic public sphere that is accessible and reasonable to all men and women without retreating to a formal, purely procedural discourse rationality.[5]

With regard to the discussion of the EU constitutional contract that has been going on in the meantime, it appears as if Europe has lost its memory. It's as if this memory has been sacrificed to that progressive cultural amnesia that evidently many Europeans take for real progress.[6]

The preamble of the EU constitutional contract is concerned with the spiritual and moral climate of Europe, in short, the European ethos. This ethos is described there exclusively in terms of universal attributes like "cultural, religious, humanistic" which are divorced from history. But there is no way to determine the European ethos without historical remembrancing, without identifying and securing the historical-cultural deep structures of Europe! Yes, democracy is rooted in consensus, but the democratic ethos is rooted in remembrance. This remembrance makes it possible to account for how the "heritages" (culture, religion, humanism) cited abstractly in the EU constitution did not develop in isolation but interpenetrate each other, shap-

---

[5] Cf. my new book: *Memoria passionis. Ein provozierendes Gedächtnis in pluralistischer Gesellschaft* (Herder - Freiburg, 2006)

[6] At the end of this "progress" stands the biotechnological "human experiment" that no longer allows itself to be constrained by normative appeals to remembrance. In the public dispute over the "human image" and "values," Christianity emphasizes that human beings are not only subjects of their own experimentation, but more fundamentally subjects of their own memory. Christianity does this in support of a politics of memory which objects to the looming total self-reproduction of the human being in biotechnological experiment. For this (anamnestic) politics, the human person is and remains more and other than the last, not yet fully experimentally fixed bit of nature. Finally, in this public dispute the currently prevailing discourse politics can only prevent itself from being overpowered by an ever-expanding biopolitics through relying on a memory-sharpened semantic addressing the theme "human being."

ing the European ethos in a crisscrossing of mutual criticism and inspiration. Finally, it is no accident that the secular state (the state whose secularity derives from its guarantee of religious freedom and protection of neutrality) arose in a particular historical cultural sphere shaped by the Jewish-Christian heritage.

In this sense the practical religious freedom that arose in secular Europe also has biblical roots. They lead finally not to a non-religious Europe but to a religiously plural Europe. These biblical roots show through, for example, in the understanding of the Reformation Churches as "religions of freedom" and on the Catholic side the lately (too late?) declared readiness to unconditionally respect the "the sanctity of conscience" in public religious discourse. This formulation, partly derived from a papal Encyclical, is affirmed by the small but momentous "Decree on Religious Freedom" of the Second Vatican Council in which the Catholic Church orders and subordinates the abstract right of the truth to the right of the person in truth. Shouldn't this biblical heritage be expressly named in the preamble to a European constitution--and precisely in the interest of normatively securing full practical religious freedom and the pluralism rooted therein?

III.

I would like to add two comments. One refers to the situation of the Church in a Europe threatened by the spell of cultural amnesia. The other concerns the meaning of *memoria passionis* as a provocative remembrance in the struggle for the future of humanity in an age of cultural amnesia.

First

The "dialectic of secularization" suggested above leads in any case not to a public sphere free of religion but to a public sphere characterized by pluralism of religions and worldviews. In this situation, it seems to me a new and elementary danger for Christianity is emerging: it is not so much (or at least not primarily) the danger of the secular state extrinsically imposing a privatization of Christian faith; it is much more the danger that Christians under the anonymous pressure of a religiously pluralistic public sphere increasingly will privatize Christianity themselves and thereby call into question their identity and mission. European Christianity is threatened not just by the danger of self-secularization but more precisely the danger of itself privatizing whatever cannot be secularized.

This is why for several years I have been trying to develop a deprivatization program under the heading of a new "political theology."[7] This political

[7] The new political theology should not be confused with those former "political theologies" like the "classical" three-fold division of theology - mythical, natural, political theology - familiar since the Sto-

theology should break open any self-privatization by modern theology in reaction to the challenges of modernity, particularly the challenges of the Enlightenment and secularization. It also addresses a second phase of deprivatization by overcoming the tendency of the Christian Church to privatize itself.

Is our European world, a world in which the project of modernity has succeeded, a strictly post-traditional society? Admittedly one cannot revitalize dead or withered traditions by showing how necessary they really would be or all that they might achieve - for instance in the face of that collective angst and uncertainty which often times overlay and paralyze public discourse today. The real issue is different and goes something like this: Are there at the margins of modernity, in the transition to the postmodern, still institutions which understand themselves as accumulated memories, as the public encodings of a long-term cultural remembrance, as providers of a storehouse of memory for structuring diffuse life-worlds that cannot be mastered purely discursively? Are there still institutions that can effectively get control over what has become a reflexive engagement with traditions and bring the indispensability of traditions from aporetic formulation to political and cultural validity? Are there still institutions which can serve as carriers and mediators of a pre-discursive point of reference? Are there still such institutions, and if there are, don't religious institutions especially belong among them? And doesn't the "Elephant's memory" of the Church also belong there?

Admittedly such a definition of classical religious institutions can only with difficulty evade the suspicion that it is a negligent idealization. It is - in the perspective of the Christian religion - only through witnessing that the religious institution, the Church, brings together publicly in herself that which her remembrance of faith compels her to: the indivisible unity of love of God and love of neighbor, of a passion for God and compassion, of remembering God in remembrancing the suffering of others. The church as an institution must in its (liturgical) representation of the authority of God always also represent, embody, and proclaim its own subordination to the undeniable authority of those who suffer.

Second

Does there not exist a danger that a Europe which openly admits its biblical roots will increasingly find itself trapped in the global struggles of religion and culture? The first thing to ask is this: What is it that could prevent our globalized world from imploding into uncontrollable religious and cultural

---

ics. If this new political theology must be assigned a place in this three-fold division, it would belong to "natural" (that is, philosophical) theology. See J. B. Metz, "Politische Theologie," in *LThK*, 3rd ed., 8, 392-394.

strife (here Christianity, there Islam, here the West, there the Arab world)? What is it that that can bring our world together peacefully during these times of globalization? I will attempt an extremely brief reply.

The proposition of a fundamental equality among all human beings - the deepest and still most unsatisfied assumption about humanity - has a biblical basis. The moral implication, adoptetd by Christianity and proclaimed in its message of the indivisible unity of the love of God and the love of neighbor, is this: There is no suffering in the world that does not concern us. This proposition refers to the recognition of an authority that is reasonable and accessible to all human beings: the authority of those who suffer, of unjust and innocent suffering. It is an authority which obliges all human beings before any consensus and agreement and which therefore neither culture and religion nor the Church can subvert or relativize. For this reason the recognition of this authority would be that criterion which is able to orient religious and cultural discourse in a globalized world. It would ground an ethos of peace for a pluralistic and globalized public sphere. And a European politics that acknowledges this biblical legacy with its demand for compassion (as well as the Greek legacy of theoretical inquiry and Roman antiquity's legacy of republican legal thinking about rights and the state) would be more and other than the mere executor of the market and technology and their so-called practical constraints in these times of globalization.

Translated by John K. Downey and Steven T. Ostovich

Where is God?

JOHANN BAPTIST METZ - THEOLOGY OF THE MISSING GOD

Tiemo Rainer Peters

Johann Baptist Metz was born ten years after the end of the First World War and ten years before the organized pogrom of *Kristallnacht*. As we learn from him, no one, least of all theologians, has the right to ignore such dates and try to do theology with his or her back turned to history. We must read his work, therefore, as a theological witness to his times, as reflecting those relationships that still challenge us today.[1]

Reason and Revelation

It is evident that this line of thinking comes above all from Karl Rahner, Metz's teacher. Rahner's central achievement was to break through scholastic theology towards 'the subject,' to crack open "the rock of a scholastic objectivism."[2] Bringing Rahner's transcendental Idealism "down to earth" and developing a theology of the subject in history and society is the qualitatively new step by which Metz changed theology.

Metz, like Rahner, grasped that all theology is at its deepest level talk of humanity and anthropology. He worked at this fundamental level, fully conscious that this is the one way to counter Feuerbach's critical unmasking of religion. And as Rahner began by going back to Thomas and offering a subversive interpretation of Thomistic thought, Metz adopted the same theological strategy: no theology would be a match for modernity until it returns critically to its foundations and reformulates its traditional modes of thinking in a new way.[3]

But was it possible to respond to the questions put by modernity within the Thomistic metaphysical epistemology? Was it possible to see in the subject's "pre-apprehension" of the "absolute hiddenness" of God the (Kantian) conditions of possibility for human perception, action, and experience? Or isn't even this God still at issue in experience? Must not the contemporary

---

[1] See T. R. Peters, *Johann Baptist Metz. Theologie des vermißten Gottes,* Mainz 1998.

[2] See J. B. Metz, *Glaube in Geschichte und Gesellschaft* (cited as *GGG* henceforth), Mainz 1977, 199: "This theology (Rahner's) has cracked open the system of scholastic theology on the 'subject.' It has pried the 'subject' out of the rock of objectivism in which scholastic theology was locked tight. 'Subject'...indicates the human person in the history of his or her experience...In this way Rahner elevated religious biography to an objective topic of dogmatics."

[3] See J. B. Metz, *Christliche Anthropozentrik: Über die Denkform des Thomas von Aquin*, München 1962.

question of the subject be grasped and respected as a problem of social processes of emancipation and of social priorities and possibilities before one can make theological use of it?[4]

Rahner's theology therefore had to be rendered historical and his essentially transcendental concept of "pre-apprehension" had to be brought under an interactive theory-practice dialectic. Briefly put: modernity (including Marx) had to be taken into theological consideration in a more concrete and effective manner.[5] Only, how can theology, which unchanged will not survive, open itself up to modernity at its deepest level? Hasn't theology for too long been put into modernity's service? In the end, won't it have to stand by its commitment to revelation and thereby make itself altogether superfluous?

Where Rahner remained dubious regarding the effectiveness of biblical mediations, Metz renewed the direct appeal to biblical tradition, albeit in a manner no longer familiar in Catholicism. He took seriously in its historical concreteness and provocative nature what had long (and since Hegel seemingly irrevocably) become "speculative": the Jewish-Christian memory of God as it is bound up [for Christians] with the "*memoria passionis et resurrectionis*," the remembering, "anamnestic" knowledge of the death and resurrection of Jesus Christ.[6]

Metz's systematic and fundamental theology returns to the historical, that is, to revelation as transmitted in stories and not only in concepts. This can be done (pace Lessing and Kant) if it can be shown, as Metz does, that the biblical stories of salvation and liberation belong not to the superceded and outmoded prehistory of reason, but rather to those premises of reason and

---

[4] *GGG*, 61f: "The human person exists (according to Rahner) as a pre-apprehension [*Vorgriff*] of God, and this pre-apprehension is the necessary precondition that makes possible knowledge and behavior. I am ignoring for the moment that it is difficult for a political theology of the subject not to recognize in such a specification of 'the human person' the anthropology of a society still fundamentally defined by religious goals…It is only being asked whether this pre-apprehension itself has anything to do with history, that is, whether the pre-apprehension itself has temporal structures. Put another way, does this transcendental anthropology take into account that this person who pre-apprehends exists entirely historically?"

[5] See J. B. Metz, "Unterwegs zu einer nachidealistischen Theologie," in Johannes B. Bauer (ed.), *Entwürfe der Theologie*, Köln 1985: 213f [translated in *A Passion for God*, ed. and trans. by J. Matthew Ashley, New York/Mahtowa, NJ: Paulist Press, 1988, pp. 34, 36]: "The first challenge (by Marx) is an epistemological one and touches upon the question of the relationship of knowledge and interest. Are there interests that are capable of being true…Truth is either truth for all, or it simply does not exist. In this sense the new political theology speaks of a universal or universalizable interest that is founded in the biblical traditions themselves: this is 'the hunger and thirst for justice,' for justice for all, for the living and the dead, for suffering present and past."

[6] *GGG*, 95: "Christianity does not introduce God after the fact as a 'stop-gap' in the dispute about the future; it seeks much more to make present the memory of the crucified Lord, this specific *memoria passionis*, as a dangerous remembrance of freedom in the social systems of technological civilization."

freedom that have been hidden and repressed (especially where a view of reason in terms of technological progress holds sway).[7]

At the limit of metaphysical possibilities and idealistic mediations of religion, there is a path that, responding to biblical truth, leads not behind or above reason but into reason itself in its anamnestic deep structure - there, where the very possibility of knowing lies.

Political Theology

Metz was determined to engage in the intellectual discussions of the time. Following the Second Vatican Council, the first elements of his theology read like a list of priorities derived from a variety of discursive relationships: between Marxists and Christians (*Paulusgesellschaft*), Protestants and Catholics, and with community reformers of every stripe. The key words and connecting concepts for the most part remained vague until he gave them theological clarification which made them impossible to elide and even at times unforgettable: "the world in its worldliness" (*Weltlichkeit der Welt)*, the church as "institution of the critical freedom of faith," "dangerous memory," "redemption or emancipation," "utopia or eschatology"; and later: "mysticism and politics," "bourgeois/liberal and messianic religion," "church of the people - church for the people," "basic community church," "caretaker church," "polycentric church," etc. Nowhere the slightest departure from apologetic precision: "The name of God stands for the belief that the utopia of liberation in which all become human subjects is not purely a projection - which is what it would be if there were only utopia and no God."[8]

The "new" political theology has nothing to do with the "old" version of Carl Schmitt, not even as its mirror-image.[9] It is a critical- and corrective-concept charging the theologies of the 1960s with forgetting history and society and points to the urgent need for a praxis-oriented hermeneutic. And in

---

[7] *GGG*, 98: "Christian memoria insists that the history of suffering does not belong simply to the prehistory of freedom, but that it is and remains an inner moment of the history of freedom. The imagination of future freedom nourishes itself on the remembrance of suffering; freedom corrupts where sufferers are treated more or less as a cliché and degraded. Christian memoria...thereby becomes...a dangerous and liberating memory over against the constraints and mechanisms of dominating consciousness and its abstract ideal of emancipation." See J. B. Metz, "Anamnetische Vernunft," in *Zwischenbetrachtungen im Prozess der Aufklärung*, Festschrift für J. Habermas, Frankfurt/M. 1989.

[8] *GGG*, 65.

[9] J. B Metz, "'Politische Theologie' in der Diskussion," in *Diskussion zur politischen Theologie*, ed. H. Peukert, Mainz/München 1969:267-301; 272: In its concern with the transcendence and freedom of "God's rule, theological talk of the dominion of God is the beginning of the secularization and relativization of every existing form of political domination; it is above all else the origin of the criticism of all those forms of political domination that understand themselves as 'absolute,' that is, as beyond and setting aside the history of human freedom."

an ideological-critical clarification: every theology is already political in that it knowingly or unknowingly pursues particular interests, mediates a world-view, and transmits and influences a temporal consciousness. It must give an account of these if it wants to remain free which is to say honest.

The Enlightenment and its traditions of thought were invited (although not Freud) to set forth from within their own perspective their questions for and criticism of theology: finally an open (and public) dispute! Horkheimer and Adorno with their critique of "instrumental," purely technically enlightened reason saw themselves trusted and engaged just like Walter Benjamin with his progress-critical mediation of theology and historical materialism; less so Habermas, not Foucault, certainly not Althusser. Dialectic was demanded, not universal pragmatics, and clearly not structuralist materialism. Too philosophically laden? Yes, in Bonhoeffer's sense: "The mark of a good theology is that it gets the blood of good philosophy boiling." Highly speculative, to be sure, despite all its social ambitions. Grounds enough, incidentally, for liberation theology, which otherwise would happily (and entirely correctly) appeal to political theology, to go its own way and assign the social sciences a bigger role in theological theory development.

The Struggle for Eschatology

Metz's thinking could be said to be dominated by the "eschatological proviso." Twentieth century theology would no longer be able to beg off the eschatological question given the way it was posed by so sincere a spirit as Franz Overbeck and kept alive by Karl Barth. This conviction also was held by Jürgen Moltmann, who followed a Protestant approach in developing his liberating and influential "Theology of Hope." Could this theology recover the political decisiveness misunderstood in liberalism and lost in "Kerygmatic Theology"? Or does it not threaten to evaporate in a utopian hope, which already in Bloch's category of "Novum," a category enthusiastically received by Moltmann, could not be contained? Bloch remains (alongside Benjamin) directly relevant here.[10] In the end, this is a matter (hardly recognized by Rahner and not dealt with already by Barth or Moltmann) of following through on the 19th century task: preserving eschatology in its unwieldiness and radicalism and not delivering it over to Idealism or to a Darwinian "logic of evolution." The whole question of eschatology has to be put in motion again.

[10] See in general *GGG*, 149-158: "Hope as Imminent Expectation, or the Struggle over Lost Time. Untimely Apocalyptic Theses."

And this is precisely where the concept of memory assumes its place in theological criticism. Isn't "Our Hope," Metz asked in the 1975 Würzburger synod document of that same name, already outlined biblically as a memory? A memory bound up with stories of discipleship, stories that concentrate hope in narrative? And is such a memory, far from needing to be transfigured, rather deeply "dangerous," a memory of a "cry" and the lament of the oppressed and the victims? Metz in this way concretizes hope and radicalizes it in its apocalyptic structure. It is taken as true again and reclaimed theologically as what it always has been for the sufferers and persecuted of the messianic era: "imminent expectation."[11]

One would like just to grant many of Metz's claims, but that would mean only one had read through some things too quickly: his theology constantly (initially under the rubric of "concupiscence") spoke of misery, guilt, and death; in the middle of its discussion of freedom it thought of "asceticism"; and its messianic expectation connected to the "solidarity with the dead in memory." Some things were expressed in so intimate and lovely a way - about the Passion and the "hour of Christ," "poverty of spirit," the sadness and comfort of religion, about the "path of discipleship" and the question of the "time for ordination" - that theological applause drowned out his questions and criticism. Where this began in trying to become clear, how it was meant to be systematic, what conditions were needed for it to work, for what price all this - hope, memoria, discipleship ("one can not live without thoughts of the parousia, without imminent expectation"), in short, Jewish-Christian "religion" - can be had: that is, under the foundational accepting of apocalyptically limited time - that is where the consternation often was as great as the confusion and unbounded theological indignation.

Cry unto God

Metz has allowed himself to be ever more (and more deeply theologically) stamped by Judaism - this is his "anti-Idealism," his "anti-mythologism." And the catastrophe of Auschwitz has marked his theology. Not that this was the case from the beginning. A socially repressed past first had to be admit-

[11] J. B. Metz, *Zeit der Orden? Zur Mystik und Politik der Nachfolge*, Freiburg/Breisgau 1977, 79: „Discipleship cannot be lived without thoughts of the parousia, without imminent expectation. Whoever forgets this destroys discipleship, or rather, is complicit in silently destroying and mutilating it, because they cannot maintain permanently their intensity of action. Discipleship corresponds to an existence in radical hope with an apocalyptic sting." And 82f: "The suffering suffused expectation of the Day of the Lord leads neither to an apocalyptic dream dance in which all practical demands of discipleship would be forgotten and evaporate, nor does it pursue a senseless radicalism for which prayers of longing and expectation can only be transparent forms of denial or self-deception. Even more the dangerous discipleship lived in imminent expectation resists an inconsequential, pious, always only self-regarding enduring reflection as it presses to action and gainsays any postponement of discipleship."

ted and made present here. Indeed a "belated" memory, but when the Sho'a was made present, then theology had to look at itself entirely anew: as "after Auschwitz." And with no desire to be other than this. A systematically challenging and programmatic endeavor: "Obviously, there is no meaning of history that can be saved with one's back turned to Auschwitz, no truth of history that can be defended with one's back to Auschwitz, and no God of history to whom one can pray with one's back to Auschwitz."[12]

Metz learned from Karl Rahner what is decisive: the determination and intensity to stick with the theme of "God" and to gather all theological power around it. Nevertheless, Metz emphasizes that where Rahner says "God" and closes his eyes at the same time, Metz wants to practice a mysticism of "opened eyes." In order to say "God" now rightly and all the more resolutely? No - rather to see God is missing! In this absence, precisely here, will God's "enduring," "inexpressible hiddenness" (Rahner) be asserted politically-theologically.

The negativity of this disturbs many. Others, however, are annoyed by how every "suffering unto God" is resisted and the monstrous "deus impassibilis," the God incapable of suffering, is insisted upon. One cannot actually grasp what Metz's insistence is about so long as the point of his polemical theodicy is misunderstood. Metz argues in the arena where talk of God is threatened by aporias that cannot be worked through imminent to theology; where a "faith" reigns that enervates every real expectation and longing and that chokes off at the root every cry of revolt so that from the get-go "the terrible dignity of human suffering" is fundamentally violated.[13]

Against a "religion" that is not only more "bourgeois/liberal" but nihilistic, a religion that currently comports itself as myth- and idol-happy, Metz mobilizes Jewish-Christian monotheism with a decisiveness that consciously ignores the sophistications of all Christologies and theologies of the cross (including his own!). And indeed, it is pious but theologically ruinous self-deception to think that Christian speculation can succeed cut off from and undisturbed by the specifically messianic question: "Where is God?" When will God "interrupt" unbroken time?

Metz confronts a Christianity that in many ways has long offered comfort and (private) compensation for the delayed parousia with the "suffering unto God" - which is far less familiar and self-evident than an all too "adaptable"

---

[12] J. B. Metz, "Unterwegs zu einer nachidealistischen Theologie," 218 [*A Passion for God*, 40.]

[13] J. B. Metz, "Unterwegs zu einer nachidealistischen Theologie," 220 [*A Passion for God*, 42]: „In contrast to some important and influential contemporary theologians, this approach certainly recognizes…a *suffering unto God*, but it does not really recognize a *suffering in God* or a *suffering between God and God*. For try as I may, I cannot understand how such discourse does not either on the one hand betray itself in a (no matter how sublime) doubling of human suffering and human powerlessness, that is, leads to a Gnostic externalization of suffering in God; or how such a theological explanation does not violate the terrible dignity of human suffering."

and “flexible” modern theology proposes for belief. The piety of lament, a mysticism of God’s distance, of the first commandment.

An effective theological skepticism and a heightened sensibility for all that is unresolved mark this theologian. His inclination to let himself be stirred from outside rather than from the inner world of theology and his readiness (and need!) to continually re-learn, moreover, is in the end a sign of a missing confidence that his type of theology will ever be done with its objective insignificance and marginality.

His texts are brief, broken down into the shortest imaginable and most precise form (“Religion: Interruption”), always powerfully expressed, confrontational, and pointed; often only sketchily carried out. Metz thereby disdains simulating as an author what is in fact no longer possible: Christianity as a unified whole, as uninterrupted continuum, as clerical power, as a theoretically closed system.

His theology is the urgent, obstinate, discreet expression of an abandonment (Mark 15:34); not an entire loss, but an agonizing absence. Theology of the missing God.[14]

Translated by John K. Downey and Steven T. Ostovich

---

[14] See T. R. Peters, *Mystik, Mythos, Metaphysik. Die Spur des vermißten Gottes*, Mainz/München 1992.

ABANDONED BY GOD? REFLECTIONS ON THE MARGINS OF THEOLOGY*

Jürgen Manemann

On 11 December 2002 Pope John Paul II held his usual General Audience. This time it set off a shock wave in the media. A collective gasp had issued from the faithful gathered at that audience. Why? John Paul II had asked the question whether it could be that God had abandoned humankind. Referring to the prophet Jeremiah, the Pope lamented the great tragedy of the silence of a God who no longer reveals himself and, having grown weary of human antics, seems to have to shut himself up in his heaven.[1] If this is the case, what can we do? John Paul II went on to invoke the salvific power of memory: the task before humankind is to remind God of his promises. Journalists racked their brains: had the Pope become an apocalyptic preacher or were these ideas simply the expression of a syndrome common among the old: doubt.[2]

As the reactions to this speech indicate, this question, the question of whether humankind has been abandoned by God, is profoundly disturbing, even scandalous. What is so upsetting? In order to understand the agitation and the challenge - the novelty - of this question we need to begin with theodicy.

The "Why-Question"

The question "Why?" asked in the face of human suffering, what is known as the question of theodicy, has been a perennial concern of theology. What is the point of this question? In which direction does it point those who ask it? The question of why - as is commonly said - points us toward a reason, a rational ground. "Every reason" says philosopher Christoph Türcke, "calms, quiets a 'why' with a 'because'.... The 'why' is the *agent provocateur* of all reasons."[3] But this "why" is double-edged: it offers, on the one hand, the door to the realm of reasons, and on the other hand it leaves no reasons in peace.[4] Theology constantly offers strategies for calming and quieting our questioning. Its systematic

---

* Jürgen Manemann, *Rettende Erinnerung an die Zukunft. Essay über die christliche Verschärfung*, Mainz 2005, 48-66.

[1] Johannes Paul II, General Audience of 11 December 2002, in: http://www.vatican.va/ holy_father/john_paul_ii/audience/2002/documents/hf_jp-ii_aud_20021211_en.html

[2] "Von Gott verlassen," *Der Spiegel* 3 (2003).

[3] C. Türcke, *Fundamentalismus – Maskierter Nihilismus* (Springe 2003), 29.

[4] Türcke, 29.

theoretical approaches incorporate any disorder into an ever more comprehensive order; its privatizing theories understand evil as simply a failure to grasp the good, thus making evil an incapacity; its theoretical notions of original sin interpret evil as punishment for Adam's Fall.[5] But all of this effort over all the years has not managed to silence the question: "Why?"

Every question signals the direction of its answer. The Why-Question aims for a foundation, for certainty. It is a question about reasons. But can this search for reasons, for a sure footing, be a question about the biblical God? Doesn't this question lead us away from God? The biblical God does not guaranty a response to our need for security but leads us in the other direction, into uncertainty. Abraham was famously told he should set out without knowing where he was going, his slave was even forbidden to look back toward his home. The freedom of this uncertain exodus is a risky freedom, a freedom which can either fail or be transformed into a productive homelessness. So, how can we break through the inherent coping mechanisms of the why-question?[6]

The "Where-Question": Local Amnesia in German Theology

There is a danger of normalization in the "why-question": it may serve to stabilize present relations and alienate humankind from the biblical God. There is a danger that concrete situations and particular subjects will recede into the background. One need only glance at the contemporary theological debate over theodicy. It is not unusual that diverse collective and individual sufferings be dealt with in *one single* proposal and that the question of suffering - not of the actual sufferings - be finally reduced to a problem of logic.[7] But theodicy must never conceal suffering. The theodicy question must never be asked without asking about those who actually suffered. Why does theology constantly forget to attend to its real and concrete location? Or more precisely: why is theology in Germany still unable to see itself as "after Auschwitz"? What is the reason for this lapse of memory?[8]

---

[5] On this ordering see: H. Kessler, *Gott und das Leid seiner Schöpfung* (Würzburg 2000), 22-40.

[6] For an understanding of how these coping mechanisms operate see: H. Lübbe, *Religion nach der Aufklärung* (Graz/Wien/Köln 1986).

[7] M. Striet, "Versuch über die Auflehnung. Philosophisch-theologische Überlegungen zur Theodizeefrage," in: H. Wagner (Hg.) Mit *Gott streiten. Neue Zugänge zum Theodizee-Problem* (sec. ed., Freiburg/Basel/Wien 1998), 48-89.

[8] J. Manemann, *"Weil es nicht nur Geschichte ist" (H. Sherman). Die Begründung einer fragmentarischen Historiographie des Nationalsozialismus aus politisch-theologischer Sicht* (Münster 1995).

"After Auschwitz"

In 1944 the philosopher Theodor W. Adorno wrote, anticipating well the time after 1945:

> The idea that after the war life will return to "normal" or that culture can be rebuilt - as if the rebuilding of that culture were not itself a negation - is idiotic. Millions of Jews have been murdered and this should be an interlude and not the catastrophe itself? What is this culture waiting for anyhow?[9]

In theology it wasn't for decades after 1945 that this question was taken up. Finally Johann Baptist Metz asked his teacher Karl Rahner after the Second World War:

> Why have you theologians never really talked about this catastrophe in your theology? Why does the abyss of suffering confronting us appear only as the echo of the thunder, a passing storm already over and done with? Why does one see in our theology little or nothing of the history of human suffering?[10]

These questions are still relevant today. The Jewish philosopher Walter Benjamin brings these two quotations to a point: "That everything goes on as usual is the catastrophe."[11]

Benjamin summarizes the drama of "going on as usual" in the ninth of his theses "On the Concept of History":

> There is a picture by Klee called *Angelus Novus*. It shows an angel who seems about to move away from something he stares at. His eyes are wide, his mouth is open, his wings are spread. This is how the angel of history must look. His face is turned towards the past. Where a chain of events appears before *us*, *he* sees a single catastrophe which keeps piling wreckage upon wreckage and hurls it at his feet. The angel would like to stay, awaken the dead, and make whole what has been smashed. But a storm is blowing from Paradise and has been caught in his wings; it is so strong that the angel can no longer close them. The storm drives him irresistibly into the future, to which his back is turned, while the pile of debris before him rises toward the sky. What we call progress, is *this* storm.[12]

---

[9] Th. W. Adorno, *Minima Moralia: Reflections from Damaged Life*, trans. E. F. N. Jephcott (London 1978).
[10] J. B. Metz, *Welches Christentum hat Zukunft? Dorothee Sölle und Johann Baptist Metz im Gespräch mit Karl-Josef Kuschel* (Stuttgart 1990), 23.
[11] W. Benjamin, "N [Re The Theory of Knowledge, Theory of Progress]," trans. Leigh Hafrey and Richard Sieburth, *Benjamin: Philosophy, Aesthetics, History*, ed. Gary Smith (Chicago: University of Chicago Press, 1989), 64.
[12] W. Benjamin, "On the Concept of History," *Selected Writings, Volume 4: 1938-1940*, ed. Howard Eiland and Michael W. Jennings, trans. Edmund Jephcott and others (Cambridge, MA and London: Belknap Press of Harvard University Press, 2003), 392.

This understanding emerges from a specific tradition Benjamin has mentioned earlier in Thesis VIII:

> The Tradition of the oppressed teaches us that the "state of emergency" in which we live is not the exception but the rule. We must attain to a conception of history that accords with this insight. ... The current amazement that the things we are experiencing are still possible in the twentieth century is *not* philosophical. This amazement is not the beginning of knowledge - unless it is the knowledge that the view of history which gives rise to it is untenable.[13]

If one wants to question radically, then one must begin asking questions in a way that does not stifle questioning, that is, questions must be asked which do not already contain their answers, but instead cut across our own set ways of thinking. In this way we can break the momentum of "going on as usual." A theology which is not content with the one-dimensionality of systems generates questions of this kind. To break through this systematic one-dimensionality theology must change its point of view and attend to the experience of those who see with different eyes: the fallen and the saved. And these questions come not from wonderment, not from philosophical astonishment, but rather from desperation.

The pioneering Russian philosopher Leo Schestow tells the following legend: There is a story about the angel of death, who comes down to human beings in order to remove their souls from their bodies - and this angel is completely covered with eyes. It happens:

> that the angel of death, if he wants to take a soul, makes sure that he comes early, that the hour has not yet struck for this person. He does not touch that soul, does not even show himself, but as he departs leaves behind for him or her two of his countless eyes. And then that person suddenly begins to see something totally new - beyond what everyone sees and more than what he himself saw with his old eyes. He sees new things in a new way, not just as a human being but as a being from "another world." He sees that the new is not "necessary" but "free," that it simultaneously is and is not, that it appears in its vanishing and vanishes as it appears.[14]

Human beings see with new eyes when they are confronted with death or with a life that has not even been lived. Both of these bring human thought to the point of despair and compel the admission that "no one knows where life ends and death begins and whether or not what seems to be life, might be death and what seems to be death, might be life."[15]

---

[13] Benjamin, 392.
[14] L. Schestow, *Auf Hiobs Waage. Über die Quellen der ewigen Wahrheiten* (Berlin 1929), 44.
[15] Schestow, 50.

What must we do to move theology to a position where it is exposed to life's realities? The theological task consists primarily in making heard the voices of the fallen and the saved. But such voices cannot really be woven into a theology. As a note found amid the ashes at the Auschwitz crematoria makes clear: "Know what happened, do not forget - and still you will never know."[16]

The Voice of a Survivor

An event reported by Elie Wiesel in his memoir *Night* will serve as a starting point for our reflections.

> When we returned from work one day, we saw three gallows on the assembly grounds. We lined up. The SS stood around us with their menacing submachine guns; the usual ceremony. Three trussed up candidates for death, among them a little boy, the angel with the sad eyes.
> The SS seemed more anxious and worried than usual. To hang a child in front of thousands of spectators was no small matter. The camp commander pronounced the sentence. All eyes were on the child. He was ashen but quite still and biting his lip. The shadow of the gallows covered him completely.
> This time our camp kapo refused to act as hangman. Three SS men stepped up to take his place.
> The three condemned got on their chairs together. Three necks were placed in nooses at the same time.
> "Long live freedom!" yelled the adults.
> The child was silent.
> "Where is God, where is he?" asked someone behind me.
> At a signal from the camp commander the chairs were tipped over.
> Absolute silence prevailed throughout the entire camp. On the horizon the sun was setting.
> "Hats off!" bellowed the commandant? His voice sounded hoarse. We cried.
> "Hats on"
> Then we began the walk-by. The two grown-ups were no longer alive. Their swollen bluish tongues hung down. But the third rope did not hang motionless: the light child was still alive. …
> For more than half an hour he hung there and struggled in death throes between life and death before our eyes. And we had to look him in the face. He was still alive as I walked by him. His tongue was still red, his eyes not yet lifeless.
> Behind me I heard the same man ask:

[16] M. Blanchot, cited in E. Weber, "Nach denken als Nach-denken: Anamnesis," in: M. Meyer/M. Hentschel (Hg.), *Lévinas. Zur Möglichkeit einer prophetischen Philosophie* (Gießen 1990), 256-276, 256.

> "Where is God?"
> And I heard a voice in me answer:
> "Where is he? There - he is hanging there on the gallows. ..."
> That evening the soup tasted like corpses.[17]

Wiesel does not ask "why" this happened but rather "Where is G-d?" And he goes on: "There - he hangs there on the gallows. ..." Theologians have interpreted this passage to mean that this God on the gallows is the God that suffers with us: Jesus in Auschwitz.[18] This reading imposes a Christian interpretive framework on the account and threatens to stifle questioning. Why don't Christian theologians conclude that the phrase "on the gallows" indicates the death of God? God, then, would have died with the small child.[19] However, instead of allowing this sort of disruptive statement, theologians remove the stinger. And all too frequently talk about the suffering God, the God who suffers with us, threatens to exalt suffering because victory over suffering is assumed. Talk of suffering and compassion is only serious if - as Johann Baptist Metz insists - it also includes the possibility of failure in its calculations. To speak of suffering without the possibility of failure is to aestheticize suffering.[20]

Some theologians seem to be anxious about the possibility of arriving at "unexpected conclusions" (Leo Schestow). This anxiety can be seen today in German neo-idealistic theological paradigms. These theologies treat freedom as central but barely mention liberation. What sort of freedom is it which does not aim primarily at liberation? A disconnected and de-contextualized talk about freedom. It is no wonder that talk about the idea of freedom seems increasingly insignificant. Such an abstract, subjective conceptualization can easily be buried by objective social biases. Furthermore one may ask how seriously such a theology of freedom takes its talk of freedom and its stress on the necessity of free will. If talk about freedom were really to be taken seriously, then a theology of freedom would also have to consider that human beings might move farther and farther from God and that finally God himself - in recognition of this freedom - might simply leave human beings on their own. But these theologians of freedom recoil from such a radical possibility. It is surprising that those very theologians who moved human freedom into the foreground, should actually be the most frightened of freedom, and would prefer to make freedom into a system of thought to be "obeyed."

---

[17] E. Wiesel, "Die Nacht," in *Die Nacht zu begraben, Elischa* (Frankfurt/Berlin 1987), 9-153, 92-94.
[18] See J. Moltmann, "Jesus in Auschwitz," in: J. Manemann/J. B. Metz (Hg.) *Christologie nach Auschwitz. Stellungnahmen im Anschluß an Tiemo Rainer Peters* (Münster ^{2}2000), 104-109, 105-106.
[19] For other meanings see R. Boschki, *Der Schrei. Gott und Mench im Werk von Elie Wiesel* (Mainz 1994), 85-91.
[20] See J. B. Metz, "Theodizee-empfindliche Gottesrede," in *Landschaft aus Schreien. Zur Dramatik der Theodizeefrage* (Mainz 1995), 81-102, 93.

Theology asks the "why-question", but seldom the "where-question" not least because of its desire for secure ground on which to stand. The Jewish tradition is different. There this latter question is always present. We see an example of this in a parable from the middle ages:

> In some obscure village in central Poland, there was a small synagogue. One night, when making his rounds, the Rabbi entered and saw God sitting in a dark corner. He fell upon his face and cried out: 'Lord God, what art Thou doing here?' God answered him neither in thunder nor out of a whirlwind, but with a small voice: 'I am tired, Rabbi, I am tired unto death.'"[21]

This parable tells us how God has become tired of human cruelty. "Perhaps He was no longer able to control it and could no longer recognize His image in the mirror of creation. He has left the world to its own inhuman devices and dwells now in some other corner of the universe so remote that His messengers cannot even reach us."[22]

On the Track of the Missing God

Theological questioning must never gloss over the tragedy of concrete human suffering. But can theology be done in a way that it exposes itself to suffering and moves the testimony of victims to the center? Theologians need to do theology in such a way that they will not have to be ashamed of themselves before the dead. On the one hand, this means that whoever writes and thinks about catastrophes may not present injustice abstractly because abstract concepts overwhelm any concrete response. On the other hand, it would be nothing less than usurpation and mockery if they so identified with the victims that they spoke as if they were the victim. Talking this way about the death and desertion of God, amounts to re-victimizing the victims and doubling their suffering. Bearing witness to the testimony of the fallen and the saved means avoiding closure, keeping the question open and at issue rather than settled. Anything else would be an affirmation of suffering and hopelessness. For hope is given to us "only for the sake of those with no hope."[23]

How can we speak about being abandoned so that we are not simply expressing a loss but an "agonizing absence" (Peters)? Political theology risks attempting this balancing act under the rubric of the "track of the missing God" (Peters). Rahner's talk of the mystery of God is here given a negative spin.

---

[21] Cited in: G. Steiner, *The Death of Tragedy* (New York 1963), 352-353.
[22] Steiner, 353.
[23] W. Benjamin, "Goethe's Elective Affinities," *Selected Writings, Volume 1: 1913-1926*, ed. Marcus Bullock and Michael W. Jennings, trans. Stanley Corngold (Cambrigde, MA 1996), 356.

Metz transforms the proposition of Thomas that "To know God means not to know him" into "To know God means to miss him."[24]

How can we express our sense of missing God? Asking the question of the missing God means abandoning the objective outsider's perspective as the final horizon for formulating questions and seeking answers. The questioner affected by suffering will ask about God quite differently. The question "Where is God?" would be construed as meaning "When will God get here?" A theology that asks the question "When will God get here?" moves beyond theodicy. The question of "why" often aims at calming and justifying, while the question of "when" aims at the end, at help. It is the more radical and more dangerous question. And an extremely profound Christological question. One thinks of Mk 15: 34 ("My God, my God, *where* have you gone?") or of the cry from the Apocalypse of John that ends the New Testament: "Maranatha. Come, Lord." A theology of the missing god would be an expression of longing for God but not of being hopelessly forlorn.[25] And with the "where" question it provokes the question of time. A theology of missing God is thoroughly apocalyptic: it was the apocalyptic traditions which had asked the "where" question ("Wo bleibt Gott?") most radically. It is no surprise, then, that theology continues to marginalize apocalyptic traditions.

Yet apocalyptic belongs at the center of Christological thought, as a brief overview of New Testament formulae shows: "The oldest formula of early Christianity and so the oldest statement of early Christianity went: 'God, who has raised Jesus from the dead,' in other words, 'God has raised Jesus from the dead.'"[26] (1 Thess 1:10 and passim)

Ancient Israel knew nothing of belief in the resurrection of the dead. This idea was born in the tensions of the early Jewish apocalyptic vision of the world. The first Christians drew this belief into their interpretation of early Judaism's apocalyptic movement and into their own theology.[27] For this reason talking about the resurrection means keeping its apocalyptic horizon in view. This apocalyptic horizon - here I risk using the singular - is about the darkening of the present, about taking seriously and without avoidance the rupture of catastrophic events that calls into question reading the present in terms of a salvific past. What is commonly called Jewish apocalyptic arose in a time of unspeakable oppression (roughly between the 2nd century BCE and the 1st century CE, the period between Daniel in the First Testament and the Apocalypse to John in the Second Testament), a time that could no longer be diagnosed and understood simply in terms of the past.

---

[24] T. R. Peters, Johann Baptist Metz. *Theologie des vermißten Gottes* (Mainz 1998), 30/31.

[25] Peters, 156.

[26] K. Müller, „Die Rede von Jesu Auferstehung. Eine Erinnerung an die von Gott befristete Zeit," in: J. Manemann (Hg.), *Jahrbuch Politische Theologie*. Bd. 3: Befristete Zeit (Münster 1999), 18-34, 22.

[27] Müller, 27.

Against the Apocalyptic Blindness of Theology: Hope is not Optimism[28]

The apocalyptic perspective, which introduces a radical temporal index into theological thought, can be read as a message about the limits of time. For Christians such a view of time is fundamental, as Jewish philosopher of religion Jacob Taubes remarked in an interview: "Any one who believes he thinks in a Christian way and believes he can do so without attending to the limitation of time is an idiot."[29]

To think in a Christian way, in a way that would not dodge the "where-question" and the problem of our having been deserted by God, always means to think apocalyptically. It was the protestant theologian Ernst Käsemann who first pointed out the loss of apocalyptic and its marginalization in the theology of the 1960's:

> That the church's theology has continued to see its task as getting beyond apocalyptic is not debatable. ... New Testament scholars may wish to ask what price we are paying for that and what risks we are taking so that we theologians might become the heirs of systematic Greek thought. One pays a price for leaving behind apocalyptic.[30]

Apocalyptic entails hope. Why, then, is the hope to which it testifies avoided? Fear of disappointment and failure. This fear can be seen throughout the whole of society. People increasingly deny themselves hope. Optimism - which according to Heiner Müller is simply a lack of information[31] - has replaced hope. Optimism costs us nothing, commits us to nothing, binds us to nothing, and never disappoints.

Hope should not be confused with optimism - a cheap hope which costs nothing. Costly hope is a hazardous affair that risks disappointment and failure. For this reason the opposite of hope is not despair but apathy. Hope does not mean certainty. The hope we are talking about here leads to instability and uncertainty. This instability and uncertainty should not be confused with the instability and uncertainty which result from our contemporary social disintegration. They are not due to that furious mobility which creates a globalized and stressful world, a world defined by computer terminals and connectivity in which portability and lack of attachment to any particular place have become ends in themselves. This motion for the sake of motion congeals into a blind

---

[28] See: J. Manemann, *Politischer Anti-Monotheismus. Carl Schmitt und die Politische Theologie* (Münster 2002).

[29] J. Taubes, in F. Rötzer (Hrsg.), *Denken, das an der Zeit ist* (Frankfurt 1987), 318.

[30] E. Käsemann, „Zum Thema der urchristlichen Apokalyptik", in ibied. *Exegetische Versuche und Besinnungen* II (Göttingen 1965), 105 Anmerk. 5.

[31] See H. Müller zit. n. D. Grünbein, Bogen and Leier, in: H. Müller, *Ende der Handschrift. Gedichte* (Frankfurt 2000), 99-116, 113.

readiness at the service of organizational productivity. But hope should not be thought of as the reward for those who are mobile, for those successful global vagabonds and tourists to whom the future belongs.[32] The hope we are talking about is not the hope of those who value the future because they have a future. Hope would only be hope, if it is for those who no longer even dare to speak. Such a hope stands at odds with a society in which those who have fallen under the wheels of mobilization are allowed to drop through the holes in the net, a society in which death itself has become an embarrassment.

This accelerated society tolerates neither the permanent nor the truly new. Everything dissolves into motion. This motion does not (as is often maintained) express itself in openness, because it supported by an image of endlessness which is committed to extending the present into the future. "Endlessness" is not an expression of hope for the other but a threat. It indicates a provisional condition, a situation of flux in which everything becomes just one small piece in the flow. This movement does not want an end. Embracing this movement becomes the sign of a society's readiness for the future. The future becomes the criterion for the present in such a way that both are merely synonyms for being in motion. And so the present evades the challenge of legitimation because the future needs no legitimation: it is always right, it is always stronger.

Limit Thinking

Apocalyptic hope is different. It refuses to have anything to do with "going on as usual." Apocalyptic thought understands time neither as an eternal recurrence nor as an extended present, but rather as a limited span. Time has an end. Apocalyptic thinking is historical thinking, because history is only history within a limited period, whether this period is understood as a "time of waiting"[33] or as a "reprieve".[34] There is a sense of urgency: this time is running out. Apocalyptic time is not a casual, carefree time but a time of distress.[35]

Jacob Taubes once described the tenor of apocalyptic with the following story:

> In 1956, after the suppression of the popular rebellion in Hungary a refugee came to Vienna seeking asylum. He was told immediately by the authorities at the border crossing that he could not stay in Austria - a country which had given shelter to many refugees. They mentioned Yugoslavia, West Germany, Switzerland, Canada, and Australia as other possible places of refuge. They pointed

[32] See Z. Bauman, *Unbehagen in der Postmoderne* (Hamburg 1999).
[33] P. Sloterdijk, *Eurotaoismus. Zur Kritik der politischen Kinetik* (Frankfurt 1989), 280f.
[34] On the notion of "reprieve," see: J. Manemann, "Beschleuniger wider Willen? Zur Katechontik Carl Schmitts," in: *Jahrbuch Politische Theologie* Bd. 3, 108-123, 108.
[35] See J. Taubes, in: F. Rötzer, 317.

> these out to the refugee on a nearby globe. He turned the sphere around himself and after a short pause asked: 'Don't you have another globe?'[36]

Apocalyptic is that yearning for another globe. It seeks to break through the dominant view of history. Apocalyptic envisions a standpoint outside of what is called history.

Apocalyptic thinking is thinking in a state of exception; it is thinking in exceptional times. It radically alters one's entire perspective. This "exceptional thinking," includes opposition to any relativizing or sanctioning of human suffering. Apocalyptic thought is something completely new arising in the face of the "radical eclipse of the horizon of the future".[37] For those with an apocalyptic vision, the only hope lies within this limited time - and the limiting power is God.

Those who think apocalyptically share the view of Benjamin's *Angelus Novus*. They cannot turn away from the wreckage of history. They see "a single catastrophe which keeps piling wreckage upon wreckage" (Walter Benjamin), a heap of debris rising to the sky. For them history has no final goal - unless it is the threat of the ultimate discontinuity: the destruction of the entire world. Refusing to make sense out of what is essentially senseless, apocalyptic thinkers protest the illusion that history is reasonable, meaningful, progressive, and just. The fulfillment of history is not found in its goal, but in its interruption: "And I saw a new heaven and a new earth; for the first heaven and the first earth had passed away, and the sea was no more." (Rev 21:1) Apocalyptic is based on trust and confidence: a trust that God remembers those without hope and a confidence that God will, in a new act of creation, bring the history of these hopeless ones to its "end."[38]

Apocalyptic from below

Unlike Hegel, apocalyptic thinkers do not see history as the locus of the Last Judgment. They revolt against the idea that the blood of the victims is dried by a process of evolving meaning.[39] To perceive the past apocalyptically is to look at it as unfinished, open. This presupposes a crazy stretching of the sense of time to meet two demands: to go back into the past and to transform (*Aufhebung*) what happened. This perspective comes from a sense of danger. It is on the basis of this danger that the apocalyptic thinker perceives the flow of time -

---

[36] R. Faber, "Das ist die Synagoge, in die ich nicht gehe." Über politisch-religiöse Witze, in: Faber (ed.), *Politische Religion - religiöse Politik* (Würzburg 1997), 331-349, 332.
[37] K. Müller, *Studien zur frühjüdischen Apokalyptik* (Stuttgart 1991), 56.
[38] On this see: Müller, *Die Auferweckung Jesu - eine Erinnerung an Gottes befristende Macht,* 34.
[39] See: A. Finkielkraut, *Die vergebliche Erinnerung. Verbrechen gegen die Menschheit* (Berlin 1989), 45.

not conceived abstractly and quasi-naturalistically, but seen clearly in terms of the origin of this understanding of time: the apocalyptic thinker knows who's running the show, who sees to it that everything "goes on as usual" (Benjamin) and insures that catastrophes continue to be perpetuated. Apocalyptic thought abandons the biological and social feeling for time and instead champions its interruption and sublation (*Aufhebung*). As Johann Baptist Metz has written, in apocalyptic time life-time and world-time are not divided from each other[40], but rather are introduced to a moral understanding of time. Such an understanding of time speaks against any notion of the future which claims that what will be tomorrow is more important than what was yesterday. Apocalyptic raises the absurd claim to turn time upside down putting itself on the side of the vanquished. It resists any understanding of time in which history slowly disintegrates like an atomic half-life.

Uncovering Domination

Apocalyptic thinking is sensitive to catastrophe but not in a pathological way of "loving" it. Günther Anders warned of an apocalyptic blindness which allows human beings to become voyeurs on their own downfall.[41]

As thought that is sensitive to catastrophe, apocalyptic is not just about the end of time, but also about memory. The verb "apokalyptein" means "to expose" or "uncover" and this uncovering is essentially a matter of memory. The apocalypse is "remembering an earlier generation who at the moment of greatest danger, without denying or dissembling, held on to courage and hope while uncovering the logic of the dominators."[42] It focuses on the urgent contemporary question: Who fears (or should fear) the apocalypse? Its announcement of the future exposes the unjust conditions of the present - a legacy from the prophets.

The apocalyptic texts of the Bible contain no specific historical timetable, though the history of apocalyptic movements shows how often they are so misunderstood. Their potential for danger does not lie in this misunderstanding (as a timetable), but rather in the violent fantasies which it seems apocalyptic texts cannot do without. They are infused with the biblical claim "'Vengeance is

---

[40] See: J. B. Metz, "Hoffnung als Naherwartung oder der Kampf um die verlorene Zeit. Unzeitgemäße Thesen zur Apokalyptik," in: Metz, *Glaube in Geschichte und Gesellschaft. Studien zu einer pratischen Fundamentaltheologie* (4th ed., Mainz 1984), 149-160. Further: Metz, "Theologie gegen Mythologie. Kleine Apologie des biblischen Monotheismus," in: *Herder Korrespondenz* 1988, 187-193. Also: T. R. Peters, *Mystik - Mythos - Metaphysik. Die Spur des vermißten Gottes* (Mainz, 1992), 54-73.

[41] See G. Anders, *Die Antiquiertheit des Menschen*. Bd. 1: *Über die Seele im Zeitalter der zweiten industriellen Revolution*, München [5]1980, 233-353.

[42] J. Ebach, Apokalypse. Zum Ursprung einer Stimmung, in: *Einwürfe* 2 (1985), 5-61, 11.

mine' says the Lord."[43] Also, since apocalyptic texts are based on an expectation of universal judgment, a postmortem tribunal, they themselves participate in the history of violence, as indicated by their origins: These texts are not just a protest against but also a reflection of violence.[44]

Apocalyptic thinking is not, as is often claimed, anti-ethical. On the contrary, it is the condition for the possibility of any ethic: in a situation of hopelessness, apocalyptic allows an impossible spark, a flash that radically relativizes the present situation. Apocalyptic is waiting, waiting for the hidden, coming, power that saves. This waiting "does not become petrified by the daily absurdities and atrocities, if it turns into urgent expectation, if it mobilizes the power of salvation, if it develops the unused possibilities for making things better."[45] So waiting, expectation, becomes not the guarantee of fulfillment but the condition for it. It sees the world truly, because only those who still expect something can see it coming[46] - and only those who expect something posses a genuine knowledge of history: they know that what is has not always been so, that it could have been different and so can become different. To see the world apocalyptically does not mean to perpetuate negativity. Such thinking is not about a pessimistic metaphysics of history, but a change of perspective: "Where a chain of events appears before *us*, *he* [the apocalyptic thinker] sees a single catastrophe which keeps piling wreckage upon wreckage and hurls it at his feet." (Benjamin). In order for the vanquished to reclaim their unclaimed rights to history, apocalyptic thinkers tear away the ideological veil with which a progressive theology (nowadays formulated as the ideological demand to become thoroughly modern) attempts to stifle the sigh of the creature.

Apocalyptic versus Katechontik[47]

The apocalyptic visionary opposes anyone who practices so-called *Realpolitik*, who "does not for one second think or wish that the world were any different than it is," and who "is obsessed by the desire of *doing things* [*Dinge zu tun*],

---

[43] Ebach, 25-26.

[44] See Ebach, 44-45.

[45] C. Türcke, "Abwarten," in: F. Hager (ed.), *Geschichte Denken. Ein Notizbuch für Leo Löwenthal* (Leipzig 1992), 137-140, 139.

[46] Türcke, 139.

[47] "Katechontik" refers to the concept of the "Restrainer" (*katechon*) in 2 Thessalonians 2. There the katechon is the human power that limits the disruptive effects of evil and mitigates suffering during the period the parousia is delayed. The historical referent remains unclear. The connection to political realism is that God has withdrawn from involvement in history, so politics has become a human activity oriented not to the good of justice but to power, i. e., the "restraining" power against the threat of political chaos. The concept of the katechon is important to Carl Schmitt's political theology - see, for example, Carl Schmitt, *Glossarium: Aufzeichnungen der Jahre 1947-1951* (Berlin 1991), 63 (entry for 19.12.47).

indifferent to the content of such action."[48] And so one might put it apocalyptically with Erich Fried: "Whoever wants the world to remain as it is, does not want it to remain."

Apocalyptic thinking is sensitive, compassionate. "To feel means to be involved."[49] And so it can not afford the luxury of an academic indifference to the world: it remembers the unredeemed hope of the vanquished. It always returns to the question of those abandoned by God: "When is God coming?" "How long must we wait?" "Where is God?" These questions are not a denial of God, but an affirmation of God. They are not utopian dreams. "The name of God," as Metz says, "stands for the belief that the utopia of liberation in which all become human subjects is not purely a projection - which is what it would be if there were only utopia and no God."[50] Later on Metz emphasizes how different this is from a utopia by alluding to prayer: No one prays to a utopia![51] The place (topos) referred to here is a place that can be experienced in this world but still be different from it, what Michel Foucault calls a Heterotopie, a place, as Levinas puts it - "beyond being," in the sense that it "happens otherwise than being."[52] He marks a place bound up with a specific "heterochronology," that is, it happens in a circumscribed space of time. In so far it belongs to the experience of this different place, the Heterotopia is the interruption of the conventional feel of time.[53] This place in which according to Levinas time shatters, is the place of discovery of humankind in its nakedness. This vulnerability of others signals a being deserted by God and compels me to action because only I can help the other person.

Apocalyptic sees a glimmer of hope in despair because to despair means not to be indifferent; it is the last bastion of hope. Apocalyptic is not about *malum physicum*, not about the *malum metaphysicum*, but rather about the *malum morale* and the concomitant theological malady of being cut off and separated from God. For this reason the apocalyptic Jesus, as Metz says, asks God to be God. The target is a new and radical "revival of the ancient trust in ...God as the Lord of history"; to "enter the place which no theology of salvation history can measure where God's plans are laid."[54] "The experience of the absence of God makes clear the urgent necessity for his presence…."[55]

---

[48] T. W. Adorno, "Education After Auschwitz," *Critical Models: Interventions and Catchwords*, trans. Henry W. Pickford (New York 1998), 198.
[49] A. Heller, *Theorie der Gefühle*, Hamburg 1980, 19.
[50] J. B. Metz, *Glaube in Geschichte und Gesellschaft*, 65.
[51] J.B. Metz, *Glaube in Geschichte und Gesellschaft*, 65
[52] E. Lévinas, *Jenseits des Seins oder anders als Sein geschieht* (Freiburg/München 1992).
[53] On this concept in Foucault: M. Foucault, Andere Räume, in: K. H. Barck/ P. Gente/ H. Paris/S. Richter (Hg.), *Aisthesis. Wahrnehmung heute oder Perspektiven einer anderen Ästhetik* (Leipzig 1990).
[54] K. Müller, *Studien zur frühjüdischen Apokalyptik*, 106.
[55] J. Ebach führt den Satz jedoch weiter: "… die Erfahrung der Anwesenheit Gottes macht den Schmerz seiner Abwesenheit um so größer." (J. Ebach, „Tags in einer Wolkensäule, nachts in einer Feuersäule. Gott wahrnehmen," in: *Merkur: Nach Gott fragen. Über das Religiöse*, 9/10 (1999), 784-794, 786.

Sensitive God-Talk

Where is God? When is God coming? At the end of his General Audience John Paul II expressed the hope that abandonment might be the seed of a new beginning.[56] The apocalypse knows about the "darkening of heaven's light", of the "eclipse of God" (M. Buber), of the silence of God. It is said in the Revelation of John "When the Lamb opened the seventh seal, there arose a silence in heaven for about half an hour. ..." (Rev 8:2) And now, this can be taken to mean that "the hour of the earth has come ... the silence in heaven leads us to look for God on earth ... the silence in heaven directs our collective attention to the earth."[57]

At the end of the Apocalypse of John we find the cry: "Come, Lord Jesus!" (Rev 22:20) - the prayer for God to be God.[58] Apocalyptic thinking does not offer solutions. On the contrary! It sharpens problems and points to the way in which questions about God and suffering should be asked. That which is called history is not what history should be. John sees this very clearly. He looks for a history beyond history, for a history which happens differently, for a counter-history. This counter-history is described metaphorically as the sealed book. "The problem is that no one is able to open and read. This frightens and troubles the writer of the Apocalypse: 'At that moment I cried.' The persecuted community cannot explain why they are persecuted and oppressed. To *this* community John would like to promise a hope that does not pass over the materiality, the embodiment, of human life: 'He will wipe away the tears from their eyes.'" This is to emphasize that these acts of God are only for those, "who have tears in their eyes, those who have compassion and weep over the oppression and wailing of these people and hope with them to the end."[59]

Translated by John K. Downey and Steven T. Ostovich

---

[56] John Paul II, General Audience of 11 December 2002.

[57] P. Richard, *Apokalypse. Das Buch von Hoffnung und Widerstand. Ein Kommentar*. Luzern 1996, 118.

[58] See J. B. Metz, "Theodizee-empfindliche Gottesrede," 99. Metz early on worked through the expectation-character of the language of prayer (see Metz, "The Courage to Pray," in Metz and Karl Rahner, *The Courage to Pray,* New York 1980). Jürgen Werbick also notes that the language of prayer leads the theodicy problem back to the question, "How long yet?" His differentiation of the two directions of questioning is first of all (analytically) meaningful, but there is a danger that the two aren't really related to each other (see J. Werbick, "Der Glaube an der allmächtigen Gott und die Krise des Bittgebets," in *Berliner Theologische Zeitschrift* 1/2001, 40-59.

[59] P. Richard, 236.

Memoria Passionis & Cultural Amnesia

READING TEXTS OF TERROR: MYSTICAL IMAGINATION AND POLITICAL CONVICTION

Bruce T. Morrill, S.J.

Introduction

In 1985 Johann Baptist Metz published a programmatic essay concerning three crises that have contributed to the necessity of political theology as a post-idealist fundamental theology for the North Atlantic Church in these late-modern times: the challenge of Marxism, the catastrophe of Auschwitz, and the struggle of the so-called third world or "culturally polycentric world."[1] These three constitute a crisis for theology - which in the twentieth century had come largely to be done in neoscholastic and transcendental-idealist veins - by together amounting to the insistence on the essentially historical (and not merely historistic) character of humanity and, therefore, on the essential function of history in doing *Christian* theology. Marxism's discovery of the world as a historical project wherein people become the subjects of their own histories not only awakened the "fateful theme"[2] of history for Judaism and Christianity but also cast an unrelenting epistemological light on the question of truth by demonstrating how interest always conditions knowledge. The historical event defining the contemporary German context for theology for Metz is symbolized in the name Auschwitz, a crisis that cannot possibly be integrated into any grand theology of history, a fissure disrupting any self-contained theological synthesis. While Auschwitz undeniably carries a unique historical, and therefore ethical, weight for Metz's German church, the crisis of which it speaks nonetheless constitutes part of the global twentieth century phenomenon that philosophical theologian Edith Wyschogrod has identified as the cataclysm, "the void exposed by the event of mass annihilation of persons within ever more compressed time frames, a void that remains indescribable and yet constitutes the unique moment, the entry of the nihil into time."[3] That Metz himself has come to this more global awareness is evident in the third (historical) crisis he has

---

[1] Johann Baptist Metz, *A Passion for God: The Mystical-Political Dimension of Christianity*, ed. and trans. J. Matthew Ashley (New York: Paulist Press, 1998), 33 [Note: This particular chapter of the book was originally, "Unterwegs zu einer nachidealistichen Theologie," in *Entwürfe der Theologie*, ed. Johannes B. Bauer (Köln: Verlag Styria, 1985), 209-233].

[2] Metz, *A Passion for God*, 36.

[3] Edith Wyschogrod, *An Ethics of Remembering: History, Heterology, and the Nameless Others* (Chicago: University of Chicago Press, 1998), 14. For an exploration of Wyschogrod's theory in relation to Metz's theology, see Bruce T. Morrill, "Anamnetic Action: The Ethics of Remembrancing," *Doxology* 17 (2000): 3-22.

identified, namely, that the increasing demographic and ethical centrality of the third-world church forces social conflicts to "the center of ecclesial and theological awareness."[4]

If Metz is correct - as I believe he is - in insisting that embracing the history of suffering in the context of a world church constitutes the essential condition for doing theology at the turn of the twenty-first century, this epochal shift carries a number of serious new challenges. Not the least among these resides in the fact that academic theology necessarily remains the work of the written word, of written texts, even as it learns from Metz's fundamental practical theology that the faith it seeks to understand is a praxis. Doing theology in and for a world church not only reiterates the role of hermeneutics but also actually heightens the ethical demands on the hermeneutical dimension of practicing theology. The desire to seek solidarity with the poor in a world church meets significant problems concerning truth and justice requiring analysis, to employ the hermeneutics of Gadamer and Ricoeur, not only of the world of the text itself but also the world behind the text (the social-political-historical context of the author and narrative) and the world in front of it (the same for the reader). How does the theologian responsibly seek to make these worlds meet in the pursuit of service to a world church?

This essay is an exploration into how the solidarity that political theology envisions for late-modern Christianity takes practical shape through the particular medium of the written text. My concern is with how the contemporary, well-educated, socially secure North Atlantic believer is able to read texts that testify to horrific human suffering. Specifically, I propose to examine the testimonial narrative of Rigoberta Menchú, the Guatemalan winner of the 1992 Nobel Peace Prize, and, more briefly, the Passion Narratives in the Gospels so as not to be immobilized by their terror but, rather, to be moved with a desire to encounter God in suffering humanity. Menchú's story and the Passion Narratives each bear both mystical and political dimensions, even though the former might be thought of more in political terms and the latter, as mystical. In considering the Guatemalan story we shall see how a narrative of suffering, even one with a politically testimonial intent, relies not only on symbol and performativity for its viability as a persuasive text (the majority of academic engagement with this text has been in the new disciplines of literary criticism and performance theory) but, I shall argue, draws from a Christian mysticism nourished by biblical faith - a dimension of her narrative largely ignored, if not denigrated, by most American academics. A close reading of certain parts of the text, as well as consideration of the academic and political controversies that have surrounded it, will invite reflection on the role and function of memory in religious and political praxis. Such a close investigation into the content and analysis of a contem-

---

[4] Metz, *A Passion for God*, 43.

porary narrative of solidarity in suffering, however, cannot but affect the theologian. As Metz has stated: "Whoever talks about God in Jesus' sense will always take into account the way one's own pre-formulated certainties are wounded by the misfortune of others."[5] My political-theological study of Menchú's controversial narrative will, therefore, lead me back to the biblical source of faith, inviting consideration of how contemporary scholarship concerning the accounts of Jesus' death carries the promise of a social-political hope, even as the Passion Narratives draw from deep mystical, prophetic wells for the images that draw us into solidarity with Christ in his suffering and death.

I hope the reader will not become frustrated when I report, nonetheless, that a further, extended word of introduction is required before diving into the worlds of these texts. As shall become evident in my exposition below, I myself bring a specific worldview before Menchú's narrative, one comprised not only of my social-political status - Caucasian, U.S. citizen, academician - but also of a particular way of doing Roman Catholic theology - primarily, as a liturgical theologian. This approach to theology, which attends to the content and practice of the Church's rites as a primary source of theology, has a pervasive influence on how I read texts. Thus, I offer first a brief excursus into how this liturgical theologian conceptualizes the praxis of faith, an approach that begins from the mystical but cannot neglect the ethical, so as hopefully to render my account of reading the texts of terror more intelligible.

Mysticism and Politics: A Liturgical Prolegomenon

Christian faith, no mere assent to ideas, is only genuinely known as a way of life, a praxis, an ongoing immersion in the paschal mystery. The salvific content of the paschal mystery is most fully revealed in the church's celebration of its liturgy, especially the sacraments of Eucharist and Baptism. The performance of liturgical worship, however, far from being an end in itself, is for the purpose of revealing our entire lives as an ongoing act of worship, of glorifying God by sharing in God's creative and redemptive action in our world. Perhaps the most prominent metaphor for our entrance into the life of faith is Saint Paul's description of baptism as our being buried with Christ in death, "so that, just as Christ was raised from the dead by the glory of the Father, so we too might walk in newness of life" (Rom 6:4).[6] Having no sooner made this indicative proclamation of our death to sin in Christ, Paul immediately goes on to exhort believers not to allow sin to have any power over us (6:14). This is but one way of describing the mystery that *is* the

[5] Metz, *A Passion for God*, 2.
[6] Biblical quotes are taken from *The New Revised Standard Version*.

Christian life of faith, a life patterned on Christ's God-given mission of redemptive solidarity with a suffering world. For his having faithfully carried out that mission even to death, God raised Jesus from the dead, making him the source of life for all who would embrace faith in him as a praxis of *following* him.[7]

What prevents a Christian life patterned on redemptive suffering from being an exercise in divine-human sadomasochism[8] is our ongoing surrender to the paschal mystery, a tragically beautiful dialectic of mysticism and ethics.[9] If what sustained Jesus of Nazareth in his mission - especially as its social-ethical implications caused increasing conflict with religious and political authorities - was his mystical relationship with God, so too Christians sustain lives of solidarity with the suffering by their mystical practices of prayer and liturgy. The Eucharist, most importantly as celebrated on the Lord's Day, is the source and summit of the Christian life,[10] the enacted, lived proclamation of the Lord's death as the very revelation of God's life for the world. What so often threatens the possibility of knowing the joyful character of such a life is the loss of the tensive quality of the paschal mystery, the awareness that Christ's suffering and death are only redemptive because of the revelation of who he is - and, therefore, who God is for us - in his resurrection. Hence, the centrality of eucharistic worship as the weekly revelation in word and sacrament of ourselves and our world as the ongoing story of God's redemptive presence and action among those who suffer. The Sunday Eucharist, the original Christian feast,[11] draws together into one body, the living body of Christ, all of our lives of prayer and service in union with all the world's struggling search for and unnamed encounters with God.

When Paul teaches, "For just as the body is one and has many members, and all the members of the body, though many, are one body, so it is with Christ" (1 Cor 12:12), he wants believers to understand that their lives are now bound in solidarity with all Christ's members: "If one member suffers, all suffer together with it; if one member is honored, all rejoice together with it" (1 Cor 12:26). The challenge for Christians in the late-modern world lies in comprehending the scope of this one body of Christ with its many members. Following the dogmatic ecclesiology of the Second Vatican Council, we know that Christ's members, the church, cannot be limited to the Roman

---

[7] For an analysis, informed by the hymn in Philippians 2, of this kenotic Christology in Metz's *Followers of Christ: Religious Life and the Church*, trans. Thomas Linton (New York: Paulist Press, 1978), see Bruce T. Morrill, *Anamnesis as Dangerous Memory: Political and Liturgical Theology in Dialogue* (Collegeville: The Liturgical Press, 2000), 34-40.

[8] See Dorothee Soelle, "A Critique of Christian Masochism," in *Suffering*, trans. Everett Kalin (Philadelphia: Fortress Press, 1975), 9-32.

[9] See Johann Baptist Metz, *Faith in History and Society: Toward a Practical Fundamental Theology* (New York: Seabury Press, 1980), 70-77; and Edward Schillebeeckx, *Church: The Human Story of God* (New York: Crossroad Publishing, 1991), 66-99.

[10] See *Sacrosanctum concilium*, no. 10.

[11] See *Sacrosanctum concilium*, no. 106.

Catholic Church (even as it subsists therein), nor merely to Christian ecclesial bodies but, rather, embrace the breadth of humanity in this world.[12] The mission of the church, the mission of all its members, is a compassionate solidarity with the joys and hopes of all people, especially the poor and suffering.[13] As Edward Schillebeeckx argued more than two decades ago, the global proportions of systemic human suffering, as well as our awareness thereof through the telecommunications media, do not allow contemporary North Atlantic Christians a merely domestic, provincial, let alone nationalistic, view of the poor who constitute the suffering members of Christ's body. For this reason, Christian holiness today is necessarily a political holiness, a life of witnessing to God's universal salvific will for suffering humanity.[14] What distinguishes social-political action as a work of Christian solidarity is its mutually informing relationship with mystical activities of prayer and, especially, the liturgy: "Politics without prayer or mysticism quickly becomes grim and barbaric; prayer or mysticism without political love quickly becomes sentimental and irrelevant interiority."[15]

To posit the mutual relationship of mysticism and politics as fundamental to Christian faith today - as has not only Schillebeeckx but also Metz, Gustavo Gutiérrez, and others - leaves open the question of how that relationship is put into practice. The answer necessarily takes shape differently in various, specific social-historical contexts. Gutiérrez has described the remarkable joy characteristic of the eucharistic celebrations in Christian base communities struggling for justice in Latin America: "No superficial glee, this; no empty 'joy' born of unawareness of the reality of oppression and suffering. This is Easter gladness - joy that passes through death and pain, in intense, profound hope."[16] Gutiérrez judges this to be the fullest realization of eucharistic sharing in Christ's death and resurrection; the prayerful praxis of liturgy proves the key source for knowing Christ the Liberator in the difficult struggles the poor must carry on in society. Metz has repeatedly argued that these base communities of the Southern Hemisphere are the exemplars of political spirituality to the universal church.[17] The problem for those of us in the North, however, concerns how, in the *koinonia* of this world church, we are to benefit from and build upon the mystical-political praxis of our

---

[12] See *Lumen gentium*, nos. 14-16.

[13] See *Gaudium et spes*, no. 1.

[14] Edward Schillebeeckx, *The Schillebeeckx Reader*, ed. Robert J. Schreiter (New York: Crossroad Publishing, 1984), 272.

[15] Schillebeeckx, *The Schillebeeckx Reader*, 274. For an extended study of Schillebeeckx on this point, see Bruce T. Morrill, "Practicing Political Holiness: The Call to a Life of Contrasts in the Work of Edward Schillebeeckx," *Doxology* 18 (2001): 71-94.

[16] Gustavo Gutiérrez, *The Power of the Poor in History*, trans. Robert Barr (Maryknoll: Orbis Books, 1983), 107.

[17] See Johann Baptist Metz, "Communicating a Dangerous Memory," *Communicating a Dangerous Memory*, ed. Fred Lawrence (Atlanta: Scholars Press, 1987), 41; *The Emergent Church: The Future of Christianity in a Post-Bourgeois World*, trans. Peter Mann (New York: Crossroad Publishing, 1987), 82-94; and *A Passion for God*, 4-5, 39, 44-45.

poor Latin American sisters and brothers. While the lackluster quality of liturgy in North America and Europe continues to be problematic both in terms of its prayer and its ability to nourish ethical praxis,[18] nobody would reasonably argue for attempting to replicate in the North the liturgical celebrations that are the self-realizations of the poor in the South. Perhaps, however, one way for the Northern believer to receive as grace the mysticism of the Latin American poor lies in prayerfully meditating on the witness of their accounts of the praxis of faith in concert with whatever sources from the repertoire of tradition (biblical, liturgical, artistic) have become native to one's own mystical praxis. Such has been the experience of my own theological quest.

Reading a Testimonial of Terror: The theological context of the reading

From the moment of its initial publication in Spanish in 1983 and then its appearance in English translation in 1984 *I, Rigoberta Menchú: An Indian Woman in Guatemala* quickly gained status as the premiere example of "testimonial literature" within the discipline of Latin American studies, as well as "a cornerstone of the multicultural canon"[19] of North American higher education. Latin Americanist scholars began identifying nearly three decades ago an original type of writing emerging from marginalized peoples, a form of "resistance literature" whereby the subaltern narrator gives personal testimony to the suffering, injustice, and struggle experienced by her people so as to gain sympathy and support for their cause of liberation. The person giving the testimony (most often a woman) usually speaks the account to an anthropologist or some other scholar, who then attempts to convey the narration as accurately as possible in printed text.[20] The scholarly significance of testimonial literature lies in its ability to reorder the subject-object relationship between ethnographers and indigenous peoples; its hybrid structure, fitting the categories of neither autobiography, biography, nor historical novel neatly; and its ability to "militate against the increasing postmodern concerns that realism and representation are dead."[21] The Menchú text has proven so popular in such collegiate departments as anthropology, history, and literature across North America due to the compelling way in which the narrator conveys in the first person the bitter reality of her Quiché (Mayan)

[18] For a discussion of this problem, including engagement of Metz's writings on the topic, see Morrill, *Anamnesis as Dangerous Memory*, 5-16, 50-61.
[19] Robin Wilson, "Anthropologist Challenges Veracity of Mulitcultural Icon," *The Chronicle of Higher Education*, 15 January 1999.
[20] See Stacey Schlau, "Rigoberta Menchú, Chronicler," *National Women's Studies Association Journal* 3 (1991): 262-277, at 262-263.
[21] Georg Gugelberger and Michael Kearney, "Voice for the Voiceless: Testimonial Literature in Latin America," *Latin American Perspectives* 18 (1991): 3-14, at 4-11.

people. While controversy over the veracity of key passages in the book has raged in recent years, professors, far from abandoning the book, have used it to explore further issues concerning the nature of the spoken and written word, the impact of politics on literature, the social construction of individuality and communal identity, and so forth.

I myself became engaged with *I, Rigoberta Menchú* both as a research scholar, preparing a doctoral exam in ritual and performance theory, as well as a fledgling college teacher, preparing a course in political theology for undergraduates. Having first learned of the book as a notable bridge between oral and written performance, I skimmed its content and, discovering Menchú's status as not only a Guatemalan Indian but a Nobel peace laureate (1992), decided to assign it as one of the biographical narratives for my nascent course, "Religious Experience: Suffering, Politics, and Liberation." The book, a first-person account from the Christian base community movement in Latin America, would provide images and stories to animate the undergraduates' subsequent reading of a text in liberation theology by brothers Leonardo and Clodovis Boff.[22]

When I first read the book in the summer of 1994 I found myself, like so many others, riveted by Menchú's descriptions (as transcribed and edited by Marxist anthropologist Elizabeth Burgos-Debray) of the hard but rewarding life in her native mountain village, the brutal working conditions on the coffee plantations near the coast, her degrading experience as a maid in the capital city, and the mounting danger and then catastrophic visitation of the Guatemalan civil war upon her people. Menchú interspersed this quasi-historical narrative with explanations of the folklore, religious beliefs and customs of her people, all the while asserting that she was also withholding secrets her people are sworn to guard from the totalizing consumption of wider society. While Rigoberta's account of the hardships of her people were at times difficult for me to stay with, it was when I began reading the protracted grizzly account of her brother Petrocinio's public torture and execution that I became unsettled and distressed, feelings which would return as I read of her mother's prolonged rape, torture, and death.

When I reached the chapter recounting her brother's torture and death I could no longer read in the silence of my room. The terror was too much to endure alone or even to bear as an interlocutor with Rigoberta. I began playing a recently acquired CD of Maurice Duruflé's *Requiem*, exquisitely recorded by the Symphony Orchestra and Boys Choir of Vilnius, Lithuania. For me the climax of this recording of the work occurs in the fourth of its eight movements, the *Pie Jesu*, in which soprano soloist Grazina Apanaviciute (b. 1940) begins in soft but stalwart supplication to the Lord Jesus, mounts a crescendo beseeching rest for the dead that by its own beautiful

[22] Leonardo and Clodovis Boff, *Salvation and Liberation*: In Search of a Balance between Faith and Politics (Maryknoll: Orbis Books, 1984).

force bears already the assurance of the Lord's presence and compassionate response, and finally recedes into a quiet dwelling upon the Latin words for "rest eternal." My reading of the terrifying text in the secure comfort of my sunny room had become a performance in concert with Menchú's narration, the Lithuanians' musicality, and Duruflé's composition.

I mention the specific recording of Duruflé's *Requiem* because from my initial listening I had found the performance powerfully nuanced to the point of being genuinely prayerful, and yet I also found myself speculating on the fact that, given the recording's date in the early 1990s, the performers (adults and children) had grown up and lived behind the Iron Curtain. What stories did these singers, musicians, and conductor themselves bear? How could the world of war into which the soloist Apanaviciute was born and raised in the Baltics, as well as the Stalinist-Soviet rule of her homeland, not have contributed to the passion with which she sang her *Pie Jesu*? What lives of faith - religious or otherwise - might these Lithuanians have practiced or were practicing still? Duruflé, I was motivated to learn, wrote his *Requiem* in the wake of the Second World War. When asked why the *Dies Irae* figured so minimally in his composition, he had remarked that more than enough wrath and terror had already been performed in the war. Drawing on the serene beauty of the Gregorian chants, he wrote his *Requiem* in prayerful honor for his fallen countrymen, for whom he wished only peaceful rest. In minimalizing the *Dies Irae* he was making the historicity of the terror of World War II a constitutive element of his aesthetic work. By employing the Gregorian requiem chants as the basis for his modern composition Duruflé also made the believers who had practiced the Christian traditions for death down through the centuries a part of its every performance.

Encountering the narrative as a mystical-political testimony

It remains for me to describe my engagement with Menchú's account of her brother's and mother's deaths, accounts that I found draw heavily on biblical images of the Suffering Servant, the Passion Narratives, and the Second Book of Maccabees. Menchú thereby joins her people to generations of faithful martyrs who have gone before. She begins the horrible story of her brother's torture and death by noting the date, 1979, setting the demise of Petrocinio, a catechist and political organizer, squarely in a period when the clash between the military-backed land developers and indigenous resistance fighters caused the army to react "in such a way that confrontations, killings, torture, and massacres [became] part of a generalized social experience."[23] Rigoberta places her brother's suffering and death not only in the context of

[23] Marc Zimmerman, "Testimonio in Guatemala: Payeras, Rigoberta, and Beyond," *Latin American Perspectives* 18:4 (1991): 22-47, at 29.

a large group of rebels whom the army had rounded up for public execution, not only in the context of events that led to more than a million Guatemalan Indians fleeing or being displaced from their homes by the mid-1980s, but also in the context of biblical faith and narrative, centered around the crucified Christ.

In explaining the origins of her brother's demise Menchú recounts a Judas-like betrayer: "a *compañero*, a person who'd always collaborated and who had been in agreement with us. But, they offered him fifteen *quetzals* - that's to say fifteen dollars - to turn my brother in, and so he did."[24] The army seizes Petrocinio as he is walking with a girl. They bind his hands and drive him with kicks "over rough ground where there were stones," and Rigoberta states, "My brother fell, he couldn't protect his face. The first part of him to begin to bleed was his face."[25] The testimony thus rings of the imagery of the Stations of the Cross, with the Christ-figure falling repeatedly, his face in need of Veronica's cloth. Rigoberta (without explanation) introduces the girl's mother at her side, such that the two women follow along as witnesses, not unlike the women in the Passion Narratives (Mark 14:40-41; Luke 23:27,55; John 19:25): "They were risking their lives by following my brother and finding out where he was being taken."[26] The military men berate the women with propaganda that amounts to a sort of trial of Petrocinio for the women's benefit, telling the women that as a communist and subversive he deserved to die, phrases reminiscent of words spoken against Jesus in his trials before the Sannhedrin and Pilate.

As Rigoberta turns to the details of Petrocinio's torturous execution, she echoes passages of the Suffering Servant poems of Deutero-Isaiah. "It's an unbelievable story"[27] (Isa. 53:1: "Who has believed what we have heard?"). "When they'd done with him, he didn't look like a person any more. His whole face was disfigured with beating, from striking against the stones, the tree trunks"[28] (Isa. 52:14: "Just as there were many who were astonished at him - so marred was his appearance, beyond that of mortals"). This soliloquy-like plaint initiates Menchú's pages-long description of the army's interrogation and unthinkable series of tortures inflicted on the body of her brother and numerous other people, several of whom her brother, she says, recognized as "catechists … who'd been kidnapped from other villages and were suffering as badly as he was."[29] The army demands to know why Petrocinio carries a Bible, why priests and nuns are subversives, whether the

---

[24] *I, Rigoberta Menchú: An Indian Woman in Guatemala*, ed. and intro. Elizabeth Burgos-Debray (New York: Verso Books, 1984), 173.

[25] *I, Rigoberta Menchú*, 173.

[26] *I, Rigoberta Menchú*, Consider the resonance with John 20:13, Mary of Magdala at the tomb: "[The angels] said to her, 'Woman, why are you weeping?' She said to them, 'They have taken away my Lord, and I do not know where they have laid him.'"

[27] *I, Rigoberta Menchú*, 173.

[28] *I, Rigoberta Menchú*, 173.

[29] *I, Rigoberta Menchú*, 174.

"whole community" is related to the guerrillas. Later, in the final scene of public execution, the commanding officer declares the prisoners subversives, Cubans, and communists (Isa. 53:12b: "[he] was numbered with the transgressors"). The body of Menchú's account of her brother's ordeal functions as a testimony to the persecution of the Christian base communities in Guatemala, a movement that, in the language of liberation theologians is a praxis of mysticism and politics that identifies the members with the suffering Christ.

The account is framed by a closing scene that once again proves an extended meditation informed by Christian scripture and tradition. Once the victims have been burned to death before the forcibly assembled, terrified populace, the people move forward to take possession of the bodies. The cowardly army recedes. Rigoberta meditates on her mother's suffering with an image inspired by the tradition of the *pieta*, as well as the thirteenth Station of the Cross: "My mother was half dead with grief. She embraced her son, she spoke to him, dead and tortured as he was. She kissed him and everything, though he was burnt." Rigoberta does not neglect the role of the assembly, the faithful community: "I said to her: 'Come, let's go home.' We couldn't bear to watch, we could not bear to keep looking at the dead. ... So we had to go, to leave it all behind and leave off looking."[30] One is reminded of Luke 23:48: "And when all the crowds who had gathered there for this spectacle saw what had taken place, they returned home, beating their breasts." As in the Passion Narratives, the forces of nature likewise give a dark response to the cosmic-historic disaster (Matt. 27:45,51; Mk. 15:33; Lk. 23:44-45): "And it started to rain; it rained heavily."[31]

The ensuing chapters of the book are about the deaths of Rigoberta's father during the revolutionaries' siege of the Spanish embassy in Guatemala City, and of her mother, whom the army kidnapped in 1980. The account of her mother's death I find highly reminiscent of the martyrdom of the mother and seven sons in 2 Maccabees 7. Like the faithful, courageous Jewish woman in the biblical story, Rigoberta's mother has also first been made to witness the deaths of at least two sons, and her own death is as terrible as their fates. After repeatedly raping her the army "shaved her head," tried to coerce a confession and denunciation of the movement from her, "cut off her ears ... cut her whole body bit by bit," and so on.[32] The ordering of bodily mutilation is likewise the king's response to the seven sons' refusals to denounce their Jewish practices (see 2 Macc. 7:4, 5,7). After desecrating Rigoberta's mother's corpse, the army "left a permanent sentry there to guard her body so that no-one could take it away, not even what was left of

---

[30] *I, Rigoberta Menchú*, 180.
[31] *I, Rigoberta Menchú*, 180.
[32] *I, Rigoberta Menchú*, 198.

it"[33] - an image that evokes the political-religious conspirators' concern about the body of the dead Jesus in the Passion Narratives. Might Menchú intend the reader's association of her mother with the crucified Christ? She closes the chapter by reporting that dogs feed on the corpse. It was left there in the elements for months until it utterly disintegrated, was totally gone. One can hear in this conclusion the johannine women's distress over the disappearance of Jesus' corpse. Menchú's description of the scavenging dogs will return later when I discuss current scholarship on the Passion Narratives.

The ethical imperative of reading

The solitary reading of any text, whether aloud or in silence, is itself an act of performance. My act of reading *I, Rigoberta Menchú*, while solitary, was not in isolation from an array of historical "communities": Guatemalan indigenous peoples, Christian base communities, the Lithuanians, French, and all who had endured, died in, and lived beyond World War II, people behind the Iron Curtain, generations of Western believers celebrating requiem masses, and American undergraduate students with whom I would soon engage the Menchú book. I read, moreover, in the company of Jewish biblical martyrs (those of the Maccabeean and Jesus movements) and, most significantly, the Suffering Servant figure of Christ, as portrayed in Deutero-Isaiah and the Passion Narratives. Reading a text of terror requires, it would seem, a multi-faceted performance, a recourse to art and image, poetry and music, prayer and worship, scripture and tradition, just as these resources were (and are) essential to the one who produced the text herself. In Gadamerian and Ricoeurian terms, the world the reader creates in front of the text can only come about by engaging the world within, behind, and even ahead of it.

The introduction of hermeneutical theory, however, points to ethical issues of reading, issues concerning valid readings, that one simply cannot avoid. Was my reading of *I, Rigoberta Menchú* - a reading I would describe as a prayerful, paradoxically consoling, if not a quasi-liturgical experience - valid? To what end? Or in drawing upon such an array of historical figures, religious-musical resources, and biblical imagery - with the redemptive suffering figure of Christ pervading them all - had I subverted the power of the *testimonio* by ameliorating the startling alterity of the marginalized woman and people who would want to "speak" to me? How does my reading of this text function both mystically and politically? How do those two categories relate within the performance of reading itself and in relation to other practices, both political and mystical, by me as a first-world Christian? And, specifically, what is the relationship between my performance of reading *I,*

[33] *I, Rigoberta Menchú*, 199.

Rigoberta Menchú and my participation in the church's liturgy? In raising these issues I need first to report further some of the North American scholarship about testimonial literature so as, then, to proffer my own analysis of the role of such textual and liturgical performances in the life of a mystically-politically committed faith.

How to Read Testimonio: Scholarly Debate and Theological Response
Scholarly Debate

Although from the time of its initial publication the subject of much lively - and highly sympathetic - scholarly debate in scores of conference papers, scholarly articles, book chapters, and dissertations, *I, Rigoberta Menchú's* controversial character reached its greatest notoriety in late 1998 when the *New York Times* published a cover story, "Nobel Winner Finds Her Story Challenged," along with the subtitle, "Tarnished Laureate." Picking up on U.S. anthropologist David Stoll's book-length study which led him to conclude that Menchú's book "cannot be the eyewitness account it purports to be,"[34] the *Times* sent its own investigative reporters to interview people in Guatemala who would, in the newspaper's estimation, be in a position to judge the veracity of Menchú's narrative. Not surprisingly, the *Chronicle of Higher Education* picked up on the controversy within weeks, with articles, essays, and letters to the editor on the topic appearing well into 1999. Highlighted was the evidence that Menchú must have fabricated several of the key experiences and episodes of her narrative: her working as a child on the oppressively exploitative coffee plantations, her lack of any formal education and only recent acquisition of Spanish, the nature of the land dispute unsettling her people and, most notably for this present paper, the detailed account of Petrocinio's public execution.

Scholars had from the start acknowledged and discussed the genre of Menchú's narrative as *testimonio* in terms of her speaking in the first person *singular* as witness to a reality she shared in the first person *plural*.[35] Repeatedly noting how in the opening lines of the book Menchú declares her story to be not merely about herself but her entire people,[36] academicians have enjoyed extended inquiries and debates into how the *testimonio* amounts to an original form of literature, breaking the paternalistic, heroic,

[34] Larry Rohter, "Nobel Winner Finds Her Story Challenged," *New York Times*, 15 December 1998, A1.
[35] "[T]he *testimonialista* gives his or her personal testimony 'directly,' addressing a specific interlocutor. ... The speaker does not speak for or represent a community but rather performs an act of identity-formation which is simultaneously personal and collective." George Yúdice, "*Testimonio* and Postmodernism," *Latin American Perspectives* 18 (1991): 15-31, at 15.
[36] "My name is Rigoberta Menchú. I am twenty-three years old. This is my testimony. I didn't learn it from a book and I didn't learn it alone. I'd like to stress that it's not only *my* life, it's also the testimony of my people." *I, Rigoberta Menchú*, 1.

hegemonic genres of the Western autobiography and historic novel.[37] In the dozen years of this scholarship prior to the internationally publicized charge against Menchú's personal moral character,[38] various analysts acknowledged and discussed the ways in which Rigoberta's narrative synthesized a range of her people's experiences much wider than her own individual or personal ones (to use utterly modern, if not postmodern Western academic categories). This very quality of her text contributed to its cause for study as an original political-literary form.

The key to the uproar over the *Times* and *Chronicle* stories and, by association, Stoll's book was how they amounted to charging Menchú with being a flat-out liar, with the *Times* article taking little to no account of the years of scholarly analysis concerning *testimonio*'s obviously strong political, persuasive intent. A little over a month after the *Times* article broke Menchú acknowledged to the press that her portrayals of her family members' deaths were not based on her witnessing them with her own eyes and that she had more education than she depicted in her testimonial. She nonetheless remained unapologetic, the *Times* reported, for the "truth" about the injustice and oppression her people suffer, a truth she sought to bring to a world audience.[39] At the end of that *New York Times* article Stoll claimed he never intended to accuse Menchú of lying.[40] Some professors view Stoll's work, beginning with his dissertation at Stanford, as providing a correction to Northern academicians' uncritical reading of texts in support of leftist revolutionary movements in Latin America.[41] Others hold a darker opinion of Stoll's intentions. One article in a magazine published by Duke University Press claims that Stoll announced the publication of his *Rigoberta Menchú and the Story of Poor Guatemalans* "by stating that the 'liar' Rigoberta Menchú would finally be unmasked."[42] Another voice in the Northern academic minority has been Denish D'Souza who, while on the faculty of Stanford, denounced the Menchú book as part of the university's multicultural

[37] See Yúdice, "*Testimonio*,"16-18, 27.

[38] Indeed, the *New York Times* contacted the director of the Norwegian Nobel Institute, asking whether the Institute planned to revoke Menchú's 1992 Nobel Prize. See Rohter, A10.

[39] "Ms. Menchú said today that the central reality for her was that her father, mother and at least two brothers were all murdered by Government security forces during the ferocious violence that descended on Guatemala's Indian communities in the years before her book was published - all facts that have not been disputed. 'I didn't find anything in these reports that changes the fact that my people are dead,' Ms. Menchú said. 'And that is my truth.'" Julia Preston, "Guatemala Laureate Defense 'My Truth,'" *New York Times*, 21 January 1999, A8.

[40] "'That would be to dismiss her morally, and that is definitely not my view,' [Stoll] said. 'You can understand and defend her narrative strategy, of folding others' experience into her own, making herself into a kind of all-purpose Maya. She was in an emergency situation. She was trying to bring down pressure on the Government and the army. To do that, you have to make a complicated situation seem simple.'" Preston, A8.

[41] See "'Historical Truth' vs. 'Narrative Truth' in Rigoberta Menchú's Autobiography," Letters to the Editor, *The Chronicle of Higher Education*, 12 February 1999.

[42] Dante Liano, "I, Rigoberta Menchú? The Controversy Surrounding the Mayan Activist," *Hopscotch* 1 (1999): 96-101, 98.

general-education curriculum. Now a research scholar at the American Enterprise Institute, D'Souza has continued to criticize the academic value of the book, notably using a metaphor from Christian tradition to condemn its social-political purpose: "Rigoberta is a modern Saint Sebastian, pierced by the arrows of North American white male cruelty; thus her life story becomes an explicit indictment of the historical role of the West and Western institutions."[43]

The views of those both negatively and positively critical of Rigoberta Menchú's *testimonio* certainly provide evidence for the narrative's power to elicit a political, social-ethical response from its Northern readers. Indeed, among the vast majority of scholars who write supportively of the book a major topic of concern is the nature or type of truth this textual genre conveys. A survey of letters to the editor in the *Chronicle of Higher Education* in the wake of that journal's and the *New York Time's* explosive 1998-1999 articles, as well as scholarly articles written since then,[44] yields the following pairs of opposed categories: literal truths versus larger truths, fact versus fiction, collective memory versus history, narrative versus legal testimony, narrative truths versus historical truths, strict veracity (of modern autobiographies) versus embroidered facts (of testimonials). The authors of the essays in which these dialectics function must take a moral/ethical position on the social-political conditions in Menchú's native Guatemala and perhaps, by extension, on those of the entire Third World. A scholar's position in this regard carries, as well, one's judgment concerning the social and political positions of the citizenry and government of the United States. Issues of class and gender and, dare I say, religious commitment come into play. In a word, the debates over the veracity of Menchú's *testimonio* shed as much light on the ethical thought-world of us academicians as on Rigoberta herself, leaving open the question of our ability to allow her and her people genuinely to confront us, as well as our ability to join them in a ethically viable solidarity. If the genre of *testimonio* is what marginalized, oppressed peoples need in order to elicit help from those who enjoy, even take for granted, the quotidian privileges and powers they experience as rights on the basis of their economic and political locations, then must not we who read such texts, while doing so critically, not maintain a position of respect for the strategies their narrators find essential to conveying the "truth" of their situations?

Doris Sommer, a professor of Latin American literature at Harvard, in a 1995 essay explores Rigoberta's repeated assertions that she is withholding much information from the reader, her interlocutor, out of respect for the

---

[43] "Nobel Peace Prize Winner Has Other Claim to Fame," *The Chronicle of Higher Education*, 28 October 1992. See also, Wilson.

[44] See especially, Patrick Smith, "Memory without History: Who Owns Guatemala's Past?", *The Washington Quarterly* 24 (2000): 59-72.

Mayan people's traditions and, Sommer seems to judge, as a strategy to elicit sympathy and support. Elucidating at length the ethical quandary generated for the reader by the secretive-disclosive tension in Menchú's narrative, Sommer arrives at this quandary:

> Do I continue to think about testimonials as a subgenre of the autobiography, and so to take their strategic coyness as a permissible departure from the familiar genre; or does the departure constitute a generic and political difference? Evidently this presents another moment of tension between *can* and *should*. At what political and aesthetic price might I favor one generic category rather than highlight the nagging lack of fit? Does the difference boil down to an ethical imperative? Should I defend the difference as an extension of Rigoberta's own cultural self-defense, even in the face of an apparent overlap with a familiar form? Again, the question finally may be undecidable outside of tactical concerns. Some readers will prefer to project themselves in familiarly heroic autobiographical terms through this apparently available text; and others will take note of its warnings against appropriation.[45]

While Sommer makes an important contribution to the ethical inquiry into the academician's reading of this testimonial, she seems to privilege Rigoberta's Mayan tradition as the sole authentic cultural source of Rigoberta's alterity or "difference" from North American academia. I would argue, however, that this is to neglect another fundamental social-cultural source for Rigoberta's ethical strategy in narration, namely, biblical Christian tradition.

[45] Doris Sommer, "No Secrets," in *The Real Thing: Testimonial Discourse and Latin America*, ed. Georg M. Gugelberger (Durham: Duke University Press, 1996), 132-157, at 148-149.

Theological response

I find Menchú's narrations of her brother's and mother's protracted, torturous deaths anything but coy, not only in terms of the excruciating detail with which she describes their terrors but also the (to me) obviously open use she makes of biblical imagery and texts to persuade the reader - at least the Christian reader as a subset of potential Northern sympathizers - to join in solidarity with her people's cause. I must confess to finding Sommer inordinately skeptical or even jaded about the role of Christian faith in Rigoberta Menchú's life and, thus, its role in Rigoberta's political strategies. Sommer discusses Rigoberta's Christianity as one of several strategies for forming revolutionary alliances, a matter of Rigoberta's rejecting institutionally committed, conservative Catholic priests and nuns while, "careful to keep opportunities open,"[46] providing a positive description of "some" nuns and priests who converted to the cause of the oppressed. I assume that the opportunities Sommer implies here consist of supportive liberal Christians to the North. Sommer never acknowledges Rigoberta's repeated self-identification as a catechist, nor her application of that title to her martyred brother. Could Sommer's seemingly jaded estimation of Menchú's appropriation of Christianity as one among "multiple unorthodoxies"[47] for her testimonial discourse contribute to Sommer's utter ignoring of Rigoberta's use of Christian scripture and tradition as crucial sources not only in her narrative-textual strategy but for her very life itself?

The ethical burden of Sommer's laudable argument - that Menchú's textual secrets prohibit any easy identification of the Northern academician with the Mayan woman and her people - need not be defeated by the Christian reader's identifying with Rigoberta's mystical meditation upon the agonies of her tortured and executed people. Finding myself so deeply moved by the stories Rigoberta crafts by means of biblical symbolism and texts, I do not thereby immediately, facilely identify with her or the victims. I do not intimately whisper back to her, "I know exactly what you mean. I feel the same pain." I do not, I cannot because the very nature of biblical faith in Christ, of traditional faith in the paschal mystery, of faith in the historical-political event of his torture and execution as the revelation of God's identification with all victims prohibits it. To participate in the church's liturgy is to know that the totality of identification with and, thereby, the redemption of all human suffering resides and comes forth only from the God of Jesus Christ in the power of their Spirit. We know, as we go to the liturgy as the summit of our lived praxis of faith and from it as the source for our continued following of the Servant Christ, that of the fullness of that redemption "seated at the right hand of God" humanity still only partakes some small share,

---

[46] Sommer, "No Secrets," 154.
[47] Sommer, "No Secrets," 154.

revealed in the pieces of the one loaf repeatedly broken, the one cup poured out. To be baptized into Christ's death is to join in the divine-human project of Christ that is not yet completed in history - be it the broken, sinful history of any one of our lives or that of all the world - but which nonetheless is experientially known in ethical and liturgical moments of solidarity in suffering.[48]

Drawing appreciatively on Sommer's work as a literary theorist, one can say that the Christian identification with victims of oppression and sin is one of metonymy, of identification-through-relationship.[49] This is a tricky point, for Sommer opposes metonymy to autobiography, by which she means the heroic substitution of one for all others, an identification-through-substitution for which she considers Christ to be a prime example. The Christ of biblical-liturgical faith, however, does not simply represent and totally sublimate all human suffering but, rather, is now a life-giving Spirit[50] animating a body with many members, none of whom, as St. Paul teaches, can presume to dispense with the others, especially others in their concrete, historical suffering. Yet Sommer is right in pointing toward the totalizing way in which Christianity has so often, in its institutions (including the sacraments) and its leaders and the faithful, used the figure of Christ, even the corpus on the crucifix, as an evasion of social-ethical praxis. I conclude, then, with a brief consideration of the Christian tradition concerning Jesus' death, especially to argue how current biblical scholarship on the Passion Narratives promises new support for the mystical-political role of these narratives in the lives of contemporary believers.

Witnessing to Jesus' Execution: Redemptive Solidarity in Suffering

Anyone acquainted with the scholarly, ecclesial, and pastoral debates repeatedly sparked by modern biblical scholarship for more than a century has most likely recognized in my rehearsal of the controversy surrounding Menchú's *testimonio* issues concerning Scripture as well: questions of historical fact, narrative integrity, collective identity, the literary nature of realism, representation, symbol and myth. Pervading all these issues, whether concerning the Bible or contemporary testimonials, is the question of truth itself, a problem that can only be entertained and discussed by differing parties if they recognize that the very notion of truth bears with it some form of commitment. As Metz has so rightly pointed out, Marx's observation con-

---

[48] "For the sacraments are anticipatory, mediating signs of salvation, that is, healed and reconciled life. And given our historical situation, at the same time they are symbols of protest serving to unmask the life that is not yet reconciled in the specific dimension of our history." Edward Schillebeeckx, *Christ: The Experience of Jesus as Lord*, trans. John Bowden (New York: Crossroad Publishing, 1981), 836.

[49] Sommer, "No Secrets," 146.

[50] See 1 Cor. 15:45.

cerning knowledge's dependent relationship upon interest constitutes an important epistemological contribution to the question of truth, even as the new political theology rejects any reduction of truth to mere relevance.[51] The contextual reality of truth-as-commitment animates current Catholic biblical scholars' disagreements over the direction they think their discipline should take. This is no less the case in reading *I, Rigoberta Menchú*. The debate over the veracity of the text sheds as much light on the readers, on the world in front of the text, on the political world of North American scholarship, as it does on Menchú's motives and narrative strategies.

The reader of the text must always ask: What do I want to hear in this story? Why do I want to hear this story? What am I listening for? Such questions always need Sommer's insistence (drawing from but going beyond postmodern methodology) that difference genuinely be respected, that in reading the Other we not seek a self-serving intimacy, resulting in the failure to "distinguish doing good from feeling good."[52] To seek honestly some measure of truth in the reading of the text - whether Rigoberta's or the gospels' narratives of terror - requires a conscious articulation of the reader's desires so that both positive and negative intentions can be acknowledged, so that ethical imperative not be distorted, let alone avoided.

What disposes me to hear the story? Why do I want to listen to what Rigoberta has to tell? The ethical imperative of that question motivated my writing the political-liturgical prolegomenon to this essay. I desire to meet the God of Jesus in the mystery of suffering. I do so politically and ethically with the paschal mystery as source and summit[53] of the quest - a liturgically animated approach to the Christian quest for truth Metz has articulated, namely, the biblically traditional association of truth with an interest in universal justice, justice for the living and the dead.[54] For this reason, I believe, I was especially drawn into hearing perhaps the most controversial of episodes for those who question, if not reject, the veracity of Menchú's book, namely, the terrifying chapter recounting her brother Petrocinio's torture and execution. Although memory can always be deceiving, I am confident in my recollection that as I read that chapter for the first time I quickly found Rigoberta to be fashioning the story as a passion narrative, as a performance in which she could grapple with the horror and unspeakable loss of her brother by proclaiming the events of his cruel demise as the revelation empowering solidarity for a people on a mission. Without attending here to details, I can report that as I first read the chapter I was well aware that the sequence of events was disjointed, as was her own placement as witness to them throughout. I recognized that she was constructing a narrative drawing

---

[51] See Metz, *A Passion for God*, 35-36.
[52] Sommer, "No Secrets," 140.
[53] See *Sacrosanctum concilium*, no. 10.
[54] See Metz, *A Passion for God*, 35-36.

upon multiple images from Christian scripture and tradition, and was doing so, it seemed (and still seems) to me in order both to find the wherewithal to stay with the terror of the event and to share it with the Christian reader/interlocutor in a way that would elicit one's sympathy with the cause of her people. Indeed, literary theorist Georg Yúdice argues that, just as participants in the Christian base communities reinterpret and apply the Bible to their lives, "testimonial writing also emphasizes a rereading of culture as lived history and a profession of faith in the struggles of the oppressed. ... [Menchú] clearly conceives of her testimonial as a kind of gospel ... ."[55] Marc Zimmerman, another Latin Americanist, avers, "[Rigober-ta's] testimonio is like that of one who is going to die, one uttered as a last will and testament to a ceremony-respecting community ... The testimonio is a sacred, ceremonial act."[56]

The key textual factor that not only sustained my reading of the Petrocinio chapter but nurtured my desire for solidarity with Rigoberta and her people was its affinity with the biblical, traditional and ritualized images of Christ's passion, images repeatedly encountered through the readings and euchology of Holy Week, the musical heritage of not only church hymnody and chant but also classical compositions of oratorio and requiem, and contemplative reading of the gospels in the tradition of Ignatius Loyola's Spiritual Exercises. My reading of Menchú's book has, in turn, "wounded" (Metz's phrase[57]) the politically uncritical ideas I had largely assumed about that repertoire of mystical symbolism, reorienting how I read the biblical Passion Narratives so as to try to understand how they function redemptively for people today. It has likewise piqued my interest in current methodological debates over viable objectives for scripture scholarship, the latest quest for the historical Jesus, and implications of historical-critical scholarship for the ecclesial reading of the gospels.[58] The question of greatest interest to me concerns the extent to which the Passion Narratives are literary constructions interpreting Jesus' death in terms of Jewish biblical traditions, that is, "prophesy historicized," and to what extent they recount events that actually historically occurred. This should be of little surprise, since it so directly parallels the controversy over Menchú's account of her brother's death (as well as other parts of her book).

One biblical scholar who has constructed a complex methodology and welter of research to argue his case for why and how Jesus died is John Dominic Crossan. His work is widely noted, not only because of his associa-

---

[55] Yúdice, "*Testimonio*," 26-27.

[56] Zimmerman, 32-33. For discussion of biblical testamentary tradition in relation to cultic tradition in the Last Supper accounts of the New Testament, see Xavier Léon-Dufour, S.J., *Sharing the Eucharistic Bread: The Witness of the New Testament* (New York: Paulist Press, 1987), 85-95, 243-247.

[57] Metz, *A Passion for God*, 2.

[58] See, among others, N. T. Wright, *Jesus and the Victory of God* (Minneapolis: Fortress Press, 1996), 1-124.

tion with the media-hyped Jesus Seminar but also due to his academic peers' taking him seriously. Anything approximating a detailed rehearsal of Crossan's research and theoretical arguments about the death of Jesus and the Passion Narratives is beyond the scope of this present chapter. A succinct summary of his position, in his own words, can suffice for my present purpose:

> My best historical reconstruction of what actually happened is that Jesus was arrested during the Passover festival and those closest to him fled for their own safety. I do not presume at all any high-level consultations between Caiaphas and Pilate about or with Jesus. They would no doubt have agreed before such a festival that fast and immediate action was to be taken against any disturbance and that some examples by crucifixion might be especially useful at the start. I doubt very much if Jewish police and Roman soldiery needed to go too far up the chain of command in handling a Galilean peasant like Jesus. It is hard for us, I repeat, to bring our imagination down low enough to see the casual brutality with which he was probably taken and executed. The details in our gospels are, in any case, *prophecy historicized* and not *history remembered.*[59]

What makes me so sympathetic to Crossan's theory, as well as that of Paula Fredriksen's work in this area,[60] is my own opinion, slowly developed over many years, that the dramatic proportions and details of the Passion Narratives simply cannot be squared with the abrupt and summary way in which brutal police states and occupying military authorities deal with dissidents, peasants (whether actively rebellious or among the masses caught in the middle of conflict), and outright revolutionaries. All of Pilate's agonizing over Jesus contradicts every piece of historical evidence about his character, to name but one key example. To name one other: Scripture scholars across a wide spectrum have long recognized in Barabbas a historically untenable scenario that, nonetheless, functions in a highly symbolic fashion. Then there is the ongoing historical inquiry into just what sort of Jewish authorities there were in both Galilee and Jerusalem, how they functioned in relation to their own people and to the Roman government. These issues, far from threatening my faith in Jesus' divine mission, let alone his identity, unsettle whatever perceptions of dignity or exceptional treatment (whether kind or cruel) I might want to find in his Passion. Discarding these, I find myself all the more moved, beyond reason or discourse, by the utterly gracious mercy of God in kenotically identifying with the most deeply despised and horrifically cut down. It is, indeed, "hard for us … to bring our imagination down low enough to see the casual brutality" of Jesus' abduction and

[59] John Dominic Crossan, *Jesus: A Revolutionary Biography* (San Francisco: HarperCollins, 1994), 152.
[60] See Paula Fredriksen, *Jesus of Nazareth, King of the Jews* (New York: Knopf, 2000), 232-234.

execution, but it is also essential to our faith. This is faith in the kenotic Christ.

Such historical awareness, then, does not lead to my dismissing the Passion Narratives. Far from it! Like Rigoberta, who could only grapple with the historical abduction and evidently typical, brutal, routine execution of her brother by enlisting the whole range of biblical and traditional symbols and narratives at her disposal, I enter into the reading of the Passion Narratives - whether individually in prayer or corporately amidst the liturgical assembly - as a mystical performance, a much needed mystical practice. How can she or any of us, albeit in genuinely different social-political locations, cope with the terror of evil, of human injustice and sin, but by means of some sort of faith, religious or otherwise, that keeps a person or a people hopefully committed to some truth? Belief in the divine mission of the wounded body of Christ sustains such a commitment, as Metz has written: "It is precisely because Christians believe in an eschatological meaning for history that they can risk historical consciousness: looking into the abyss."[61] The commitment intrinsically bears an ethical imperative and, in this age, political involvement. Telling and hearing passion narratives, texts of terror proclaiming divine redemption even in the painful struggle for human justice, is an at once mystical and ethical-political action.

For Rigoberta and myself faith and truth reside in Christian tradition, even as she and I and all believers across time and space draw upon biblical and other sources in distinctive but mystically bound praxes of following Jesus. The mystical binding is the Holy Spirit. A detailed discussion of the singular importance of pneumatology for today's Church and the mission of all believers is, again, beyond the scope of this essay. My point here is that the Spirit of the executed-and-risen Christ inspired Christian communities in the earliest decades to draw upon the resources of Jewish biblical tradition to construct narratives of his torture and execution that enabled them to know that God was with Jesus through it all[62] and beyond. The beyond, of course, is their life of following Christ in suffering and service, in the power of the Holy Spirit. It is, of course, our life today as well, whether in Guatemala or the United States, but always in solidarity with all of suffering humanity.[63]

With Crossan and Rigoberta we must not avoid the startling reality of the suffering even as we need to do so accompanied by all the textual, musical, and other resources of tradition at our disposal. When Crossan turns to see what finally happened to Jesus, he contemplates and then develops the following:

---

[61] Metz, *A Passion for God*, 40.

[62] While the Marcan Jesus' cry from the cross depicts his feeling of abandonment by God (15:34), still I would argue that Jesus' every breath 'til his last (15:37) is the presence and action of the Spirit of God that uniquely took possession of him from his baptism (Mk. 1:10).

[63] A book - at once scholarly and spiritual - that has inspired me in this regard is William Reiser's *Jesus in Solidarity with His People: A Theologian Looks at Mark* (Collegeville: The Liturgical Press, 2000).

> What actually historically happened to the body of Jesus can best be judged from watching how later Christian accounts slowly but steadily increased the reverential dignity of their burial accounts. But what was there at the beginning that necessitated such an intensive volume of apologetic insistence? If the Romans did not observe the Deuteronomic decree, Jesus' dead body would have been left on the cross for the wild beasts. And his followers, who had fled, would know that. If the Romans did observe the decree the soldiers would have made certain Jesus was dead and then buried him themselves [in a hasty, shallow grave] as part of their job. In either case, the dogs were waiting. And his followers, who had fled, would know that, too.[64]

The dogs at the foot of the cross: It is this governing image for Crossan's theory about the demise of Jesus and his body that Luke Timothy Johnson, one of Crossan's most energetic critics, considers an "odd insistence," one indicative of the insignificance of Jesus' death, as well as the irrelevance of institutional Christianity, this type of methodology propounds.[65] But I read Crossan in a different way here, finding a far more ethically challenging and life-provoking Jesus *for the Church* here. To embrace Crossan's reading of Jesus' death does not necessarily require a rejection of faith in God's having raised him up to be a life-giving Spirit (1 Cor. 15:45). Quite the opposite. To realize that the Son of God shared the fate of millions of forgotten victims summarily disposed of in the shallow graves of history is not to cast aside faith in Christ the Savior but, rather, to deepen our longing for him.

What we need today are readings, liturgical and otherwise, that bespeak the sheer incomprehensibility of the scope and depth of human suffering and the ongoing desire for God to meet us therein. This is a religion, to echo Metz, much more of questions than ready answers, but one not lost or without direction. It is a praxis of faith requiring theology to rely increasingly on "the supposedly weak categories of memory and narrative," thinking less in "systems concepts" and more in "subject concepts."[66] We question and search in a world revealed by baptismal faith, caught in the ongoing tension of the already-not yet revelation of salvation in Christ. Far from aimless and lacking direction, we have Scripture as the primary resource for forging the always-needed prophetic vision for the given age. But this is just another way of saying that we are responsible for tradition's being a living tradition, a tradition for the life of the world. In his later writings, Metz repeatedly utters the apocalyptic cry, "What is God waiting for?"[67] The mystical-political reading of the texts of terror turns the question back on us: What are

---

[64] Crossan, *Jesus*, 154.
[65] See Luke Timothy Johnson, *The Real Jesus*: The Misguided Quest for the Historical Jesus and the Truth of the Traditional Gospels (San Francisco: HarperCollins, 1996), 46- 48.
[66] Metz, *A Passion for God*, 3, 40.
[67] Metz, *A Passion for God*, 57-58, 63-69.

we waiting for? Why would we not seek the Christ who promises to meet us now in the suffering humanity catalogued in Matthew 25?[68] As the sole or even primary motive, the fear of final judgment has, we must admit, proven largely ineffective. We go to meet him, rather, in the suffering of our world so that we might go to meet him, the Bridegroom, who comes to us each Sunday in the Eucharist.[69] We live a mystical-political praxis in anticipation of celebrating with him and all victims of history at the heavenly wedding banquet.

---

[68] See Metz, *Followers of Christ*, 79.

[69] As Metz has astutely noted, the urgency that solidarity with the suffering, living and dead, brings to the Christian sense of time does not engender apocalyptic terror but, rather, finds sustenance when the Eucharist, as narrative remembrance of the crucified Christ "… until you come again in glory," is celebrated as a "feast of expectation." *A Passion for God*, 85. It is for precisely this reason, I believe, that the recovery of the eschatological dimension of Christian worship constitutes the most important agenda for liturgical theology today. See my *Anamnesis as Dangerous Memory*, 62-72, 92-122, 189-205. See also, Bruce T. Morrill, "The Beginning of the End: Eschatology in the Liturgical Year and Lectionary," *Liturgical Ministry* 12 (Spring, 2003): 65-74.

KNOWING CHRIST CRUCIFIED: DARK WISDOM FROM THE SLAVES

M. Shawn Copeland

> *For the word of the cross is folly to those who are perishing, but to us who are being saved it is the power of God . ... Christ the power of God and the wisdom of God* (I Corinthians 1:18).

> *How Jesus' blood for your redemption flows. See him with hands outstretcht upon the cross; Immense compassion in his bosom glows' / He hears revilers, nor resents their scorn: What matchless mercy in the Son of God! (Phillis Wheatley)*

> *The cross we bear precedes the crown we wear. To be a Christian one must take up his [or her] cross, with all of its difficulties and agonizing and tension-packed content and carry it until that very cross leaves its marks upon us and redeems us to that more excellent way which comes only through suffering. (Martin Luther King, Jr.)*

The saving word of the cross of Jesus of Nazareth stretches across the centuries and cultures to fall graciously upon the oppression and suffering of African peoples enslaved in the United States of America and their descendants - beginning with a letter written by the apostle Paul to believers in Corinth to a poem by Phillis Wheatley, the first published poet of African descent on the North American continent, to the twentieth century theologian, pastor, and civil rights activist the Reverend Dr. Martin Luther King, Jr. For more than five hundred years, the story of Jesus of Nazareth, his life, ministry, and crucifixion has formed a crucial motif in the religious lives of African-derived peoples. In the thick of slavery, lynching, segregation, and discrimination, thousands of African Americans - bond and free - fixed their eyes on the cross of Jesus as they puzzled their existence and reasons for such malicious oppression, as they pondered the agony and suffering that filled daily life, as they walked in faith and not by sight.

The enslaved peoples came to embrace the rabbi from Nazareth as one of themselves, for the cruelty of his suffering was so very much like their own. They came to know Jesus as a *friend* with whom they might share their secrets, a *savior* to whom they could entrust their hopes of freedom, a *companion* with whom they might walk through slavery's deep shadow, a *healer* who could make the wounded whole, a *fellow-sufferer* who knew in his body the sting of the lash, who had endured what was their daily portion. Bloodied and nailed to rough wooden planks, Jesus was the One who went *all the way with them and for them*. Jesus was their 'all in all,' their joy, their 'Rose of Sharon'; there was no human condition he could not meet. These women and men met Jesus' compassion with compassion, his care with care. They fell in love with him and in the paradox and promise of Jesus' life, they found their own. A compelling image of this experience is offered by an emancipated slave who said that Jesus "hooked [them] in the heart."[1]

Several contemporary African American theologians including William Jones, Delores Williams, and Anthony Pinn[2] have questioned the preeminence of the cross as an appropriately liberating model for a despised people. For these theologians, the weight of protracted black social oppression and suffering forms a 'stumbling block' for the meaning of the cross of Jesus. Quite rightly, they have exposed the totalizing impact of a *subjugating theology of the cross*, that is, a theology that tutors oppressed people to an *imitatio Christi* that violates incarnate spirit, that subjugates intellect and will, desecrates body and heart. Indeed, given more than five hundred years of chattel slavery, rape, torture, murder, lynching, and extended public abuse of black human 'others,' what might an African American theology say about the cross of Jesus of Nazareth? How can such a theology affirm the Christian God as a God of love, compassion, justice, and mercy? How can this theology operate as if the goodness of God toward *all* humankind stood as unassailable theological axiom?

In serious interrogation of "human suffering as an organizing principle for life options," these theologians conclude that black women and men should consider the totality of their communal historic experience of public suffering in light of a black humanist framework.[3] Williams never jettisons the cross, but together with Jones and Pinn advances an anthropology that affirms and justifies humanity in the face of evil. Yet, I would argue that this is a rather truncated anthropology that drives an artificial wedge between immanence and transcendence inasmuch as it limits divine agency and, thereby, resists an absolute or transcendent solution to the problem of evil. Thus, in its suppression of the unrestricted orientation of the human person

---

[1] Clifton H. Johnson, ed., *God Struck me Dead: Voices of Ex-slaves* (Cleveland, OH: The Pilgrim Press, 1969), 19.

[2] William R. Jones, *Is God A White Racist: A Preamble to Black Theology* (Garden City, NY: Anchor Press/Doubleday, 1973); Delores S. Williams, *Sisters in the Wilderness: The Challenge of Womanist God-Talk* (Maryknoll, NY: Orbis Books, 1993), and, "Black Women's Surrogacy Experience and the Christian Notion of Redemption," in *After Patriarchy: Feminist Transformations of the World Religions*, Paula Cooey, et al., eds. (Maryknoll, NY: Orbis Books, 1991); Anthony B. Pinn, *Why Lord? Suffering and Evil in Black Theology* (New York: Continuum Books, 1995).

[3] Pinn, 17.

toward self-transcendence or *being-in-love-with-God*, this position inadvertently insults the very humanity it seeks to honor and defend.

This essay challenges any displacement of the cross as well as any limitation of human transcendence. It seeks to demonstrate that a proper *imitatio Christi* constitutes not only resistance to oppression and evil, but also the affirmation and liberation of human transcendence. Such a response is rooted in a *dark* or *apophatic wisdom* that counters and confounds the knowledge of this world and its expectations. This dark wisdom may be discerned in the religious (African American Christian) approach of the enslaved people to their oppression and suffering and provides an efficacious response that contributes to an eschatological future for the whole of humanity.

In order to understand just how the enslaved people perceived the cross of Jesus, the Spirituals, the Sorrow Songs of the enslaved people, and Slave Narratives provide an indispensable resource.[4] These transcriptions of oral interviews conducted well after Emancipation present difficulties for researchers and scholars, yet remain a key source for the history of the enslaved people as told from their perspective. Historian John Blassingame states plainly, "If scholars want to know the heart and secret thoughts of slaves, they must study the testimony of the blacks."[5] The Slave Narratives allow us some access to the musings and memories of women and men who were well acquainted with hardship and pain. These narratives quite properly may be understood as a form of what Johann Baptist Metz has named "dangerous memories, memories which make demands on us."[6] When Metz first alerted us to the fundamental importance of memory as a theological category, he sought to rouse a complacent bourgeoisie from an amnesia that had filtered out oppression and social suffering in history and engaged in Christianity in but the most anemic manner. In the name of the *memoria passionis Jesus Christi*, Metz protested our forgetfulness of the human 'other,' our forgetfulness of our true freedom that can neither be derived absolutely from nor separated totally from human history.

My exposition proceeds in three parts: The first inquires the crossroad where law and religion congeal in the massive public, maldistributed, transgenerational suffering of chattel slavery. The second uncovers the wounding experience of slavery as 'time on the cross.' Here the enslaved peoples call

---

[4] For one of the major collections, see George P. Rawick, ed., *The American Slave: A Composite Autobiography* 19 vols. (1941; Westport, CT: Greenwood Publishing Company, 1972). Begun under the auspices of the Federal Writers' Project of the Works Project Administration (WPA) 1936 to 1938, this collection augments earlier oral histories begun at Hampton Institute in Virginia, Southern University in Louisiana, and Fisk University in Tennessee.

[5] John W. Blassingame, "Using the Testimony of the Ex-Slaves," 94, in *The Slave's Narrative*, ed., Charles T. Davis and Henry Louis Gates, Jr. (New York: Oxford, 1985).

[6] Johann Baptist Metz, *Faith in History and Society: Toward a Practical Fundamental Theology*, trans. by David Smith (New York: Seabury Press, 1980), 109.

up dangerous memories of suffering and brutality and link hope, future, and freedom to the passion of Jesus. The third part teases out the dark wisdom the enslaved people drew from this generative, if paradoxical, encounter with the cross. With this essay, I hope not simply to honor Johann Baptist Metz, whose intellectual and religious commitment has been of personal inspiration and encouragement, but to provoke theologians of all viewpoints and all racial-ethnic cultural backgrounds, particularly those working in the United States, to recognize the moans and musings and memories of battered and despised peoples around the globe as what Metz has called a "subversive factor in our society, the ferment for that new political life we are seeking on behalf of our future."[7]

At the Crossroad of Slavery

As the sons of Jacob betrayed, captured, imprisoned, and sold their brother Joseph, likewise sub-Saharan Africans and Arabs from the north betrayed, captured, imprisoned, and bartered away their brothers and sisters - among whom were the Igbo, Bini, Fulani, Mende, Tvi, Ashanti, Yoruba, BaKongo.[8] Children, women, and men were chained and force-marched to the Atlantic coast, only to be housed in dank places underground, then herded onto ships bound for the 'new' world. Once on board, the Africans endured filth, severe beatings, sexual assault, and immeasurable psychic trauma. Statistics suggest that from 12 to 33 percent of the captives died during the ocean voyage.[9] Although Anglo-American accounts correlate slavery in colonial history with the arrival in 1620 of a 'Dutch-man-of-war' carrying some twenty Africans, the 'peculiar institution' has murky beginnings. Slavery was the spawn of indentured servitude. When masters defaulted on time-bound contracts and attempted to extend their legal hold over men and women, white and black, it is not surprising that indentured servants rebelled. Historians cannot be precise, but sometime around 1640 in colonial America, slavery came to be associated almost exclusively and exhaustively with black bodies and black bodies came to signify enslavement.

---

[7] Metz, 119.

[8] For a discussion of some of the ethnic groups caught up in the slave trade, see Joseph E. Holloway, ed., *Africanisms in American Culture* (Bloomington and Indianapolis, IN: Indiana University Press, 1990).

[9] Philip D. Curtin, *The Atlantic Slave Trade* (Madison: The University of Wisconsin Press, 1969), 275-281. The exact numbers of Africans who were captured and/or died in the infamous "Middle Passage" or in ways related to their embarkation and were enslaved may never be known. Some scholars estimate that in the course of a two-hundred year period, 500,000 Africans or about seven percent of those caught up in the entire transatlantic trade were brought to what is now the United States, and one scholar proposes that the total may be well over forty million (See Holloway, "The Origins of African-American Culture," in *Africanisms in American Culture*; see also Albert Raboteau, *Slave Religion: The 'Invisible' Institution in the Ante-bellum South* (Oxford: Oxford University Press, 1975).

Contemporary American understanding of slavery has been shaped by a commonsense appropriation of the romanticized film version of Margaret Mitchell's "Gone With the Wind." However, in practice, slavery was neither romantic, nor uniform, but shaped by topography, agriculture, economics, and human temperament. Slavery was never exclusively Southern. At some period prior to Emancipation, men and women who lived in New York, New Jersey, Massachusetts, Rhode Island, Ohio, and Wisconsin engaged in slave-holding or slave trading. Slavery was a business and a way of life; but, most basically, it was a lie. Nearly everyone touched by slavery learned to live with it by learning to live with a lie - a monstrous moral fiction that insulted God and human nature.

Chattel slavery was not a quaint revival of the medieval feudal system. It was structured, sanctioned, interpreted, and enforced by legislation. The slave "is one who is in the power of a master *to whom he belongs*. The master *may sell him, dispose of his person*, his industry and his labor."[10] Slaves were "deemed, sold, taken, reputed and adjudged in law to be *chattels personal*, in the hands of their owners and possessors, and their executors, administrators, and assigns, *to all intents, constructions, and purposes whatsoever*."[11] These laws aimed to "erase every feature of social and human differentiation," and reify African humanity.[12]

In 1827, George Stroud published *A Sketch of the Laws Relating to Slavery in the Several States of the United States of America* in which he compiled a summary of laws in the various states that pertained to the institution of slavery.[13] The most conspicuous elements illustrate the civil condition of slavery as social death: slaves serve the term of their lives; slaves cannot testify against any white person, either in civil or criminal cases; slaves cannot be party to a civil suit; slaves are forbidden all claim on the benefits of education as well as all means of moral or religious instruction; slaves are required to submit, not only to the will of the master but to all white persons; slaves have no recourse to self-defense, and, thus are prohibited from defending themselves against the violence of the master or other whites; slaves are not exempt from the full weight of penal codes of slave-holding states; although slaves may be "considered member[s] of civil society" for the purposes of prosecution and trial upon criminal accusation, but in a manner "different from that which is observed in respect to free white persons, and

[10] William Goodell, *The American Slave Code in Theory and Practice: Its Distinctive Features Shown by its Statutes, Judicial Decisions, and Illustrative Facts* (1853; New York: Negro Universities Press, 1968), 23, author's emphasis.

[11] Goodell, author's emphasis.

[12] Hortense Spillers, "Mama's Baby, Papa's Maybe: An American Grammar Book," 82, in *The Black Feminist Reader*, ed., Joy James and T. Denean Sharpley-Whiting (Oxford: Blackwell, 2000).

[13] George M. Stroud, *A Sketch of the Laws Relating to Slavery in the Several States of the United States of America* (1827; 1857; reprint, New York: Negro Universities Press, 1968).

the difference is injurious to the slave and inconsistent with the rights of humanity."[14] These laws granted near absolute power over black human beings to white masters and, by extension, to *all* whites.

Slavery also was deeply entangled with Christianity. Christian baptism underwent syllogistic mutation: It was unthinkable to baptize slaves; blacks, Africans, were natural slaves; therefore, blacks could not be baptized. Such logic had lethal doctrinal and pastoral, moral and ethical consequences. There were political and economic consequences as well. In 1664, the lower house of Maryland asked the upper house to "draw up an Act obliging Negroes to serve *durante vita* … for the prevention of the dammage Masters of such Slaves must susteyne by such slaves pretending to be Christened."[15] It was intended that slavery should stand in perpetuity, and Christianity would be one means to that end.

The Christianization and evangelization of the enslaved peoples is a disputed and complex historical and theological question. In 1565, the Spanish established themselves at St. Augustine in what is now northern Florida and baptized enslaved Africans into the Roman Catholic Church. Less than a century later in Virginia, Anglo-American Protestant slaveholders were criticized by some Anglican clergy for their refusal to expose the Africans to the bible and to Christian baptism. And during most of the seventeenth century, Anglican clergy preached either freedom from slavery as a by-product of baptism or the admonition that one Christian should not enslave another. In opposition, other ministers argued that the Africans were 'heathens' and slavery served as a just and necessary response to heathenism. Yet, there is evidence that the enslaved peoples were affected by the evangelical preaching associated with the Great Awakening and the evangelizing mission of the Baptists and Methodists.

By the early eighteenth century, slaveholders began to maintain that Christian baptism could better equip the Africans to accept their fate. Historian Albert Raboteau has shown that white planters and ministers drew on biblical passages and spurious theological arguments to legitimate and sacralize perpetual bondage.[16] Ministers claimed that the enslaved Africans were not human; that God had foreordained black people to a life of subjugation and servitude to white people; and that because the Bible does not expressly prohibit it, slavery did not transgress divine law. Ministers advocated a Christianity that sought to unmake the God-image in Africans, to render them servile and docile, acquiescent to a divine ordination of their subjugation to whites. How sly to detach Paul's admonition from its life-setting and eschatological intent, to inscribe it onto the circumstances of the

[14] Storud, xi-xii.
[15] Cited in Raboteau, 99.
[16] Raboteau, 100.

plantation: "Slaves, obey your earthly masters in everything, not only while being watched and in order to please them, but wholeheartedly, fearing the Lord. Whatever your task, put yourselves into it, as done for the Lord and not for your masters, since you know that from the Lord you will receive the inheritance as your reward; you serve the Lord Christ" (Col. 3: 22-24).

White ministers employed the hermeneutics of sacrifice and servitude in their proslavery arguments. James Furman, a Baptist cleric from South Carolina stated: "We who own slaves honor God's law in the exercise of our authority."[17] Thornton Stringfellow of Richmond, Virginia, urged slaves to "blind compliance" to God's will, stating that "God gave special aid [to whites] to effect slavery" as part of the divine plan to bring Africans under the civilizing influence of Christianity.[18] Bishop Meade advocated a double doctrine of Jesus as the *servant-of-servants*. The double-ness of the doctrine is found in its application to both slaveholders and slaves. According to Meade, Jesus "chose the form of a servant and became the servant-of-servants, illustrating [the] blessed doctrine [of slavery] by his own meek, patient, suffering life." On the one hand, since Jesus was "faultless in word and deed toward those in bondage," slaveholders were to imitate him by perfect behavior toward those whom they held in slavery. On the other hand, since Jesus had been meek and humble, enslaved women and men were to imitate him by accepting their enslavement meekly and humbly, without protest, for God's divine will ordained their state.[19]

Yet, from a privileged hermeneutical stance emerging from their massive suffering, the enslaved peoples turned a critical eye on the hypocrisy of the Christianity of the slaveholders. One former enslaved man said:

> I often heard select portions of the Scriptures read.... On Sunday we always had one sermon prepared expressly for the coloured people .... So great was the similarity of texts that they are always fresh in memory: "Servants, be obedient to your masters - not with eye-service, as men-pleasers." "He that knoweth his master's will and doeth it not, shall be beaten with many stripes"; and [verses] of this [type].... One very kind-hearted clergyman ... was very popular with the coloured people. But after he had preached a sermon from the Bible that it was the will of Heaven from all eternity that we should be slaves and our masters are our owners, many of us left ... consid-

---

[17] Cited in Donald Matthews, *Religion in the Old South* (Chicago: University of Chicago Press, 1977), 136.

[18] Thornton Stringfellow, "The Bible Argument: Or, Slavery in the Light of Divine Revelation," in *Cotton Is King, and Proslavery Arguments*, ed., E. N. Elliott (Augusta, GA: Pritchard Abbot, 1860), 486, 493,

[19] Riggins Earl, *Dark Symbols, Obscure Signs: God, Self, and Community in the Slave Mind* (Maryknoll, NY: Orbis Books, 1993), 33.

> ering, like the doubting disciple of old, "This is a hard saying, who can hear it."[20]

But, in spite of slavocracy's *eisegesis,* the Bible came to occupy a pivotal place in the religio-cultural life of the enslaved Africans. Biblical stories, characters, themes, events, and images gave meaning and hope to the struggle of black women and men for emancipation and liberation in this world and triumph in the next. Since most of the enslaved peoples were forbidden to learn to read, their knowledge of the content and message of the bible came through public readings and sermons. Portions of biblical books or chapters were memorized, repeated, and reshaped. Purged of malicious meanings, like those mentioned earlier, these passages became the subject of meditation, reflection, and sermonic interpretation. Biblical scholar Renita Weems and sociologist Cheryl Townsend Gilkes have argued that since the enslaved peoples were not bound intellectually or morally to any *official* written text, translation, or interpretation, they created for themselves an *oral text* that displayed affinities with prophetic and apocalyptic traditions of the Hebrew Scriptures.

Thus neither Anglo-American, nor Roman Catholic Christianity mastered the totality of the religious consciousness, intentionality, and expression of enslaved black communities. For these communities' reception of Jesus owes as much to African Traditional Religions, Yoruba traditions in particular. Consider the Yoruba deity or *orisha* Elegba: It is Elegba or Eshu-Elegba who "brings divinity down to earth," who mediates between the other deities and human beings, who determines in large measure the destinies of people's lives according to their deeds, who delivers sacrifices to Olúdùmare, the Great High God.[21] Of course, there can be no identity between the protean (trickster) Eshu and Jesus of Nazareth. But the assertion insinuates inculturation and the context into which teaching about Jesus of Nazareth was received. This context constitutes *black sacred space*: It is drawn on the heart and mind and generated from those religio-cultural meanings reconfigured through blending and fusing fragments of ancient African cosmologies that were dislocated and fragmented under the stress of the "Middle Passage" and slavery.

The meeting of law and religion in the economic invention of the United States traces a brutal crossroad on ground and spirit of North American soil. When that tracing is lifted up through political ideology and chattel slavery, black children, women, and men are nailed to the cross.

---

[20] Creel, "Community Regulation and Cultural Specialization in Gullah Folk Religion," 51.

[21] Rawick, *The American Slave*, vol. 1, 47.

Time on the Cross

Asked about her suffering under slavery, Delia Garlic replied: "Slavery days was hell."[22] Slavery at once circumscribed and exploited the potential of African women and men and did so principally through objectification and instrumentalization.

By law, enslaved Africans were considered real estate, and, as such, were subject to be mortgaged, and could be seized and sold as real estate.[23] Black children, women, and men could be put up for sale at whim or need. Slave traders, slave pens, and the slave market served this function. Katie Rowe, a former slave, recalled how the Africans were handled and inspected like so much cattle: "De white men come up and look in de slave's mouth jes lak he was a mule or a hoss."[24] Free born, but kidnapped as an adult and sold into slavery, Solomon Northup confirmed this practice. Customers calling at the slave pen, he wrote, "would feel of our hands and arms and bodies, turn us about, ask us what we could do, make us open our mouths and show our teeth, precisely as a jockey examines a horse."[25] Buyers would tell slaves to roll up the legs of their pants or lift up their skirts in order inspect for blisters, signs of disease, or scars from whippings that indicate evidence of a slave's disposition toward rebellion. W. L. Bost, interviewed at Asheville, North Carolina, said that he would "hear the [the auctioneer's] voice as long [as he lived]."[26] Delia Garlic recalled how "Babies was snatched from deir mother's breast and sold to speculators. Chillens was separated from sisters and brothers and never saw each other again. 'Course dey cry. You think they not cry when dey was sold like cattle?"[27]

For the sake of the profits of the plantation, enslaved women and men were reduced to instruments of labor. Black women and men worked from sunup to sundown, usually, six days each week, and sometimes for some hours on Sundays. On some plantations, slaves were supervised in the fields by black drivers who, in turn, were under the direction of white overseers. On other estates, they worked the fields under the immediate supervision of white overseers, the plantation owner or a member of the owner's family.

There was little gender differentiation when it came to heavy labor in the field. Harriet Robinson pointed out that "women broke in mules, throwed

[22] Norman R. Yetman, ed., *Voices from Slavery* (New York: Holt, Rinehart and Winston, 1970), 133.
[23] Goodell, 24.
[24] James Mellon, ed., *Bullwhip Days: The Slaves Remember, An Oral History* (New York: Avon Books, 1988), 28.
[25] Solomon Northup, *Twelve Years a Slave*, ed., Sue Eakin and Joseph Logsdon (1853; Baton Rouge: Louisiana State University Press, 1968), 52.
[26] Yetman, 36.
[27] Yetman, 133.

'em down, and roped 'em. [And] they'd do it better'n [some] men"[28] In his travels in the Carolinas, Frederick Law Olmstead described "some thirty men and women" repairing a road:

> The women were in majority, and were engaged at exactly the same labor as the men; driving the carts, loading them with dirt, and dumping them upon the road; cutting down trees, and drawing wood by hand, to lay across the miry places; hoeing and shoveling.[29]

Ferebe Rogers identified herself as a "was a field hand," who had "come up twixt de plow handles. I weren't de fastest one with a hoe, but I didn't turn my back on nobody plowin."[30] Fannie Moore, who was interviewed at Asheville, North Carolina, said that her mother "work in the field all day and piece and quilt all night."[31] And Sarah Gruder recalled, "I never knowed what it was to rest. I just work all de time from mornin' till late at night. I had to do everythin' dey was to do on de outside. Work in de field, chop wood, hoe corn, till sometimes I feel like my back surely break. I done everythin' 'cept split rails."[32]

Interviewed in a rural area outside of Houston, Richard Carruthers recalled a rough tempered overseer by the name of Tom Hill. "[Hill] used to whip me and the other [slaves] if we don't jump quick enough when he holler and [sometimes] he stake us out like you stake out a hide and whip till we bleed … Sometime he take salt and rub on the [slaves] so [we] smart and burn … and suffer misery."[33]

Black women and men labored in the making of the material of the plantation both through production and reproduction, and, in this their instrumentalization was nearly total. Slavery thrived on the black woman's body; indeed, her body was that site in which the planter's economic desire intersected with black women's sex, sexuality, and reproductive capability. Historian Deborah Gray White observes, "Planters made sure that slave women were prolific."[34] This was more than cost cutting: after the importation of Africans became illegal in 1808, the increase of plantation capital, its laborers or slaves, depended upon internal breeding. Biology bound the black woman to capital accumulation. Given the custom of *partus sequitur ven-*

---

[28] Yetman, 252.
[29] Frederick Law Olmstead, *The Cotton Kingdom* (1861) *American History Landmarks*, ed. David Freeman Hawke (Indianapolis & New York: The Bobbs-Merrill Company, Inc., 1970), 63.
[30] Yetman, 257.
[31] Yetman, 227.
[32] Yetman, 151.
[33] Yetman, 53.
[34] Deborah Gray White, *Ar'n't I a Woman? Female Slaves in the Plantation South*, rev. ed. (New York: W. W. Norton & Company, 1999), 31.

trem - the child follows the condition of the mother - slavery devoured the fruit of the black woman's womb.

Slavery exacted a perverse physical, psychological, intellectual, and spiritual toll. Verbally and physically intimidated, the enslaved people were coerced to perform a grotesque pantomime of survival - smiling when they wanted to weep, laughing when they felt anger and rage. In 1842, Lydia Marie Child published a transcription of a lecture given by a fugitive slave who was traveling under the pseudonym of Lewis Clarke. Clarke reflected upon the answer a slave might give to the question, "Do you want to be free?"

> ... if some Yankee had come along and said, "Do you want to be free?" What do you suppose I'd have told him? Why, I'd tell him, to be sure, that I didn't want to be free; that I was very well off as I was. ... [I]f a woman slave had a husband and children, and somebody asked her if she would like her freedom, would she tell them yes? If she did, she'd be down the river to Louisiana, in no time; and her husband and children never know what become of her. Of course, the slaves don't tell folks what's passing in their minds about freedom; for they know what will come of it.[35]

Talk of freedom may have made some slaves uneasy, but not even the most unlettered women and men could be convinced that they should be objects of property only to bought and sold at whim, that they should be instruments of labor, that they should relinquish a claim on humanity. This was the case, even when instinct for self-preservation might have them publicly deny a deep desire for freedom.

It is true, that to some enslaved peoples, freedom was an awesome notion, perhaps, an unattainable condition. One freed slave admitted to an interviewer, "I've heard [the slaves] pray for freedom. I thought it was foolishness, then, but the old-time folks always felt they was to be free. It must have been something [re]vealed unto 'em."[36] Divine revelation broke through slavery's crushing reality to give life to faith and religious love; "the God of history acted within American experience, and acted with the same emancipatory purpose as depicted in the biblical Exodus."[37] As one enslaved woman cried out,

> I'se saved. De Lord done tell me I'se saved. Now I know de Lord will show me de way, I ain't gwine to grieve no more. No matter how much you all

[35] John Blassingame, ed., *Slave Testimony: Two Centuries of Letters, Speeches, Interviews, and Autobiographies* (1977; Baton Rouge: Louisiana State University Press, 1989), 152-153.

[36] Mellon, 190.

[37] Theophus Smith, *Conjuring Culture: Biblical Formations of Black America* (Oxford: Oxford University Press, 1994), 155.

> done beat me and my chillen de Lord will show me de way. And some day we never be slaves.[38]

This profession of faith is notable. The woman grasps the relation between salvation and real concrete historical freedom; she makes a direct connection between the material conditions of life (slavery and freedom), a virtuous life (divine guidance), and eternal life. In the midst of the oppression and grief of slavery, God can be counted upon to show the enslaved people the way to freedom. Secondly, the woman's profession underscores the enslaved peoples' persistent attempt to define themselves and control their own humanity and religious life. It dismisses the slaveholders continuing effort to interpose themselves between the slave and God's will.

When Delia Garlic's mother was sold away, her final words were "Be good and trust in de Lord." Commenting on her mother's exhortation, Garlic said: "Trustin' was de only hope of de poor black critters in dem days. Us just prayed for strength to endure it to the end. We didn't 'spect nothin' but to stay in bondage till we died." [39] Yet when Emancipation came, the enslaved people gave God the glory. Mary Reynolds mused:

> I sets and 'members the times in the world. … I 'members 'bout the days of slavery and I don't 'lieve they ever gwine have slaves no more on this earth. I think Gawd done took that burden offen his black chillun and I'm aimin' to praise him for it to his face.[40]

Historians Blassingame, Raboteau, and Mechal Sobel have documented the ambiguous attitudes and behavior of slaveholders in response to the religious lives of the enslaved peoples.[41] On some plantations, slaves were forced to attend white churches, sitting or standing in segregated areas. And, on other plantations, the enslaved people were permitted to hold unsupervised praise meetings, sometimes led by a 'slave' preacher. In other situations, the enslaved peoples secretly withdrew to woods, gullies, and thickets (called brush arbors or 'hush arbors') to pray and sing.

But, if some slaveholders permitted the enslaved people to hold independent and sometimes unsupervised worship services, other planters punished slaves for praying and singing. Ellen Butler's master was among the latter and never allowed the slaves to go to church. The enslaved people prayed anyway. Raboteau reports that

---

[38] Yetman, 228.

[39] Yetman, 134.

[40] Melon, 23.

[41] Mechal Sobel, *Trabelin'On: The Slave Journey to an Afro-Baptist Faith* (Princeton, NJ: Princeton University Press, 1979) and John W. Blassingame, *The Slave Community: Plantation Life in the Antebellum South* (1972; New York: Oxford University Press, 1979).

> When Thomas Jones ... grew concerned about the state of his soul, his master told him to stop moping about, forbade him to attend prayer meetings, and ordered him to stop praying. In spite of repeated and severe whippings, Jones persisted in attending Methodist class meetings and refused to promise that he would abandon prayer. Eli Johnson claimed that when he was threatened with five hundred lashes for holding prayer meetings, he stood up to his master and declared, "In the name of God why is it, that I can't after working hard all the week, have a meeting on Saturday evening? I'll suffer the flesh to be dragged off my bones . . . for the sake of my blessed Redeemer."[42]

Former slave, Alice Sewell told her interviewer that many enslaved people in her area

> used to slip off in de woods in de old slave days on Sunday evening way down in de swamps to sing and pray to our own liking. We prayed for dis day of freedom. We come four and five miles to pray together to God dat if we don't live to see it, to please let our chillen live to see a better day and be free, so dat dey can give honest and fair service to de Lord and all mankind [sic] everywhere.[43]

Enslaved women and men defied barbaric punishment in order to commune with God, "to give honest and fair service to de Lord"; from within the tightly circumscribed circle of slavery, they prayed for that which was unseen. Since the vast majority of the millions of Africans enslaved in the Americas died in the bondage in which they had lived, the very unselfishness of such prayer signifies the transcendent dimension of being human and witnesses to an eschatological hope that discredits any facile optimism before God and the condition of enslavement. Finally, the enslaved people's embrace of the cross was no act of self-abnegation, but an act signifying resistance. They were sustained by a dark wisdom: the story of Jesus is their story, the suffering of Jesus is their suffering, the vindication of Jesus is their vindication.

Dark Wisdom of the Cross

Canonized a saint of the Roman Catholic Church on October 1st 2000, Josephine Bakhita was born in 1869 in the Dagius village of Olgossa, in western Sudan. At about the age of eight or nine, Bakhita was captured and sold into slavery. The sixth and final person to claim to own Bakhita was Maria

---

[42] Cited in Raboteau, 307; Rawick, vol. 1, 17, 142.

[43] Yetman, 263.

Turina Micheli, the wife of an Italian hotelier. Years later Bakhita recalled the March day that she chanced upon a crucifix in the Micheli residence. Canossian Daughter of Charity, Sister Maria Luisa Dagnino took down Bakhita's recollection:

> In silence [Bakhita] stared at this man hanging on a cross. He seemed to gaze at her with an expression of immense suffering and infinite gentleness. 'Who are you?' Bakhita asked him. 'Why have they put you on the cross?' … Eventually Illuminato Checchini [the hotel administrator] told her about Jesus and his sacrifice on the cross. …[This] moved her deeply. By hard personal experience she knew the pain of blows, insults … being beaten and lashed with the whip until the wounds bled. … [Bakhita] said, "As I looked at the crucifix, I experienced a strange feeling which I could not explain."[44]

Like hundreds of thousands of enslaved women and men before her, Josephine Bakhita had been touched deeply by the wonder and mystery of the cross of Jesus of Nazareth. What did it mean? What did it teach them? What did it mean for the enslaved peoples to grasp Jesus as an oppressed and suffering companion?[45]

In at least three ways, Jesus of Nazareth captured the religious imagination and affections of the enslaved people. Jesus identified with and preached the gospel to those who were afflicted, poor, and dispossessed. The Spiritual marvels: "*Did you ever see the like before/ King Jesus preaching to the poor.*" The enslaved people understood the similarity of their condition with that of those also outcast and despised in biblical stories. Second, Jesus was a man of word and deed: what he says he will do, he does. Again, the Spiritual testifies: "*My Lord's done just what he said/ He's heal de sick and rais'd de dead.*" The Spiritual echoes the Gospels' reports of cures and miracles that witnessed to Jesus' transformative power for the comfort and joy of a suffering people: "*I'll tell you what de Lord done for me/He tuk my feet from de miry clay.*" "*He sot me upon a solid rock/ An 'gib me David's golden harp.*" Finally, because Jesus himself was beaten, tortured, and murdered, the enslaved peoples believed that he understood them and their suffering like no one else. They believed that he was one with them in their otherness and affliction, that he could help them negotiate this world with righteous anger and dignity. And when they sang, "*Nobody knows de trouble I've had / Nobody knows but Jesus,*" they were motivated not by despair but by love and faith.

---

[44] Maria Luisa Dagmino, *Bakhita: From Slavery to Sanctity* (Nairobi: Paulines Publications of Africa, 1993), 4-5, 42-43.

[45] Earl, 81.

We should not be surprised that the Spirituals focus on the suffering, crucifixion, and death of Jesus. The enslaved folk knew in their bodies and minds what it meant to endure suffering and abuse, and in Jesus' suffering and death they recognized their own. Slave narratives report some especially vicious types of punishment; two of these were called the *buck* and *staking*. In the *buck*, the man or woman was bent over or buckled, that is "doubl[ed] in two, until the legs were passed over [the] head, where they were kept by a stick passed across the back of [the] neck." While in this position the slave was whipped and the wounds caused by the lash were rubbed with salt and water and pepper.[46]

Staking called for the enslaved man or woman to be forced to lie face down on the ground, with arms and legs extended and tied to stakes; if the slave were a pregnant woman, a hole was dug for her extended belly. Lying in this 'X-formation,' the person would be flogged. One variation of this punishment required that the enslaved man's or woman's "hands would be tied together with a rope, which was then thrown over the limb of a tree or over a beam." The person would be "pulled up till the toes only just reached the ground, feet tied together, and a rail or fence thrust between the legs with a weight on it to keep the body at full stretch."[47]

These types of punishment were not uncommon. Hence, we may assume that the descriptive realism of the Spirituals regarding the suffering and death of Jesus draws intimately on the suffering the enslaved people endured. In the following Spiritual of lament, the enslaved folk pour out an empathy for Jesus that transcend the limitations of time and space. Jesus stood with them in their sufferings, they stood with Jesus in his.

> *They nail my Jesus down / They put him on the crown of thorns*
> *O see my Jesus hangin' high! He look so pale an' bleed so free:*
> *O don't you think it was a shame / He hung three hours in dreadful pain?*

And, there is this Spiritual about the crucifixion:

> *They crucified my Lord…They nailed him to the tree…*
> *You hear the hammers ring…The blood came trickling down…*
> *Those cruel people! Hammering!*

Consider the words of another and famous Spiritual about the crucifixion and death of Jesus:

---

[46] Earl, 81.
[47] Blassingame, 220.

Dey crucified my Lord / An' He never said a mumblin' word.
Not a word - not a word - not a word.
Dey nailed him to a tree…. / Dey pierced him in de side.
De blood came twinklin' down . . . / He bowed his head and died.
An' He never said a mumblin' word.
Not a word - not a word - not a word.

Finally, there is this most well-known of the great Songs of Sorrow:

Were you there when they crucified my Lord?
Oh! Sometimes it causes me to tremble, tremble, tremble.
Were you there when they crucified my Lord?
Were you there when they nailed Him to the tree?
Were you there when they pierced Him in the side?
Were you there when the sun refused to shine?
Were you there when they laid him in the tomb?

The enslaved people gave great attention and care in this Spiritual to represent the suffering that Jesus endured. John Lovell, the preeminent authority on the history and formation of the Spirituals, writes that the enslaved singer portrays a grave "great wrong [being] committed under the eyes of frightened or uncaring people. For the wrongs of humankind, the finger points to us all. … We are all guilty, not so much for what we do, as what we allow to happen. And without a doubt, the slave singer was including [chattel] slavery … in the bill of indictment."[48] The repeated inquiry "Were you there?" challenges each person to place him or herself at the scene of crucifixion, to acknowledge her or his collusion with evil. Lovell's comments are reinforced by the inclusion, in some variants of this Spiritual, of verses that confess, "*I wuz dere win dey nailed 'im to der cross.*"[49]

Mrs. Brown, a freed woman living near Nashville, remarked that she first heard the Spiritual, "I'm Troubled in Mind," from her father when she was a child. After he had been whipped, her father always went and sat upon a certain log near his cabin, and with tears streaming down his face sang this song:[50]

Oh Jesus, my saviour on thee I'll depend,
When troubles are near me, you'll be my friend.
If Jesus don't help me, I will surely die.
When laden with trouble and laden with grief,

---

[48] Blassingame, 304.
[49] Blassingame, 304.
[50] *Jubilee Songs as Sung by the Jubilee Singers of Fisk University* (New York: Biglow & Main, 1872), 58.

To Jesus in secret I'll go for relief.
If Jesus don't help me, I will surely die.
In dark days of bondage to Jesus I prayed,
to help me bear it, and he gave me aid.
If Jesus don't help me, I will surely die.

We may be tempted to read this as an example of relying on religion as an escape, "an opiate of the oppressed."[51] *"If Jesus don't help me, I will surely die."* Rather, this refrain is an affirmation of faith and hope, not doubt; it is an assertion of confidence, not a query.

The Inscape of Prayer

The enslaved people faced their suffering and oppression through nourishing their interior lives in prayer. One former slave stated that in prayer, "My mind gets fixed on God and I feel a deep love, joy, and desire to be with God."[52] For many of the people, to nourish and expand the inscape or essential inner quality of their spiritual lives, the deep desire for God, was an act of defiance. A man known as Praying Jacob was held in bondage in Maryland by a master of exceptional cruelty.

> Jacob's rule was to pray three times a day, at just such an hour of the day; no matter what his work was or where he might be, he would stop and go and pray. His master has been to him and pointed his gun at him, and told him if he did not cease praying he would blow out his brains. Jacob would finish his prayer and then tell his master to shoot in welcome - your loss will be my gain - I have two masters, one on earth and one in heaven - master Jesus in heaven, master Saunders on earth. I have a soul and a body; the body belongs to you, master Saunders, and the soul to Jesus.[53]

"For those who want to save their life will lose it, and those who lose their life for my sake, and for the sake of the gospel, will save it. For what does it profit them to gain the whole world and forfeit their life?" (Mark 8:35-36). Praying Jacob disarmed slavery's power over his body through an embrace of Christian discipleship and thus death had no power over him: he was a follower of Jesus of Nazareth in word and deed.

---

[51] Earl, 80.
[52] Earl, 23.
[53] G. W. Offley, *A Narrative of the Life and Labors of Rev. G. W. Offley* (Hartford, Connecticut, 1860); reprinted in *Five Black Lives* 134-135.

What the Old Slaves Knew

"The old slaves didn't know nothing about books," a freed man remarked, "but they did know God. And knowing [God] they called on him [sic] in their trouble and distress, and I can testify that [God] heard them."[54] The knowledge of God the old slaves possessed came not through intellectual training or analysis, although 'book learning' is something they desired earnestly for their children. To speak of the knowledge of the enslaved peoples as apophatic or dark wisdom is to signify a wisdom that is, at once, a counter to the specious wisdom of this world and a subjugated knowledge, a knowledge hidden from this world by an oppressed people.

What did the enslaved people know about God? What dark wisdom sprang from their massive oppression and suffering, their love of and identification with the crucified Jesus? Here is some of what the enslaved people knew about God, here is some of their dark and hidden wisdom:

• The old slaves knew themselves as "new creature[s] in Jesus, the workmanship of his hand saved from the foundation of the world." They knew themselves as "chosen vessel[s] before the wind ever blew or before the sun ever shined."[55] As one former slave related the experience of hearing God promise "I am a wall around my people, and if I call you through fire and water, come, follow me."

• The old slaves knew that no one who consumed human flesh could live: In other words, slavery was death-dealing for the slaveholder, the slave trader, all who profited from the buying and selling human beings. The cross stands as a complete rejection of violence; it is the very "inversion of force,"[56] of mastery, of dominance. Meditating on stories of Jesus' ministry to the poor and oppressed, the enslaved people understood him as a "Bringer of Life."[57] The enslaved people grasped 'the otherness' of Jesus; he, too, was a stranger in a world of death and oppression. Jesus was "God's Black Slave who had come to put an end to human bondage."[58] Jesus was for them! Jesus

---

[54] Johnson, 70.

[55] Johnson, 111.

[56] Paul Ricoeur, *Figuring the Sacred: Religion, Narrative, and Imagination* (Minneapolis, MN: Fortress, 1995), 279.

[57] Theo Witvliet, *The Way of the Black Messiah* (Oak Park, IL: Meyer Stone Books, 1985), 170. The enslaved Africans understood Jesus Christ as the Bringer of Freedom, as their Savior. This understanding was derived from two primary sources: a subtle grasp of the Scriptures and the circle of culture that gave us B'rer Rabbit, B'rer Fox, and B'rer Mockin' Bird; Ole Sister, High John de Conquer and Stackolee; Anansi and King Buzzard. From this circle of culture came the trickster, the legendary and mythic heroes and "bad men" who would not be bested. From this circle of culture came enslaved and free men and women who fought with every means at their disposal for freedom, for emancipation.

[58] James H. Cone, *The Spirituals and the Blues* (San Francisco: Harper & Row, 1972), 49.

[58] John Lovell, *Black Song: The Forge and the Flame: How the Afro-American Spiritual Was Hammered Out* (New York: Macmillan Publishing, 1972), 189.

meant that death would not be the last word, that slavery would not be the last word. The God who vindicated Jesus would vindicate the enslaved peoples and that vindication was, at once, historical and eschatological, this-worldly and other-worldly.

• The old slaves knew that the power of God in the cross was the power *to live and to love* - even when violence does its worst. One old freed woman told of her vision and experience of God's love: "I rejoice ever in the love of God. The love of God is beyond understanding. It makes you love *everybody*."[59]

• The old slaves knew that we cannot overlook affliction and loss and that the pain of such suffering lasts. Indeed, enslaved women and men wept inconsolably for the loss of children, parents, husbands and wives, nor did they forget the massive public oppression of their enslavement. Nor, were the enslaved people willing to love uncritically. But, they did not allow their pain to circumvent their freedom to love mercy, to do justice, to walk humbly with God (Micah). When the enslaved people sang *"Lord, I want to be a Christian in my heart / Lord, I want to love everybody in my heart,"* they were calling for grace to incarnate a logic radically different than human logic. Human logic is a logic of equivalence, a forensic logic - punishment is exacting and justice is limited to a fairness of sameness, an eye for an eye, hatred for hatred. The enslaved people sought grace, sought God's logic of "excess, of superabundance."[60] There could be no surrender of human agency to hatred or violence. "Beloved, let us love one another; for love is of God, and whosoever is born of love is of God and knows God; for God is love . ... Beloved, if God so loved us, we also ought to love one another. ... If we love one another God abides in us and God's love is perfected in us" (I John 4: 7-12).

• The old slaves knew that the power of God in the cross is its paradox - the unexpected, unimagined, resurrection. God's logic, divine logic, interrupts, reveals, and projects merciful love into the bleakest circumstances.

• The old slaves knew that, as one freed woman learned in her conversation with God, God is a "time-God working after the counsel of [God's] own will. In due time [bringing] all things to [fruition]."[61] The providence and compassionate care of God works in chaos and pain an order that heals and comforts, that nurtures human freedom.

The dangerous memories of suffering yield a dark wisdom that teaches us what it means to embody the seed of history, to link past and future - the ancestors and those yet to be born. The dangerous memories and dark wisdom of the enslaved people teach us a love-ethic that commends us all to love

[59] Johnson, 115.
[60] Ricoeur, 279.
[61] Johnson, 58-59.

ourselves and our own people, yet not to love others or ourselves uncritically. The dangerous memories and dark wisdom of the enslaved people teach us how to be defined by commitment in the here-and-now to the realization of the reign of God, rather than by victimization. The dangerous memories and dark wisdom of the enslaved people join ethos and cosmos to teach us not how to avoid or deny suffering, but how to "suffer suffering."[62]

[62] Paul Ricoeur, "Toward a Hermeneutic of the Idea of Revelation," 86, in *Essays on Biblical Interpretation*, ed., Lewis S. Mudge (Philadelphia: Fortress Press, 1980).

NOT IN VAIN: METZ'S MEMORIA PASSIONIS AND VIOLENCE AGAINST WOMEN

Johann M. Vento

"If you lined up all the girls who died in vain,
you could walk on their heads to hell and back again."[1]

Introduction

In seeking to discuss violence against women theologically, I have found Johann Baptist Metz to be an excellent conversation partner. Several aspects of his theology correlate well with the experience of victimization and bear much fruit when examined in light of the problem of violence against women. These include his argument for the need for a political theology, his understanding of human subjectivity and intersubjectivity, of suffering and suffering unto God, and of the function of memory, narrative, and solidarity in his practical theological anthropology.[2] I will focus on Metz's sense of eschatological urgency, especially as it is expressed in his insistence on the importance of the memory of suffering, as the starting point for a theological praxis in response to the problem of violence against women.

In a passage describing the poetry of Ernesto Cardenal, Metz is also describing the ideal function of a theology that is practical, political, and mystical. I quote this passage in full because it expresses what I believe to be one of the most important tasks for theology in the face of the problem of violence against women: theology must be a praxis of saving victims, past and present, from the obliteration of their subjectivity by the "conversation of the victors." According to Metz the political poetry of Cardenal:

> seeks not only to unmask, not even exclusively to accuse, above all it seeks to *save*. Its basic stance is not aggression, but rather 'protection'; it seeks to protect, to rediscover that which as victim of our domineering civilization has long been forgotten or repressed; whatever in the conversation of the victors (which often advances itself as the language of God) has long since become speechless and dumb. It seeks to recall not only what has succeeded but also

[1] Shawn Colvin, "Object of My Affection," *Fat City*, audio compact disc, Sony, 1992.

[2] For a discussion of the relevance of Metz's understanding of suffering unto God to the experience of victimization, trauma, and recovery see Johann M. Vento, "A Feminist Appraisal of Metz's Mysticism of Suffering Unto God," *Horizons* 29 (Spring 2002): 7-22.

> what has been ruined, not only the realized but also the lost, and attempts thus to direct itself against the monotonous victoriousness of reality as it has come to be.[3]

In this essay I will argue that the patriarchal image of women as appropriate victims of violence constitutes a "conversation of the victors" that numbs us to the horror of violence done to women. The memory of the suffering of victims is needed to restore the sense of outrage at what has been ruined and lost and to allow for a praxis of resistance to "the monotonous victoriousness" of violence against women.

While the causes of this violence are complex, they share a rootedness in a fundamentally patriarchal view of women, particularly women's sexuality. This viewpoint is sometimes quite explicit, but in our context often disguised and unacknowledged. It is nevertheless effective in creating and sustaining an environment that is hostile to women's flourishing. The insidiousness of the patriarchal justification for violence against women means that each of us is to some extent molded by it. That it might seem extreme to call our culture hostile to women's well-being shows the extent to which we are habituated to the image of women as appropriate victims of violence.

Our immersion in a culture that provides the conditions for violence against women represents a particular form of cultural amnesia. And because we are under its spell, we are desensitized to the horrors of the problem of violence against women. This cultural amnesia has formed in us a "moral callousness" regarding the violence itself and its victims.[4] Because of this callousness, we have lost our ability to feel the outrage appropriate to the phenomenon of violence against women and therefore to be in solidarity with victims. It is with this aspect of the problem in mind that I wish to engage Metz's emphasis on the memory of suffering. In order to speak of this problem theologically, we need to begin with a praxis that removes our calluses and that allows us our outrage. In what follows, I will discuss the severity of the problem of violence against women and examine the moral callousness that surrounds this problem in our culture. In the second half of the essay, I will argue that the eschatological urgency of Metz's theology, expressed in his understanding of the function of the memory of suffering, gives a theological vocabulary to the need for outrage and the starting point for a theological praxis to save "all the girls who died in vain."

---

[3] Johann Baptist Metz, *The Emergent Church: The Future of Christianity in a Postbourgeois World*, trans. Peter Mann (New York: Crossroad, 1981), 99.

[4] Mary D. Pellauer, "Moral Callousness and Moral Sensitivity: Violence Against Women," in *Women's Consciousness, Women Conscience: A Reader in Feminist Ethics*, ed. Barbara H. Andolsen, Christine E. Gudorf, Mary D. Pellauer (San Francisco: Harper & Row, 1987), 33-50.

Severity of the Problem of Violence against Women

Violence against women has been a pervasive problem throughout history and in almost every culture. It represents a form of mass suffering that dehumanizes its victims, its perpetrators, and all of us who ignore or avoid it. Rape, battering, and childhood sexual abuse occur in epidemic proportions and have devastating effects for their victims, their families, and society as a whole. The statistics regarding violence against women in the U.S. alone provide an example of this pervasiveness. Thirty-one percent of American women report that they have been physically or sexually abused by an intimate partner.[5] The FBI estimates that one in ten women will be physically abused by their husbands in marriage. Thirty percent of women murdered in 1990 were killed by their husbands or partners.[6] In 2000, 1,247 women were killed by a husband or boyfriend.[7] According to the American Medical Association, an estimated four million women each year are victims of severe assaults by intimates. Further, women battered by intimates account for one-third of all women admitted to emergency rooms. Estimates of the number of battered women who are also raped by their abusers range from thirty-three to forty-six percent.[8] One in three women in the U.S. will be sexually assaulted in their lifetime.[9]

Childhood sexual abuse, also shockingly widespread, is particularly damaging to its victims, because it occurs so early in life. One in four girls and one in six boys will be victims of sexual abuse before the age of sixteen.[10] Studies show that childhood sexual abuse dramatically increases the likelihood of a host of other problems, including mental illness, early unwanted pregnancy, drug addiction, risk of HIV infection, eating disorders, prostitution, and participation in the pornography industry.[11] More than half of women who have been raped were victimized for the first time before the age of eighteen. These women were twice as likely to report being raped as an adult.[12]

---

[5] Center for the Prevention of Sexual and Domestic Violence, "Domestic Violence," available at www. faithtrustinstitute.org/Domestic-Violence/index.htm. Accessed December 31, 2004.

[6] National Clearinghouse for the Defense of Battered Women, *Statistics Packet,* Philadelphia, 1994.

[7] Center for the Prevention of Sexual and Domestic Violence, "Domestic Violence," available at www. faithtrustinstitute.org/Domestic-Violence/index.htm. Accessed December 31, 2004.

[8] National Clearinghouse for the Defense of Battered Women, *Statistics Packet.*

[9] Center for the Prevention of Sexual and Domestic Violence, "Sexual Violence," available at www. faithtrustinstitute.org/Domestic-Violence/index.htm. Accessed December 31, 2004.

[10] Center for the Prevention of Sexual and Domestic Violence, "Child Abuse," available at www. faith-trustinstitute.org/Child-Abuse/index.htm. Accessed December 31, 2004.

[11] Pellauer, 42.

[12] U. S. Department of Justice, "Full Report of the Prevalence, Incidence, and Consequences of Violence Against Women," November 2000, available at www.ncjrs.org/txtfiles1/nij/183781.txt. Accessed August 1, 2003.

The effects of violence against women on its victims can be dramatic and far-reaching. Severe or ongoing abuse through childhood sexual abuse, rape, or battery often result in the condition diagnosed as post-traumatic stress disorder (PTSD). This is a physiological condition with serious psychological consequences for victims. It is characterized by loss of memory, somatic disorders, night terrors, eating disorders, self-mutilation, the inability to act in the interest of one's own well-being, to experience concern for others, and to trust God, self, and others. One researcher describes the effects of PTSD as "psychic death" and "soul murder" which destroys the very identity of the victim.[13] Women who are victims of such severe trauma require long periods of recovery with explicit attention to regaining the sense of self lost through violence and its aftermath. Such recovery is possible, but only if others hear the stories of the victims, express outrage at what has happened to them, take their traumas seriously, and denounce the crimes against them without qualification.[14]

Moral Callousness

Although acts of rape and battering, and even to some extent, certain forms of pornography, are acknowledged as crimes in our context and are publicly denounced and at times prosecuted, violence against women thrives, because it finds its source and sustenance in deeply rooted cultural attitudes and practices that are not widely questioned, even in what some refer to as a "post-feminist" environment. Although the roles of women in our society have undergone dramatic shifts in the past forty years, the prevalence of pornography, rape, and battering demonstrates the durability of the belief that females are appropriately dominated by males and that this domination requires violent enforcement. That is, despite the advances of women, patriarchal assumptions and attitudes about women and women's sexuality perdure in varying degrees in our context. Patriarchal views form a "common sense" that simultaneously contributes to the problem of violence against women and feeds off of it.

These assumptions continue to thrive unchallenged, because they so often escape explicit acknowledgement. According to Margaret Miles:

> The most pervasive foundations of violence against women are so ordinary, so unexceptional, and therefore so unnoticed that they are seldom challenged.

[13] Elizabeth Waites, *Trauma and Survival: Post-Traumatic and Dissociative Disorders in Women* (New York: Norton, 1993), 22.

[14] For a discussion of the traumatic effects of violence against women and a description of the process of recovery, see Judith Herman, *Trauma and Recovery: The Aftermath of Violence - from Domestic Abuse to Political Terror* (New York: Basic Books, 1992).

> Pornography, an industry larger than the record and film industries *put together*, may be enormously important as the major eroticization of violence in our culture, but there are other rationalizations of and support for violence against women. These are more superficial in that they lie more on the surface of American culture; at the same time they are more foundational in that they are built into the assumptions and institutional structures of American culture in the family and child-rearing, in educational institutions, and in churches, synagogues, and government.[15]

This subtle yet effective patriarchal common sense engenders a moral callousness that manifests itself in many forms: ignoring or trivializing the prevalence or severity of crimes such as childhood sexual abuse, rape, and battering, understanding these as primarily private issues, blaming the victims, and glorifying images that link sexuality and violence. All of these are based on deeply rooted cultural assumptions that denigrate and demonize women and women's sexuality.

Our moral callousness toward violence against women manifests itself in rationalizations for rape and battering that allow us to trivialize these issues, ignore their patriarchal foundations, and distance ourselves from their horror. Two examples of such rationalization are the myth of the rapist as sociopath, and the tendency to blame victims. These rationalizations effectively say to women, "yes, violence is a problem, *but* ... it is not really very common ... it is the result of a few sick men ... you asked for it."

Although it is common to think only "sick" people would rape, researchers who study both the attitudes of convicted rapists and those of the general population, consistently find that there are few differences in their views of rape and have concluded that men who rape are no more sociopathic than men in general.[16] Rather, rape is a learned behavior that is the "end point in a continuum of sexually aggressive behaviors that reward men and victimize women."[17] Blaming the problem of violence against women on the psychological state of a few men rather than seeing it in the larger context of patriarchal beliefs about the value of women distances us from the problem and allows it to be privatized. We do not need to examine generalized sexual aggression in our culture if we so tidily dismiss its most extreme forms as aberrant.

Moral callousness is also evident in the tendency to blame the victim. Victims and their advocates often report ways in which male behavior is

---

[15] Margaret R. Miles, "Violence Against Women in the Historical Christian West - The Visual and Textual Evidence," in *Shaping New Vision: Gender and Values in American Culture*, ed. Clarisssa W. Atkinson, Constance H. Buchanan, and Margaret R. Miles (Ann Arbor: UMI Research Press, 1987), 15.

[16] Diana Scully and Joseph Marolla," 'Riding the Bull at Gilley's:' Convicted Rapists Describe the Rewards of Rape," in *Violence Against Women: The Bloody Footprints*, ed. Pauline B. Bart and Eileen Gail Moran (Newbury Park, CA: Sage Publications), 28.

[17]Scully and Marolla, 42.

blamed on women. Elizabeth Waites describes the "double bind" in which women are expected to be attractive to men, or compliant with men's desires, on the one hand, but are blamed for being too provocative or too weak in regard to male violence on the other:

> When a man responds to [a woman] by being sexually aroused but controlled and respectful, she is admired as an artful creature. When a man responds to her by being sexually aroused but out of control and contemptuous, she is vilified as being a female vampire, deserving of harassment, rape, or any other abuse she receives.[18]

Victims of rape are often questioned as to their own actions during the attack. If a woman resists the attack and sustains injury, she is told that she should have been more passive. But a woman's lack of resistance, out of fear of greater injury, is often seen as her consent. Liz Kelly concludes that "whatever choices women make, they are likely to be told that they should have done the opposite."[19] Surprisingly it is often women who participate in blaming the victim. We often hear questions such as, Why doesn't she leave him? What was she doing out at that hour? Why did she dress that way? If we can convince ourselves that violence only occurs to women who do those things we would never do, we can feel a safe distance, and again ignore the pervasiveness of violence against women and the attitudes that support it.[20]

The myth that rape and battery are private problems caused by relatively few aberrant men and the willingness to blame women for their victimization are examples of patriarchal rationalizations for violence committed against women. They allow us to distance ourselves from rape and battery and therefore prohibit solidarity. Further, they serve to deny women's experience and victimize them once again. Ruth Seifert notes that patriarchy reserves for itself the power to name and define women's experience. When violence against women is defined as trivial, as private, or as invited by women, "women's experience and therefore women's subjectivity is being extinguished."[21] Thus a vicious cycle emerges in which patriarchal values provide the condition for acts of violence against women by defining them as appropriate victims, women are objectified further through acts of violence against them, and afterward their subjectivity is questioned as their experience is trivialized.

One of the primary factors in our moral callousness toward violence against women is our habituation to the association of sexuality with vio-

---

[18] Waites, 57.
[19] Liz Kelly, *Survivng Sexual Violence* (Minneapolis: University of Minnesota Press, 1988), 84.
[20] Miles, 26.
[21] Ruther Seifert, "War and Rape: A Preliminary Analysis," in *Mass Rape: The War Against Women in Bosnia-Herzegovina*, ed. Alexandra Stiglmayer (Lincoln: University of Nebraska Press), 67.

lence, which is propagated by explicit pornography and increasingly by mainstream entertainment and advertising. As a form of public discourse pornography is a powerful voice that propagates the belief that women are appropriate victims of violence. In the common wisdom, pornography is wrong because it depicts illicit sex. But that understanding prevents us from recognizing the basic message of pornography and its influence on the culture as a whole. The depiction of sex or even of sexual violence is not in and of itself pornographic. Pornography is "verbal or pictorial material which represents or describes sexual behavior that is degrading or abusive to one or more of the participants *in such a way as to endorse the degradation*."[22] Pornography propagates the association of sex with degradation of and violence toward women. While pornography is officially proscribed in our culture it flourishes, and while most people might say that they do not use or are not influenced by pornography, the basic connection that pornography makes between sex and violence is increasingly pervasive in mainstream media. We buy products everyday that play on this connection.

While preparing this article, I came across a prime example of this association in a report on the local nightly news.[23] The report was about a park in Las Vegas where men pay to "hunt" naked women with paint ball guns. The park itself turned out to be a hoax designed to sell a series of "reality videos" portraying such hunts. Ads for the "Hunting for Bambi" video entice customers to watch "Bambies" who "are ready to be chased down and shot like dogs."[24] The videos show successful "hunters" posing with their kill, the men in hunting gear, the nude, bloodied women in postures evoking a slain animal. These videos convey the message, common to pornographic material in general, that hunting, harming, or killing women is sexy, that women and women's sexuality are "animalistic" and appropriate objects of contempt, that this contempt is normal and its expression through violence a healthy activity. It is sport. It is fun.

The pornographic image of women is widely available in several media. "Adult Entertainment" is big business. Its annual profits of eight to eleven billion dollars per year outpace the mainstream film industry.[25] Moreover, it is not limited to materials commonly categorized as pornographic. Images of women as sexual property and as fit objects of violence abound in mainstream entertainment and especially in advertising. Images that reduce women to specific body parts, or that animalize or mechanize women's bod-

---

[22] Helen Logino, "Pornography, Oppression, and Freedom: A Closer Look," in *Take Back the Night*, ed. Laura Lederer (New York: William Morrow and Company, Inc., 1980), 43.

[23] "WB17 News at Ten," July 8, 2003. See also "Hunting for Bambi," available at www.-wherestheoutrage.org/art_83.html. Accessed July 27, 2003.

[24] "Hunting for Bambi," available at www.wherestheoutrage.org/art_83.html. Accessed July 27, 2003.

[25] T. L. Stanley, "Porn Crosses Over to Media Mainstream" *Advertising Age* 75:4 (January 26, 2004), available online through Academic Search Premier Database.

ies, portrayals of women with hands and feet bound, with bloodied noses, frightened women cowering in corners, women buried alive, naked women posing as corpses sell everything from shoes to cologne to cars.[26] In most of these images, the women are dressed provocatively and with glamorous make-up - these ads are meant to evoke sex. One shows a topless young woman, hands over breasts, with a hunted expression on her face advertising a skateboard and sport clothing brand called "Serial Killer." These ads make explicit use of what so many mainstream music videos, films, television reality shows, etc., also bank on: the fundamentally pornographic image of women as appropriate victims of violence, especially sexual violence.[27] This imagery is used so widely because it sells; on some basic level, it makes sense to us. We are not outraged. We are not even indifferent. We buy it, literally and figuratively.

The prevalence and severity of violence against women and the tragedy of its effects are frequently unnoticed or trivialized. Crimes of violence against women are commonly viewed as the private problems of a relatively few aberrant individuals or of women who are not smart enough to protect themselves. We are largely unaware of the extent to which our own sensibilities about women, sexuality, and violence are formed (or de-formed) by the image of women as appropriate objects of violence. In Metz's terms, with regard to violence against women, we are inured to the "conversation of the victors" and "the monotonous victoriousness of reality as it has come to be." Metz's theological project is developed to rescue human subjectivity from this kind of moral callousness toward victims. The memory of suffering as Metz understands it and the eschatological vision that it is meant to nourish are necessary to destabilize the deeply imbedded common sense patriarchal notions that feed violence against women, to stir in us the outrage that is appropriate to such a destruction of human well-being, and to prompt us toward a theological praxis to resist violence against women.

Metz's Eschatological Urgency and the Memory of Suffering

An urgent tone pervades Metz's work - an intense and unyielding stance. This tone is rooted in his understanding of theology as practical and performative. It's urgency derives from his insistence that theology interrupt the status quo with the story of the victims. Metz's theology seeks to jar, unsettle, disturb, and convince. Metz explains the urgency of his theology in his argument for an eschatological sense of time. "It is time for it to be time," he

---

[26] For a gallery of such images, see the website of media watch-dog group About Face, available at www.about-face.org.

[27] Logino, 43.

urges (quoting Paul Celan) in the face of a sense of unending evolutionary timelessness, which numbs the desire for and pursuit of justice.[28] For Metz, struggling for a more just world is pointless in the grip of evolutionary time in which we can only expect more of the same. In this connection he quotes Teilhard de Chardin, "We go on asserting that we are awake and are waiting for the master. But, if we were honest, we would have to admit that we expect nothing at all."[29] If Christians live in real expectation of a future whose content is the kingdom of God, we experience "the pressure of time," which "does not deprive responsibility of its power, but provides it with motivation."[30] According to Metz, to expect God's promised future is to struggle for it; to have hope for the world is actively to shape it.[31] To do theology as a Christian is to do that which will lead one into conflict with whatever in society stands counter to the subjective agency of all. It is to bring discomfort to the comfortable in the process of giving voice to the voiceless and making visible what has been erased.

An expectation of a future "whose content is the kingdom of God" will involve the ability to see the injustice of the present. In order to hope and struggle for the rescue of what has been lost, we must first recognize the loss and confront the full pain of it. In the case of violence against women, we need to resist the moral callousness that protects us from that pain. We need to feel the outrage that has been subdued by the common sense attitudes and assumptions that determine our response to violence against women. Hope for the future that elides the suffering of the past and present is a cheap hope that cannot nourish praxis but only numbs us further to the suffering of others. The memory of suffering guards against such a weak or easy hope. Metz's understanding of the function of the memory of suffering helps to clarify how we might allow the memory of women's suffering to form us and to engender the kind of outrage appropriate to destabilizing the "monotonous victoriousness" of violence against women.

The Memory of Suffering

Metz argues that memory is formative of human identity as subject. Memory's role in identity formation is located in its capacity to call the present into question and to offer hope for transformation. Conversely, the loss of memory is the loss of identity. For Metz, it is particularly the memory of

---

[28] Johann Baptist Metz, *Faith in History and Society*, trans. David Smith (New York: The Seabury Press, 1980), 175.
[29] Metz, *Faith in History and Society*, 179.
[30] Metz, *Faith in History and Society*, 176-177.
[31] Johann Baptist Metz, *Theology of the World*, trans. William Glen-Doepel (New York: Herder and Herder, 1969), 150.

histories of suffering, the memories of what has been lost, of the defeated in history that preserve human subjectivity. These are dangerous memories that serve as the ground for criticism of the status quo and the impetus to transformation. These memories are "turned against the victory of what has become and already exists."[32]

For Metz, the memory of the suffering, death, and resurrection of Christ is the primary dangerous memory for Christians. It reveals God's will to save even those already dead. The memory of the suffering of Jesus is the foundation of the promise of future freedom for everyone: "We remember the future of our freedom in the memory of his suffering …."[33] For Metz, the message of the resurrection is change, the announcement of a fundamentally new era, announced in the new man, Christ. It is important to see Metz's understanding of the function of this memory in terms of his eschatological orientation. He speaks of the function of the Christian *memoria* to disclose what is still to come. Metz sees the coming of the kingdom of God announced in the suffering, death, and resurrection of Jesus as a dialogue between the "existing lack of humanity and a humanity that is really possible"; between suffering humanity and "an essentially human way of life"; between Good Friday and Easter Sunday.[34] The memory of the suffering, death, and resurrection of Jesus provides a way of reflecting on human suffering as the "point at which the proclamation of the new and essentially human way of life that is announced in the resurrection of Jesus can begin."[35] From this Christian *memoria* emerges an expectation of a more human future, a future of freedom. For Metz, this reflection on a future of freedom has a practical effect in Christian subjects:

> … the Christian *memoria* becomes a memory which shocks us out of ever becoming prematurely reconciled to the facts and trends of our … society. It becomes the dangerous and liberating memory over against the controls and mechanisms of the dominant consciousness ….[36]

The memory of Christ's suffering, death, and resurrection implies that the meaning of the victims of history has not been decided by the victors. This memory holds out hope to all that the meaning, value, and freedom of each human being, even those long dead, is yet to be realized in history, has yet to "make a claim on history."[37] For Metz there can be no real hope for a redeemed future without a hope for the redemption of the past. In this way, the

---

[32] Metz, *Faith in History and Society*, 171.
[33] Metz, *Faith in History and Society*, 111.
[34] Metz, *Faith in History and Society*, 112.
[35] Metz, *Faith in History and Society*, 112.
[36] Metz, *Faith in History and Society*, 113.
[37] Metz, *Faith in History and Society*, 76.

Christian *memoria* calls into question the status quo, and it challenges Christians to struggle to change unjust situations. Faith in the Christian *memoria* can have a "critically liberating force" because it acts

> 'contra-factually' in making us free to bear in mind the sufferings and hopes of the past and the challenge of the dead. It allows not only a revolution that will change the things of tomorrow for future generations, but a revolution that will decide anew the meaning of our dead and their hopes. Resurrection mediated by way of the memory of suffering means: The dead, those already vanquished and forgotten, have a meaning which is as yet unrealized.[38]

Metz's understanding of the function of the memory of suffering is an essential antidote to the moral callousness surrounding the problem of violence against women in our context. We need to be "shocked … out of ever becoming prematurely reconciled to the facts and trends of our … society" - shocked out of our moral callousness. The memory of women's suffering and victimization has the capacity to destabilize the received patriarchal attitudes and assumptions that feed the problem of violence against women and at the same time obscure it. An emphasis on the memory of suffering opens the way for a focus on the deformative effects of violence against women.

The insight that moral sensitivity is based on the ability to empathize with others is not exclusive to Metz or to our own age. Feminists have long known of the formative capacity of awareness of the suffering of others and of the danger of its opposite. Mary Pellauer quotes Mary Wollstonecraft in her "A Vindication of the Rights of Women" of 1792, where she declares that "[t]hose who are able to see pain, unmoved, will soon learn to inflict it."[39] The consciousness raising groups of the sixties and seventies in the last century allowed women to share their stories of oppression to practical effect: the birth of an influential wave of the feminist movement. In her discussion of our tendency to distance ourselves from victims of violence, Margaret Miles argues for the power of empathy with the suffering of others:

> How do we claim as our own the experience of another human being? How do we feel experiences we have not had? Feminist author Emily Culpepper once responded to these questions with a simple but profound reply: "We tell each other our stories." In the commitment to listening with empathy and speaking with honesty, the experience of another woman can become one's own experience. The ability to feel the pain of others can then become an ethical resource, empowering women to overcome isolation, individualism, and fear.[40]

---

[38] Metz, *Faith in History and Society*, 113.
[39] Pellauer, 49.
[40] Miles, 26.

It is the eschatological horizon of Metz's understanding of the power of the memory of suffering that sets what Metz is saying apart from a more general sense of the importance of empathy in moral reasoning. Further, its lends a specifically theological and mystical dimension to the need for outrage in the face of violence against women. His eschatological sense brings to bear on the present the past history of suffering, the Christian *memoria*, and the future promised by God, all of which together function to indict any present situation of injustice and servitude.

Metz's eschatological focus on the memory of the dead has the capacity to disrupt the moral callousness, in its many forms, that governs our response to violence against women. Metz calls for a passionate solidarity that settles for nothing less than the redemption of all. He urges the memory of suffering as a praxis on behalf of the dead and not only in the interest of current struggles. The memory of the suffering of those who have been defeated and hope for their rescue are what form for Metz a Christian subjectivity. Our own identity as subjects and the hope of our own salvation is tied up with exactly this: the memory of the dead and their sufferings and hope for *their* rescue, for *their* redemption. To say that the sufferings of all victims will be redeemed and that all will be made whole and to expect that as a real, imminent future is not rational. It is a mystical stance that can only be accepted in faith and nurtured by memory in solidarity. But it is a mystical stance with *practical* intent and function. The memory of the suffering of the dead and the hope in *their* future destabilizes that which oppresses, because it prevents us from acquiescing to "reality as it has come to be." It allows the victims to make a claim on us and on our current praxis, and it demands a different future. It restores our humanity as it produces a counter-cultural sensibility that allows us to see, name, and resist that which obliterates human subjectivity. It provides a radical hope that can sustain the praxis of attentiveness to the full negativity of radical suffering.

So, as Emily Culpepper says, it is imperative that we tell each other our stories of suffering. But with Metz, we must acknowledge the need for telling the stories of the suffering of the past as well, and of a very different future for "all the girls who died in vain." Such telling and hearing requires community. Metz is known for claiming the church as a necessary vehicle of the Christian *memoria* as dangerous memory.[41] His insight that a community with historical memory is required to resist the prevailing logic of the victors is compelling. Indeed, so pervasive is the common sense of patriarchy, so perfect its ability to suppress alternative visions of reality, that sustaining an opposing vision of women's well-being requires the power and support of community where memories of suffering are preserved and narrated. We

[41] Metz, *Faith in History and Society*, 92.

know from the experience of women recovering from the trauma of victimization that supportive communities where women can share their stories of violence and hear the stories of other survivors are essential to the process of recovery.

Further, the memory of the suffering of the dead gives voice to the voiceless - thus providing a potent indictment against the apparently successful "conversation of the victors." Communities that remember the suffering of women who have gone before nurture in all members of the community a consciousness of the demonic aspects of patriarchally structured patterns of relationship and the violence to which they give rise. Remembrance of the suffering of the dead can nurture in victims a deep sense of the injustice of abuse committed against them and in the community at large a sensitivity to their suffering. Thus communities dedicated to preserving the memory of suffering of the dead communicate to women that violence done to any woman at any time is a cause of outrage and a source of sorrow for the community. Such communities can make the credible claim to be places of refuge and hope for victims. They can allow us to resist what has come to be and nurture in us a powerful, universal, mystical-political hope that can fuel our praxis in the interest of the well-being of all women and, by extension, all peoples.

Conclusion

Violence against women thrives in our culture as does the sometimes subtle, sometimes explicit, and remarkably effective patriarchal image of women as appropriate victims. Formed as we are by such an environment, our capacity for outrage at and therefore for moral sensitivity to victimization is endangered and requires an intentional discipline of attention to the suffering of women. Metz's understanding of the memory of suffering provides an apt starting point for such a praxis, especially in light of the moral callousness that surrounds the violence and its victims in our context.

Given the basis of violence against women in patriarchal norms, however, much more is needed for a theological analysis and reflection adequate to the reality of the problem. In particular a thorough-going feminist analysis is in order, not only of the dynamics of patriarchy as the basis for violence against women, but also of the ways in which Christian theology and tradition have themselves been permeated by patriarchal attitudes about women and about violence against them. Traditional understandings of theological anthropology, especially with regard to women's roles in society and church, the salutary function of suffering, the imperative to forgive, and the understanding of self-sacrifice all must be criticized and re-articulated from a specifically feminist perspective. Further, as the memory of suffering can prove useful for victims and for their communities, so can the memory of agency. Women and society as a whole also need to be nourished on stories of women triumphing over patriarchal limitations, recovering from violence, finding communities of support, and learning to flourish. These memories of agency must not be separated from the memories of suffering or they run the risk of denying once again the tragedy of violence against women. But taken together, both kinds of narratives have the capacity to nurture a sense of the injustice of the present and hope for a different future.

While an analysis of Metz's work is not enough to craft a theology that resists violence against women, it offers a great deal towards that endeavor. His call to an eschatological urgency and his focus on the memory of suffering provide necessary, though not sufficient, elements of a theological praxis that can remove our calluses, let us feel outrage, and allow us to hope. I end with a quote from Marie Fortune that expresses a longing for this kind of hope:

> To say that the way things are is not the way they have to be, to assert that violence against women is not a part of the created order, to suggest that women should not live in fear simply because of our gender is nothing less than a statement of faith in this time. There is little in our experience which tells us that women should be able to live free from fear. So we make this assertion on faith alone. As the writer of Hebrews said, "Now faith is the assurance of things hoped for, the conviction of things not seen." And after listing numerous foremothers and forefathers, the writer concludes: "These all died in faith, not having received what was promised, but having seen it and greeted it from afar, and having acknowledged that they were strangers and exiles on the earth." As women we are strangers and exiles in this patriarchal land. It is our job to speak the truth so that our daughters and granddaughters will know that the way things are is not the way they have to be.[42]

[42] Marie Fortune, "Violence Against Women: The Way Things Are is not the Way They Have To Be," in *Sexuality and the Sacred: Sources for Theological Reflection*, eds. James B. Nelson and Sandra P. Longfellow (Louisville, KY: Westminster/John Knox Press, 1994), 330.

MELANCHOLY HISTORY

Steven T. Ostovich

Memory work as a form of critical reflection is notoriously difficult. This is especially the case when writing history. Memories are imprecise. Historicism calls for history to be just the facts of what happened, but memories do not seem to have the objectivity necessary for determining the past the way it actually was. They often have "rough edges" that resist incorporation into the smooth-flowing narratives of progress and meaning that underlie the (Hegelian) philosophy of history. Memories can have a "future content" that disrupts attempts at a hermeneutic fusion of past and present horizons. They can be enmeshed in the lies we attempt to tell ourselves as we construct our sense of self and world. And yet memory also is a category of responsibility, that is, memories demand a critical response on the part of the historian. An extreme test case of this intellectual and moral responsibility: writing German history after Auschwitz.[1]

The name "Auschwitz" represents a historical trauma, a trauma that affects attempts to forge a sense of German national identity not only after the Third Reich but in light of the more recent (re-)unification of East and West. Memories of Auschwitz disrupt attempts at writing German historical identity for all the reasons listed above. The issues raised by this name affect more than just German historiography, however. Perpetrators, victims, witnesses, and their descendants all are affected by Auschwitz, and the intellectual and moral viability of modern Western culture itself is called into question here. What does one do with the memory of Auschwitz? How does one respond to this trauma in history?

Auschwitz and the Possibility of Mourning

Historians, cultural critics, philosophers and others have been turning to the language of psychoanalytical theory in working through historical trauma.

"Mourning" has become a primary trope for discussing responsibility for trauma in history: mourning is seen as a way to restore an integrated self capable of bearing responsibility. Much has been made of the German inability to mourn after the Holocaust and the end of the Third Reich. Mourning in

---

[1] On lying, responsibility, and the construction of "normalcy" in post-Third Reich Germany, see Andrew Stuart Bergerson, *Ordinary Germans in Extraordinary Times: The Nazi Revolution in Hildesheim* (Bloomington and Indianapolis, IN: Indiana University Press, 2004).

this context means working though the past as a way to take responsibility for what happened, and the inability to mourn is an avoidance of responsibility. Much now also is being made of the attempts of a postwar generation of Germans to mourn a past it is not quite sure is its own. Museums are built, sites are marked, rites are conducted - and a chancellor is elected who, born very late in the Third Reich, symbolizes the German attempt to work through the troubled past in his political actions. Again, this German experience underlines the challenge Auschwitz poses for modern thinking generally: we all seem to be searching for the closure that would identify a responsible self capable of attaining objectivity and control over against this past.

Is this possible? What can one do with this trauma? Can one understand Auschwitz in modern terms of understanding? Is it possible to master an "unmasterable past," to use Charles Maier's phrase? Isn't understanding on the model of mastering a kind of forgetting, a forgetting by means of reduction to the apparently normal flow of history of what is essentially a rupture of history? Can one take responsibility for Auschwitz by mourning the past, that is, by defining a subject liberated from it? Mourning may be possible, but is it always desirable? Does mourning reduce and contain experience to something that can be controlled and made harmless? In what follows, "melancholy" is suggested as a more responsible (intellectually as well as morally) attitude towards historical trauma.

This suggestion immediately has its own problems, problems identified by Sigmund Freud in his essay "Mourning and Melancholia."[2] The temporal index of trauma is important for Freud and for our considerations. Trauma is not a past event for Freud; rather, an experience becomes traumatic in its "afterlife" (*Nachträglichkeit*) as it inhibits responsible living in the present. Both mourning and melancholy have to do with grief attached to loss: mourning offers the possibility of working through the loss in a manner that is painful but ultimately healthy in its enabling the self to recognize the loss and thereby be liberated from the past; melancholy, on the other hand, is a pathology in which the self is trapped by the effects of the past and that puts the sufferer on the path to self-destruction. Dominick LaCapra translates Freud into the context of the Holocaust: "Freud compared and contrasted melancholia with mourning. He saw melancholia as characteristic of an arrested process in which the depressed and traumatized self, locked in compulsive repetition, remains narcissistically identified with the lost object. Mourning brought the possibility of engaging trauma and achieving a reinvestment in, or 'recathexis' of, life that allowed one to begin again."[3]

---

[2] Sigmund Freud, "Mourning and Melancholia," *Collected Papers*, vol. IV, authorized translation under the supervision of Joan Rivier (London: Hogarth Press, 1956), 152-170.

[3] Dominick LaCapra, "Revisiting the Historians' Debate: Mourning and Genocide," *History and Memory after Auschwitz* (Ithaca, NY and London: Cornell University Press, 1998), 44-45.

Mourning carries the possibility of healing; melancholy means being disabled by what Freud several times calls the open "wound."

Mourning as a model for working through the past depends on the modern understanding of the self as an autonomous individual. The goal of mourning for Freud is to help the wounded self heal and recover its ability to deal successfully with the world around it. Trauma drags this subject away from its present and disconnects it from its world. Healing through mourning is liberation to restored autonomy: "when the work of mourning is completed the ego becomes free and uninhibited again."[4] Mourning enables liberation from the past.

But this is the problem with mourning. Liberation through mourning involves reaching closure regarding the past. This presumes the past places no legitimate demand on the present that cannot be mastered and rendered nonthreatening. But doesn't Auschwitz resist mastering? Mourning presupposes the kind of autonomous selfhood that is called into question by ruptures like Auschwitz. LaCapra acknowledges there is a problem here and qualifies the work of mourning: "working through the past in any desirable fashion would thus be a process (not an accomplished state) and involve not definitive closure but a recurrent yet variable attempt to relate accurate, critical memory-work to the requirements of action in the present."[5] A lesson of Auschwitz is that closure may not be possible, and the self may remain fragmented.

This is why *melancholy* provides a better model than mourning for responding critically to historical trauma. Melancholy offers the possibility for thinking through responsible selfhood in light of ongoing rupture, of living with the open wound.

Within the Rings of Saturn

This possibility is addressed in the work of that most melancholic of twentieth century thinkers, Walter Benjamin. Benjamin's work has been described as "melancholy dialectics," as a "melancholy science" characterized by an understanding of the subject in terms of "melancholic agency."[6] Readers of Benjamin often trace this melancholy to Benjamin's reaction to the destruction of World War I. Martin Jay does not disagree with this but offers a

---

[4] Freud, 154.

[5] LaCapra, 42.

[6] See, for example: Max Pensky, *Melancholy Dialectics: Walter Benjamin and the Play of Mourning* (Amherst, MA: University of Massachusetts Press, 1993); Susan A. Handelman, *Fragments of Redemption: Jewish Thought and Literary Theory in Benjamin, Scholem, and Levinas* (Bloomington and Indianapolis, IN: University of Indiana Press, 1991), 124; and Judith Butler, "Afterword: After Loss, What Then?" in *Loss: The Politics of Mourning*, ed. David L. Eng and David Kazanjian (Berkeley/Los Angeles/London: University of California Press, 2003), 467-473.

much more specific trauma behind Benjamin's melancholy - the suicides of his friends Friedrich Heinle and Frederika Seligson on 8 August 1914 as a protest against the war. Jay claims Benjamin, "steadfastly defied all attempts to heal the wounds caused by the war...He refused, that is, to seek some sort of new symbolic equilibrium through a process of collective mourning that would successfully 'work through' the grief." This was an intentional program "to compel his readers to face squarely what had happened and confront its deepest sources rather than let the wounds scar over. Rather than rebuilding the psychological 'protective shield' (*Reizschutz*) that Freud saw as penetrated by trauma, he laboured to keep it lowered so that the pain would not be numbed."[7] This refusal to mourn is Benjamin's moral and intellectual as well as emotional response to the world he experienced. And it has a political and not just personal implication: refusal to mourn means refusal to close the books on the victims of past oppression and is a way of keeping alive the demand for justice that remembers the dead. So Benjamin's reaction is an act of responsibility and solidarity (and not the opposite).

The embrace of rupture and disdain of closure in the name of justice is evident in Benjamin's conception of history as messianic. In his theses "On the Concept of History," for example, he describes a *Jetztzeit* "shot through with splinters of messianic time" (A) in which the possibility of eschatological rupture always is present: "every second was the small gateway through which the Messiah might enter"(B).[8] Thesis IX, the famous *Angelus Novus* of history, communicates Benjamin's opposition to understanding history as progressive in its portrayal of the angel of history horror-struck in its inability to repair the historical catastrophes piling up at its feet as it is blown backward into the future by the wind called "progress." Neither is history "empty time" to be filled in with the facts reconstructed by historians. Rather, history becomes memory work, and these memories are "dangerous" as they place demands on the present in the name of the dead: "In the voices we hear, isn't there an echo of now silent ones?" (II). This means "Articulating the past historically does not mean recognizing it 'the way it really was.' It means appropriating a memory as it flashes up in a moment of danger ....The Messiah comes not only as the redeemer; he comes as the victor over the Antichrist. The only historian capable of fanning the spark of hope in the past is the one who is firmly convinced that *even the dead* will not be safe from the enemy if he is victorious" (VI). This hope is "nourished by the im-

[7] Martin Jay, "Against Consolation: Walter Benjamin and the Refusal to Mourn," in *War and Remembrance in the Twentieth Century*, ed. Jay Winter and Emmanuel Sivan (Cambridge: Canbridge University Press, 1999), 225-226.

[8] Walter Benjamin, "On the Concept of History," in *Walter Benjamin: Selected Writings, Volume 4, 1938-1940*, trans. Edmund Jephcott and others, ed. Howard Eiland and Michael W. Jennings (Cambridge, MA and London: Belknap Press of Harvard University Press, 2003), 389-400.

age of enslaved ancestors rather than by the ideal of liberated grandchildren" (XII). The task of the historian is "to brush history against the grain" (VII). The images Benjamin uses - the "arrest" of thought in a "constellation saturated with tensions," the "shock" that crystallizes in a "monad," the "messianic cessation of happening," (XVII), the "tiger's leap into the past" (XIV) - all communicate his willingness to think through rupture in history and his conviction that this thinking is necessary for understanding in general.

Complicating this picture is Benjamin's *Habilitationsschrift*, *Ursprung des deutschen Trauerspiels.*[9] This is a study of German baroque plays of mourning in which Benjamin obviously takes mourning seriously. But even here, Benjamin sets mourning in the context of melancholy. The *Trauerspiel* works by allegory, and Benjamin writes how an "object becomes allegorical under the gaze of melancholy" (183). As with history, Benjamin is concerned here with thinking through rupture and remembering the dead. He writes of the "disjunctive, atomizing principle of the allegorical" (208) and defends allegory over against the more typical concern with the symbol: the latter moves toward "totality," but the former remains "incomplete, imperfect" (186). Symbols reach for closure; allegories disturb us. Allegory settles in ruins and corpses: "Criticism means the mortification of the works ... not then - as the romantics have it - awakening of the consciousness in living works, but the settlement of knowledge in dead ones" (182). There is an anamnestic character to allegory.

Allegorical thinking and the difference between allegory and symbol have ramifications for understanding history: "Whereas in the symbol destruction is idealized and the transfigured face of nature is fleetingly revealed in the light of redemption, in allegory the observer is confronted with the *facies hippocratica* of history as petrified, primordial landscape. Everything about history that, from the very beginning, has been untimely, sorrowful, unsuccessful, is expressed in a face - or rather in a death's head" (166). As with messianic history, allegory works through "shock" and remembering the dead. The symbol works by abstracting from the historical into the eternal, an eternity which in its totality gives history a teleological meaning. Allegory, in contrast, is characterized by "an appreciation of the transience of things and the concern to rescue them for eternity" (223), and this rescue occurs only eschatologically.

These issues also show up in Benjamin's self-understanding. Mourning promises the possibility of closure with regard to a troubling past and the restoration of wholeness to the individual. The self for (and of) Benjamin,

---

[9] Translated as: Walter Benjamin, *The Origin of German Tragic Drama*, trans. John Osborne (London and New York: Verso, 1977). Osborne notes that *Trauerspiel* is more correctly translated as mourning-play and uses the German word in the text of his translation. Page references in parentheses in what follows refer to this translation.

however, remains fragmented. Gerhard Richter points out how this living with rupture is not just a necessity for Benjamin but part of the resistance to totalitarianism Benjamin intimated in his essay on "The Work of Art in the Age of Its Technological Reproducibility." Richter's *Walter Benjamin and the Corpus of Autobiography* is a sustained reading of Benjamin's three attempts to write his autobiographical self (*Moscow Diary, Berlin Chronicle*, and *Berlin Childhood around 1900*). Richter follows Benjamin's principle that "language has a body, and the body has a language" to unpack these three works corporeally in terms of "the body," "the ear," and "the eye/I," respectively. The difficulty in this project lies in the resistance of Benjamin's corporeal self to being pinned down: this self is "staged" rather than "explained.". This ambiguity is intentional and political, according to Richter. "The body prevents its reading from being organized into a closed hermeneutic system. In the moment of reading, it is in a certain sense already a corpse." The body is always fragmented, and therefore is useless to systems like fascism "that rely on presence, stability and access to stable meanings…Instead of being employable by a stable network, [the body] renounces its use value as a concept. It is always already shifting into something else."[10] Living without closure makes it possible to resist fascist appropriation of the corporeal self. Positively, for Richter, "If the forces of an occluded past and the signals of a future promise form, together with the ethical acceptance of political responsibility, a constellation within the rupture itself, then this constellation names precisely rupture's transformative potential" in a politics of remembering, hope, and "perpetual openness."[11] Political actions are neither metaphysically grounded nor procedurally justified, and yet we remain responsible for tracing their internal logic.

Political Theology and Melancholy History

Thinking though this responsibility in rupture after Auschwitz takes us beyond Benjamin to the Benjamin-influenced political theology of Johann Baptist Metz. This is a "new" political theology developed in the 1960s in the context of Marxist-Christian dialogue and as a recovery of the political dimension of faith in reaction against the popular privatization of faith in existential theology.[12] Metz begins with a "theology of the world," that is, by secularizing theological discourse. This secularizing discourse is different from the classical Christian theological abstraction wherein faith categories

---

[10] Gerhard Richter, *Walter Benjamin and the Corpus of Autobiography* (Detroit: Wayne State University Press, 2000), 158-159.

[11] Richter, 242-243.

[12] See Bernd Wacker and Jürgen Manemann, "Political Theology: History of a Concept" in this volume.

were explicated by means of Greek philosophy. Metz is much more interested in the Jewish roots of Christianity as a response to this world in all its concreteness. Metz understands the world as history and history as eschatological (under the influence of Ernst Bloch as well as Benjamin). The focus on eschatology leads Metz to the thesis: "Shortest definition of religion: interruption."[13]

Memory work has the character of what Metz calls anamnestic reason. Memories are as dangerous for Metz as for Benjamin.

There are memories in which earlier experiences break through the center-point of our lives and reveal new and dangerous insights for our present. They illuminate for a few moments and with a harsh steady light the questionable nature of things we have apparently come to terms with, and show up the banality of our supposed "realism." They break through the canon of all that is taken as self-evident, and unmask as deception the certainty of those "whose hour is always there" (John 7:6). They seem to subvert our structures of plausibility. Such memories are like dangerous and incalculable visitants from the past.[14]

One such dangerous memory is the *memoria passionis*, the memory of suffering, the paradigm of which for Christians the memory of the suffering, death, and resurrection of Jesus. Metz claims these memories have a future content that cannot be subsumed into controlling narratives of historical progress or the additive totality of empty time. Metz, like Benjamin, uses *Eingedenken* or "remembrancing" to describe memory work. More than simply making the past present through remembering, remembrancing responds to the future content of dangerous memories and the demands they put on the present. The practice of remembrancing turns to memory not simply as a window on the past but as disruptive of attempts to subsume the past under contemporary plausibility structures of personal or collective identity. This is anamnestic reason, that is, thinking as historically and politically situated and involving hope for the future that rests on "solidarity backwards" with the dead, especially the victims of oppression whose lives continue to demand justice.

Metz, too, bemoans a modern (and not just German) inability to mourn, but his own work moves beyond mourning and takes on a melancholy quality. This is clearest in his awareness of what it means to do theodicy as a German Catholic theologian after Auschwitz. Theodicy traditionally is understood as concerned with explaining how an omnipotent, omniscient, and perfectly good God can allow suffering. Metz rejects all such explanations in

---

[13] Johann Baptist Metz, *Glaube in Geschichte und Gesellschaft: Studien zu einer praktischen Fundamentaltheologie* (Mainz: Matthias-Grüneald-Verlag, 1977), 150. A new translation of this work by J. Matthew Ashley is forthcoming from Paulist Press.

[14] Johann Baptist Metz, "The Future in the Memory of Suffering," *Concilium* 76 (1972): 15.

light of Auschwitz. Christians are in no position to explain Auschwitz to themselves let alone to the Jews and other victims. Turning to the *memoria passionis* of Jesus Christ to reach closure on this issue results in a ghastly abstraction of human suffering, a reduction of suffering to an inner-Trinitarian moment, a dishonest denial of suffering. Still, silence about Auschwitz also would be wrong. For Metz, theodicy therefore becomes not explaining the ways of God to the world but presenting the suffering of the world to God - questioning God, asking God to be God, holding God to God's promises. This is the attitude of the Book of Job, although too often Christians have slipped into the position of Job's friends rather than staying with Job. "To confront Auschwitz is in no way to comprehend it."[15] Don't explain; don't justify; but question. Auschwitz, too, is a dangerous memory.

This is where anamnestic reason comes into play. Reason traditionally has been understood in terms of abstract universals. Modern reason in particular involves mastery if not domination. Auschwitz as dangerous memory cannot be thought through in these terms. As Theodor W. Adorno pointed out, after Auschwitz, "we cannot say any more that the immutable is truth, and that the mobile, transitory is appearance. This mutual indifference of temporality and eternal ideas is no longer tenable even with the bold Hegelian explanation that temporal existence, by virtue of the destruction inherent in its concept, serves the eternal represented by the eternity of destruction."[16] Or in Metz's terms, "Only as anamnestically constituted does reason prevent abstract understanding from taking progressive lack of recollection, progressive amnesia, for actual progress. Only anamnestic reason enables enlightenment to enlighten itself again concerning the harm it has caused."[17] The "universal" basis for reasoning is not some abstract idea of, for example, what it means to be human. Rather, suffering is the true universal, a universal that is historical. But this entails living without the stability of closure. "When I assert that the *memoria passionis* is the only universal category of humanity open to us, I am not thinking of a memory which only serves to affirm us or to secure our identities - rather the opposite: it calls into question our tightly sealed-up identities. It is 'dangerous' memory; it makes one rather 'weak,' it creates an open flank."[18] And this openness characterizes

[15] Johann Baptist Metz, "Christians and Jews after Auschwitz: Being a Meditation also on the End of Bourgeois Religion," in *Love's Strategy: The Political Theology of Johann Baptist Metz*, ed. John Downey (Harrisburg, PA: Trinity Press, 1999), 41.

[16] Theodor W. Adorno, *Negative Dialectics*, trans E. B. Ashton (New York: Continuum, 1995), 361.

[17] Johann Baptist Metz, "Anamnestic Reason: A Theologian's Remarks on the Crisis in the *Geisteswissenschaften*," in *Cultural-Political Interventions in the Unfinished Project of Enlightenment*, ed. Axel Honneth, Thomas McCarthy, Claus Offe, and Albrecht Wellmer (Cambridge, MA: MIT Press, 1992), 191.

[18] Johann Baptist Metz, *Hope against Hope: Johann Baptist Metz and Elie Wiesel Speak Out on the Holocaust*, ed. Ekkehard Schuster and Reinhold Boschert-Kimmig, trans. J. Matthew Ashley (New York and Mahwah, NJ: Paulist Press, 1999), 33-34.

thinking about history as well as the self. Dangerous memories call for the anamnestic reason capable of thinking through rupture and that remains ever open to interruption. Put another way, anamnestic reason maintains response-ability, that is, the ability to keep responding critically through the ruptures of dangerous memories.

Benjamin and Metz help us think about the possibility of mourning and its shortcomings. Responsibility for the past is rationally and morally essential to being human, and mourning can provide a helpful model as we work through historical trauma. But in light of dangerous memories, responsibility cannot be equated with control. Mourning as remembering is a good thing, but the very nature of what is remembered resists the closure that is the goal of memory work as mourning, that is, of working through the past as way to be liberated from it. The past has a future content that demands melancholic openness to the rupture of dangerous memories as a form of responsibility to the past, to the dead and their demand for justice.[19] It must remain possible to speak of Auschwitz, for example, in a manner that is not the practical equivalent of forgetting it by reducing it to a mere historical "fact." Melancholy may become pathological and acted out in repetition, but as Jay points out regarding Benjamin's melancholic refusal to mourn, there is a difference between "a refusal to mourn based on a denial that there was anything lost in the first place" and "a refusal to mourn that knows all too well what its object is…and is afraid that mourning will close the case prematurely."[20] Memory work requires the intellectual and moral courage to be melancholy, that is, to be open to the possibility of responding to ruptures ever again.

---

[19] See Giorgio Agamben, *Homo Sacer: Sovereign Power and Bare Life*, trans. Daniel Heller-Roazen (Stanford, CA: Stanford University Press, 1998); and Giorgio Agamben, *Remnants of Auschwitz: The Witness and the Archive*, trans. Daniel Heller-Roazen (New York: Zone Books, 1999).

[20] Jay, 237.

Second Courage

MODERN LIBERALISM, AUTHORITY AND AUTHORITARIANISM
Political Theology against Deceptive Modern Categories

Matthew L. Lamb

Totalitarianism was not of academic concern at the beginning of the twentieth century. Academics scarcely worried about the dangers of totalitarianism in, of all places, Enlightened Europe and America. Indeed, the term "totalitarianism" was not coined until the 1920's in reference to fascism and communism.[1] Tyranny (the more classical term) was to be swept away in an inevitable progress toward enlightened and liberal democratic governments. The warnings of a Plato or an Aristotle that democracies could degenerate into tyrannies seemed quaint to many at the dawn of the twentieth century.

Any effort to bring modern totalitarianism - and many would argue that only in the twentieth century with its technological achievements could we have totalitarianism - into relation with the pre-modern traditions of Christianity requires care. Moderns have ways of defining things to their own rather biased advantage, which biased definitions are hardly being deconstructed in postmodern historicism.

Another way of illustrating the problem is to recall the very heated debates in the Catholic Worker movement in the late 1930s and early 1940s. John Cogley and Jack English were two Catholic Workers who broke with Dorothy Day's pacifism and decided it was their moral duty to enlist in the war against fascism and Nazism. Dorothy Day kept worrying that armed struggle was inadequate to the real menace of totalitarianism and that our own liberal democracy could be infected by a similar pathology. Later in life Jack English remarked to me how he had failed to realize how Dorothy Day was arguing at a far deeper level than he had grasped in his younger days.[2] The level of argument was closer to that engaged by Theodor W. Adorno and Max Horkheimer in their *Dialectic of Enlightenment,* written in exile during Nazism and seeing this evil as linked, not with pre-modern darkness, but springing from the truncated character of supposed enlightened modernity. Other illustrations of this deeper level of concern and reflection are

---

[1] Hannah Arendt, *The Origins of Totalitarianism* (New York: Harcourt Brace Jovanovich, 1973). I use "liberalism" in the classic sense, which includes both liberal and conservative variations in American politics. In the light of Leo Strauss's hatred of Nazism - see Ron Rosenbaum, *Explaining Hitler: The Search for the Origins of His Evil* (New York: Random House, 1998), 395 - an important 1941 essay of Leo Strauss on "German Nihilism" has been published in *Interpretation: A Journal of Political Philosophy* Vol. 26, N. 3 (Spring 1999): 353-378.

[2] Cf. William Miller, *Dorothy Day: A Biography* (New York: Harper & Row, 1982), 313-403.

Zygmunt Bauman's *Modernity and the Holocaust* and Peter Novick's *The Holocaust in American Life*.[3]

Can the present academic and cultural attention to the Holocaust mask defense mechanisms by which liberal cultures continue to promote and extend a tyranny of tolerance, relativist nihilism, a culture of death? Could Dorothy Day's worry find its ground in the ways that national security and individualist choice now carry on the killing more subtly but no less effectively from the many arms races through the widespread legalization of abortion to euthanasia? One calls to mind Thomas Merton's "Chant to be Used in Procession around Furnaces" as it moves from German furnaces to nuclear missile silos; one could today extend its invocation of "clean cut" and "killing machines" to the aseptic abortion, euthanasia, and death-penalty procedures.[4]

Hannah Arendt warns of grave practical implications of everyday nihilism, arguing persuasively "the ideal subject of totalitarian rule is not the convinced Nazi or the convinced communist, but people for whom the distinction between fact and fiction (i.e. the reality of experience) and the distinction between true and false (i.e., the standards of thought) no longer exist."[5] Pierre Manent in a perceptive essay on totalitarianism remarks "one of the sources of the totalitarian project is found in the idea that it is possible for man to model society in accordance with his wishes, once he occupies the seat of power and possesses an exact social science and employs adequate means for this task."[6]

In this essay I shall argue that modern liberal cultures, by which I mean those cultures which draw upon the secularist political-philosophical categories of the European Enlightenment, have no way of adequately differentiating authority from authoritarianism. As a result, the efforts to deconstruct the totalitarianism of fascism, Nazism, and communism have failed to go to the roots of the problem, resulting in what Herbert Marcuse called a tyranny of tolerance, Alan Bloom called nihilism with a happy ending, and John Paul II calls a culture of death.

The first section will sketch the clear distinction between authority and authoritarianism in both pre-modern thought and Bernard Lonergan's work.

---

[3] Theodor W. Adorno & Max Horkheimer, *Dialektik der Aufklärung* (Amsterdam: Social Sciences Association, 1944); Zygmunt Bauman, *Modernity & the Holocaust* (Ithaca: Cornell University Press, 1989); Peter Novick, *The Holocaust in American Life* (New York: Houghton Mifflin, 1999).

[4] For a penetrating expose of contemporary secularist ideology on these issues, cf. Robert George, *The Clash of Orthodoxies: Law, Religion, and Morality in Crisis* (Wilmington DE: ISI Books, 2001). Thomas Merton, *The Collected Poems of Thomas Merton* (New York: New Directions Books, 1977); also *The Nonviolent Alternative: Revised Edition of Thomas Merton on Peace* (New York: Farrar Stauss, 1980).

[5] Hannah Arendt, *The Origins of Totalitarianism*, p. 474; also pp. 311-318 where she indicates how totalitarianism revealed the illusions of democratic pretensions.

[6] Pierre Manent, *Modern Liberty and Its Discontents,* edited & translated by Daniel Mahoney & Paul Seaton (New York: Rowman & Littlefield, 1998), 119.

The second section will indicate the failure of modern theories of authority to clearly differentiate it from authoritarianism, outlining Max Weber's notion of authority as domination. The final section will outline how a political theology, as Johann Baptist Metz elaborates it, offers the possibility of a recovery of theological traditions capable of illustrating his claim that tradition is constitutive of just and liberative authority.

Authority versus Authoritarianism

The difference between authority and authoritarianism is similar to the difference between love and rape. Indeed, authoritarianism not only contradicts authority, it seeks to destroy genuine authority. To equate authoritarianism with authority would be as unintelligent and irresponsible as equating rape with love. Can the traditions of secularist liberalism provide a clear and compelling differentiation of authority and authoritarianism?

My argument will be that modern liberal cultures are in a bind insofar as they have shifted the basic framework for understanding authority from a context in which wisdom and virtue provided the norms for legitimate authority to a context in which dominative power became normative and legitimacy was defined only extrinsically. Such a shift has hampered moderns from being able to discern the difference between a power that is legitimate because it is exercised wisely and virtuously, and the illegitimate use of power springing from intellectual and/or moral vice.[7] It is not that modern and postmodern cultures do not have criteria for legitimacy; it is that those criteria are always extrinsic and purely procedural, as Michael Sandel has illustrated.[8]

Take a key category for liberal political reflection: authoritarianism. It is usually defined in modern dictionaries and encyclopedias as "absolute or blind obedience to authority as opposed to individual freedom". Thus an "authoritarian political system" is opposed to "a democratic political system."[9] So it would appear as if the cure for authoritarianism is democracy. Yet the histories of democracies, ancient and contemporary, are replete with injustices stemming from blind bias and majority oppression of minorities. The question of authority in democracy is a fundamental and difficult one.[10]

---

[7] Cf. Bernard Lonergan, "Dialectic of Authority" in *A Third Collection* (New York: Paulist Press, 1985), 5-12.

[8] Michael Sandel, *Democracy's Discontent: America in Search of a Public Philosophy* (Cambridge: Harvard University Press, 1996).

[9] See *Encyclopedia Britannica, American Heritage Dictionary, Webster's, etc.*

[10] Cf. Robert Dahl, *After the Revolution? Authority in a Good Society* (New Haven: Yale University Press, 1990); Richard Sennett, *Authority* (New York: Alfred Knopf, 1980); note the tendency to seek solutions in terms of management in, e.g., Christopher McMahon, *Authority and Democracy: A General*

Bernard Lonergan provides a framework, in my judgment, for transposing a classical understanding of authority and power that finds norms in wisdom and virtue into contemporary historically conscious cultures. The importance of this transposition can be appreciated to the extent that one grasps the inability of contemporary cultures to clearly differentiate authority from authoritarianism. To simply equate authority with democracy will not do, as Socrates and countless other victims of arbitrary democratic procedures have experienced.[11]

Classical philosophy provided norms for judging those in authority by appealing to the intellectual virtues of wisdom and prudence. Socrates warns Alcibiades: "You have not therefore to obtain power or authority for yourself to do anything you like, nor has the state for itself; you must both get justice and wisdom." Discussing how ignorance and license bring on various misfortunes, Socrates continues: "And in like manner, in a state, and wherever there is any power and authority which is wanting in virtue, will not misfortune, in like manner, ensue?"[12] In Aristotle's ethics and politics one finds as well reflections on how laws and constitutions are inadequate if political authority is severed from the wisdom and justice of intellectual and moral excellence.[13]

This concern for normative judgments to guide those in authority was heightened in Judaism and Christianity. The normative judgments are to be guided, not only by human wisdom, prudence, and virtue, but also by the Divine judgment. God is no respecter of the powerful and mighty. Indeed, God enters into covenant with an enslaved and impoverished people. The covenant with Israel reveals how only the Lord can fully redeem the suffering and injustice of the chosen people. The New Covenant in Christ Jesus reveals how God's covenant and redemption are open to all peoples through the continuing mission of the Son and Spirit in the apostolic mission of the church.[14]

Theory of Government and Management (Princeton: Princeton University Press, 1997); William S. Graebner, *The Engineering of Consent: Democracy and Authority in Twentieth Century America* (Madison: University of Wisconsin Press, 1987).

[11] Cf. Ernest Becker, *Beyond Alienation: A Philosophy of Education for the Crisis of Democracy* (New York: George Braziller, 1969); Gil Elliot, *Twentieth Century Book of the Dead* (New York: Charles Scribner's Sons, 1972).

[12] *The Collected Dialogues of Plato* (Benjamin Jowett Fourth Edition, Oxford University Press, 1953) vol. 1 Appendix: Alcibiades 1 (134c and 135a-b), 673. Also Thomas L. Pangle (ed.) *The Roots of Political Philosophy: Ten Forgotten Socratic Dialogues* (Ithaca: Cornell University Press, 1987), 175-239.

[13] Cf. Ernest Fortin, *Classical Christianity & the Political Order: Reflections on the Theologico-Political* Problem (New York: Rowman & Littlefield, 1996); also, Richard Kraut, *Aristotle on the Human Good* (Princeton: Princeton University Press, 1989).

[14] Cf. Bruce Chilton & Jacob Neusner, *Types of Authority in Formative Judaism and Christianity* (New York: Routledge, 1999) but note the dependence on types originating with Max Weber; also the important work of James Burtchaell, *From Synagogue to Church: Public Services and Offices in the Earliest Christian Communities* (Cambridge: Cambridge University Press, 1992). Burtchaell provides an important dialectical history of the developments in the study of early Christianity from Luther to the present.

In both the Jewish and Christian scriptures one finds a stark recognition of the inadequacy of human efforts at virtuous living in the face of the massive injustice and evil in history. The authority and power of the Word of God revealed a prophetic wisdom and teaching that transcend and transform human living. Where the Jewish Scriptures present a range of political forms of authority (patriarchal, tribal, the judges, kingship), Christ's teaching and practice emphasizes that Christian authority is a *diakonia* or service.[15]

There are many resources in the Greek, Latin, and monastic theologians on the discernment and judgment required to exercise authority properly. Genuine authority is not authoritarian. It seeks to foster, not blind submission to arbitrary commands, but moral, religious, and intellectual excellence or virtue in those over whom one has authority.[16] In a Boston College symposium on authority, Bernard Lonergan contributed a short and incisive essay on the "Dialectic of Authority".[17] In it he retrieves the pre-modern notion that authority is "legitimate power" and that the source of power is in cooperation. Cooperation is both down through the ages, from one generation to the next, and ongoing at any given place or time. The context for a dialectic of authority, of distinguishing between genuine authority and mere authoritarianism, is the context of wisdom and discernment.

Lonergan transposes this wisdom in terms of discerning how authority is exercised according to the transcendental precepts (Be attentive, Be intelligent, Be reasonable, Be responsible). His transposition of the transcendental precepts from Aquinas's notion of wisdom are clear in his analysis of wisdom and the self-knowledge of the soul in Aquinas, who "subscribed, not obscurely, to the program of critical thought: to know truth we have to know ourselves and the nature of our knowledge, and the method to be employed is reflection."[18] Yet he realized that to bring a twentieth century reader to the explanatory theory of Aquinas, he had to articulate a new notion of wisdom "that generates the principles" grounding metaphysics, and brings to contemporary cultures the wisdom of the Greeks and medieval schoolmen, "but

[15] For authority as service, see Mt. 20:25-26; Lk. 22:25-26; also cf. Yves Congar, *Pour une église servante et pauvre* (Paris: Editions du Cerf, 1963).

[16] For just a few recent studies tapping into this vast literature, cf. Thomas DuBay, *Authenticity: A Biblical Theology of Discernment* (San Francisco: Ignatius Press, 1997); Luke T. Johnson, *Scripture and Discernment: Decision-Making in the Church* (Minneapolis: Abingdon Press, 1996); Jules Toner & George Ganss (eds.), *Commentary on Saint Ignatius' Rules for the Discernment of Spirits* (New York: Institute for Jesuit Studies, 1982); Armand Veilleux, *Pachomian Koinonia: The Lives and Teachings of St. Pachomius and His Disciples* volumes 1-3 (Kalamazoo: Cistercian Studies, 1982); Irénée Hausherr, SJ, *Spiritual Direction in the Early Christian East* (Kalamazoo: Cistercian Studies, 1990).

[17] Frederick J. Adelmann (ed.), *Authority*, Boston College Studies in Philosophy vol. III (The Hague: M. Nijhoff, 1974), 24-30.

[18] Bernard Lonergan, *Verbum: Word and Idea in Aquinas* (Toronto: University of Toronto Press, 1997), 87; see 78-104.

purged of every trace of antiquated science, formulated to integrate not only the science of the present but also of the future."[19]

Some have wondered what the place of virtues is in Lonergan's work. In fact, his notion of method is, in my judgment, a transposition of the pre-modern analysis of habits and virtues into the intentionality analysis of to-day. We have no conscious experiences of habits or faculties, but we do of our acts and the objects of those acts. From the ease with which we do sets of acts or operations, we can conclude that we have acquired a habit, good or bad. Now Lonergan's definition of method is "a normative pattern of related and recurrent operations yielding cumulative and progressive results."[20] A normative pattern of related and recurrent operations or acts is a set or sets of habits. The habits are good insofar as they yield cumulative and progressive results. Bad habits or vices can only yield repetitive and regressive results.

Authority, therefore, is legitimate insofar as it springs from an authentic cooperation across time, learning from those wise and virtuous in times past and present. Authority becomes authoritarian to the extent that the truly wise and virtuous are ignored and the cooperation springs, not from wisdom but ignorance and bias, promoting not the human good but domination and control for unjust ends.[21] Lonergan's dialectics of authority presupposes a rather drastic revision of many social theoretical categories that have been taken for granted in twentieth century analysis. Lonergan is not simply taking over the concepts of *Gemeinschaft* versus *Gesellschaft*, of community versus society, with which the social theorist Ferdinand Tönnies initiated what in later social theorists would become lists of supposed antagonisms between human spontaneity and social conformity.

For examples: Max Weber sets up contrasting ideal types of affective value-orientations in traditional or charismatic types, on the one hand, and instrumentalist rationality grounding bureaucratic types; Emile Durkheim opposes mechanical solidarity to organic solidarity; Talcott Parsons frames the basic problem of social order as how to control individuals locked in a Hobbesian "war of all against all", with a consequent extrinsicism endemic to his functionalist methods; even Jürgen Habermas contrasts and opposes a life-world to technical control increasingly dominating and colonizing the life-world; Anthony Giddens grants too many concessions to domination and constraint in social structure.[22]

---

[19] Bernard Lonergan, *Insight: A Study of Human Understanding* (Toronto: University of Toronto Press, 1992), 432 and 448.

[20] *Method in Theology* (Toronto: University of Toronto Press, 1996), 4.

[21] "Dialectic of Authority," 7-12.

[22] For a general introduction to these contrasts, cf. Gregory Baum, *Religion and Alienation* (New York: Paulist Press, 1975) esp. 41-61, 162-192. Jürgen Habermas, *The Theory of Communicative Action*, 2 vols., trans. Thomas McCarthy (Boston: Beacon Press, 1984-6); Anthony Giddens, *Central Problems in*

While it would far exceed the scope of this essay to spell out in sufficient detail these social theories, they are mentioned here only to alert the reader to possible misunderstandings. Lonergan analyzes the dynamics of developing society without invoking an instrumental rationality which dominates and controls by an authoritarian imposition of order what would otherwise be a chaotic jungle of narrow communal or tribal biases.[23] No matter how complex and specialized social institutions become, they always remain the products of human communal cooperation, whether for good or ill.[24]

Lonergan's notion of community and authority breaks with the materialism and empiricism of those who would see physical force as the source, and forcing others to obey one's commands as the carrier, of social power. Genuinely human social power - rather than reified and alienated phantoms - has its source in cooperation, and its carrier is community. Just as genuine social power expands responsibility and freedom, so genuine authority resides in such communal cooperation.[25] Contrary to much modern social theory, "it would seem to be a mistake to conceive the sociological as simply a matter of external constraint."[26] Indeed, force, constraint, and militarism reveal a failure, a terrible blindness and fear, at the core of all societies which depend on them for their social cohesion.[27] If the difference between genuine social power and authority, on the one hand, and dominative power and authoritarianism, on the other, is similar to the differences between love and rape, then social theory needs norms rooted in wisdom rather than power. Social theories today, absent wisdom, tend to reflect rather than correct the underlying alienations in modern societies.

Contemporary scholarship is only beginning to overcome a nineteenth and early twentieth century prejudice that ignored the literature on discernment and forced texts into an authoritarian framework. Indeed, it is difficult to see the meaning and practices communicated by this patristic and monastic literature through the modern and postmodern glasses we have inherited. Pierre Hadot has made this point in regard to the spiritual exercises foundational to classical philosophy.[28] When it comes to writings on discernment and the exercise of authority, it is especially important to avoid modern categories that can too easily distort the real import of the traditions.

Social Theory (Berkeley: University of California Press, 1979) and his *The Constitution of Society* (Berkeley: University of California Press, 1984).

[23] Cf. Matthew Lamb, "The Social and Political Dimensions of Lonergan's Theology" in Vernon Gregson (ed.) *The Desires of the Human Heart: An Introduction to the Theology of Bernard Lonergan* (New York: Paulist Press, 1988), 255-284.

[24] Cf. *Insight*, 477-8, 627-9.

[25] Cf. "Dialectic of Authority," 5-12.

[26] *Insight*, 215.

[27] Cf. *Insight*, p. 238.

[28] Pierre Hadot, *Philosophy as a Way of Life* (Oxford: Blackwell, 1995).

Max Weber: Authority becomes Authoritarian

In the final section of this essay I shall indicate the importance of a specifically theological solution to the problem of authoritarianism and injustice in history. In Lonergan's dialectics of authority he ends with the need, given the massive injustices and histories of suffering everywhere evident, for redemption. Intellectual and moral excellence or virtues are not adequate to the task of justifying human communities, societies, and authorities. Only God is able to redeem them.[29] As the saying goes "corruptio optimi pessima" - the corruption of the best is the worst. Contributing to the pre-history of the modern collapse of authority into authoritarianism is a long list of failures on the part of philosophers and theologians, secular and ecclesiastical authorities, in European Christendom. There was a general failure to measure up to the great intellectual, moral, and religious achievements of the truly excellent.

Those failures became rationalized and the bitter harvests of nominalism and voluntarism, of secular and ecclesiastical authoritarianism, were there for the founders of modernity to systematize in the works of Machiavelli through Hobbes, Locke, Hume, Descartes, Kant and Hegel, to Marx and Weber.[30] Lonergan has pointed out how these thinkers, by trying to rely too heavily upon empirical modern science and mathematical calculation - recall Hobbes' definition of reasoning as calculating - were unable to fulfill the Enlightenment's promise of liberation:

> There was promised that liberation of man under the rule of emancipated reason. But the implementation of that rule was entrusted to modern science; and modern science put its faith far less in the immanent reasonableness of the human spirit, far more in the embodiment of reason in experimental results and mathematical hardheadedness. So extrinsic a criterion and so abstruse a control, it can be argued, have done more for the mechanization than for the liberation of human life.[31]

For Max Weber authority is "Herrschaft".[32] Despite Talcott Parsons' valiant efforts to camouflage the Nietzschean influences on Weber with bland functionalist terminology, it is now recognized that Weber's social theoretical

---

[29] Cf. Lamb, "Social and Political Dimensions of Lonergan's Theology," 269-279.

[30] Cf. Fred Lawrence, "The Modern Philosophic Differentiation of Consciousness, or What is Enlightenment" in Fred Lawrence (ed.) *Lonergan Workshop* (Atlanta: Scholars Press, 1981), 231-279; also Alan Bloom, *The Closing of the American Mind* (New York: Simon & Schuster, 1987), 284-312.

[31] Lonergan's Foreword in Matthew L. Lamb, *History, Method and Theology* (Atlanta: Scholars Press, 1978), vi.

[32] Max Weber, *Economy and Society* translated by Guenther Roth & Claus Wittich (Berkeley: University of California Press, 1978), Volume I: 215ff.

analysis of authority is in terms of domination.[33] It coincides with his theoretical project of founding modern social theory. Max Weber constructs a complex conceptualist methodology, the terms and relations of which are fundamental to social theory. This "nest" of terms and relations establishes a framework within which most subsequent sociological analysis is developed. Value-neutrality is fundamental to the project and so is what might be termed a "truth-neutrality" if the judgment of truth requires anything more than an appeal to the data of sense. A socially normative rationality is instrumental. Conceptualist "pure types" provide the slots into which social agents and procedures are pegged. The entire section of his *Economy and Society* dealing with authority is entitled "The Types of Legitimate Domination." Central are associations (*Vergesellschaftung*); community and communal patterns of cooperation tend to be viewed as holdovers from premodern times. They are transmogrified into "traditional" types of domination.

Because normative rationality is instrumental (*Zweckrationalität),* the greater the value informing human actions, the greater their irrationality since the one acting, informed with a dedication to the goodness of what is valued, does not calculate the consequences of his actions.[34] Authority is analyzed in purely command/control terms. The one in authority is the one who dominates his subordinates, and they obey him. Authority is, to put it bluntly, social authoritarian domination as control:

> To be more specific, domination will thus mean the situation in which the manifested will (command) of the ruler or rulers is meant to influence the conduct of one or more others (the ruled) and actually does influence it in such a way that their conduct to a socially relevant degree occurs as if the ruled had made the content of the command the maxim of their conduct for its very own sake - Looked upon from the other end, this situation will be called obedience.[35]

Authority as "legitimate power" - to recall Lonergan's definition - is not defined by an attentive, intelligent, reasonable, and responsible cooperation.

The basis of legitimacy can be (1) conventional, by which Weber means traditional, affect-laden, or value-based, or (2) positive-legal, which predominates in advanced modern societies. Authority is needed since social relationships are conflictual, competitive, or selective. The first are those of

---

[33] Cf. Reinhard Bendix & Guenther Roth, *Scholarship and Partisanship: Essays on Max Weber* (Berkeley: University of California Press, 1971); Anthony Giddens, *Studies in Social and Political Theory* (New York: Basic Books, 1977); Susan Hekman, *Weber: The Ideal Type and Contemporary Social Theory* (Notre Dame: Notre Dame University Press, 1983); also Matthew Mullane, "Nietzsche and Weber on the Critique of Religion" to be published in Fred Lawrence (ed.) *Lonergan Workshop Journal.*

[34] *Economy and Society*, vol. 1: 26.

[35] *Economy and Society*, vol. 2: 946.

warfare (*Kampf*); and the competitive relations are "war by more peaceful means." Thus the third form, selective social relations, takes on the hues of a Darwinian competitive selection.[36] We see here how Weber has internalized in modern social theory the political philosophical notions of warfare as intrinsic to human life. As will be mentioned in the next section, the Enlightenment *philosophes*, responding to the European wars of religion, tended to dump religion and write warfare into human nature.[37] Since the basic types of social relationships are such, there is no room for an understanding of human beings as by nature cooperative. There is no natural basis of legitimacy but only "conventional" or "contractual".

Modern liberal democracies, for Weber, depend upon an internalized domination. What Weber saw as crucial to this entire system of modernity was the "belief in legitimacy" whereby millions and millions of human beings externally behave in ways that spread and deepen the patterns of authoritative domination in modernity. He was not interested in such value questions as what motivated this obedience.[38] In democracies we get to elect at least some of the governmental dominators.[39] But there is no constitutive role for intellectual or moral virtues, let alone theological virtues.

This absence of virtues' role is evident in the three pure types of authoritarian domination. The legal-bureaucratic is the specifically modern type of authority. It is what makes modernity function. There is an impersonal order ramifying throughout modern societies in which commands are given and followed. This is functional, formal, technical rationality par excellence. Weber sees eight fundamental categories in this type of dominative authority: rule-bound conduct, jurisdiction, hierarchy, rules as technical and normative, bureaucrats not owning means of production, persons completely indifferent to offices (cogs in machine), written forms paramount, bureaucracy the dominant form.[40]

Legal-bureaucratic rationality is present in both the modern political and modern religious (or what Weber calls hierocratic) organizations.[41] The bureaucratic aspect of this legal authority Weber calls monocratic and, in the light of subsequent totalitarianism, his praise for it is chilling:

> Experience tends universally to show that the purely bureaucratic type of administrative organization - that is, the monocratic variety of bureaucracy -

---

[36] *Economy and Society*, vol. 1: 39.
[37] Cf. Edith Wyschogrod, *Spirit in Ashes: Hegel, Heidegger and Man-Made Death* (New Haven: Yale University Press, 1985); also M. Lamb, "Christianity within the Political Dialectics of Community and Empire," in N. Biggar, J. Scott, & W. Schweiker (eds.) *Cities of Gods: Faith, Politics and Pluralism in Judaism, Christianity and Islam* (New York: Greenwood Press, 1986), 73-100.
[38] *Economy and Society,* vol. 1: 215, n. 4.
[39] *Economy and Society*, vol. 2: 948-955; 1442-1462.
[40] *Economy and Society*, vol. 1: 218-20.
[41] *Economy and Society*, vol. 1: 220-222.

> is, from a purely technical point of view, capable of attaining the highest degree of efficiency and is in this sense formally *the most rational known means of exercising authority over human beings.*[42]

This is realized in both capitalism and socialism. All emotion and value is irrelevant and should they intrude, they would be "irrational." This monocratic bureaucracy pervades all sectors of modern society: church, state, military, politics, education, and economics. It makes mass liberal democracy possible. Indeed, long before Michael Sandel would complain about procedural liberalism, Weber was indicating how there is a way in which no modern society can be a liberal mass democracy without monocratic bureaucracy. "Everywhere bureaucratization foreshadows mass democracy."[43]

The other two pure types of authority, the traditional and the charismatic, can hardly hold a candle to the efficiency of the legal-bureaucratic. Weber defines these types of authority in ways that will assure that their applications to the past and to religious phenomena will silence any ability the past or religion might have to significantly challenge modernity.

In analyzing the traditional types of authority Weber sets up the categories in such a way that one sees pre-modern societies as having little or no wisdom to pass on to us. Not efficient bureaucracy but "the sanctity of age-old rules and powers" provide legitimacy. Not impersonal social order but the person of those in authority, the rulers, is important. Gerontocracy, Patriarchalism, and Patrimonialism are ways traditional dominative authority is realized. Fiefs, benefices, etc. - everything in the sections on this type of authority breathes of musty, old regimes. Where this traditional domination occurs "It breaks down the type of formal rationality which is oriented to technical legal order." Thus modern capitalism would be impossible if only the traditional types of authority prevailed.[44]

Types of charismatic authority are, in Weber's social theory, the opposite of the legal-bureaucratic. Weber took over a specifically religious and Christian term, investing it with value-neutral connotations that would assure a contradiction between the religious and the intellectual or reasonable person. "The term 'charisma' will be applied to a certain quality of an individual personality by virtue of which he is considered extraordinary and treated as endowed with supernatural, superhuman, or at least specifically exceptional powers or qualities".[45] The occurrence of "quality" twice should warn us. Charisma is not quantifiable and so must be radically "irrational"! Indeed,

---

[42] *Economy and Society*, vol. 1: 223, italics mine; cf. also 223-226; also vol. 2: 956-1005.
[43] *Economy and Society*, vol. 1: 226.
[44] *Economy and Society*, vol. 1: 226-241.
[45] *Economy and Society*, vol. 1: 241.

charismatic domination as Weber defines it is "irrational": "Bureaucratic domination is specifically rational in the sense of being bound to intellectually analyzable rules; while charismatic domination is specifically *irrational* in the sense of *being foreign to all rules*."[46] If charismatic authorities are a danger to modern legal-bureaucratic authority, Weber in the rest of the treatment shows how charismatic dominative authority, although a threat to bureaucratic domination, need not be feared. It will inevitably be "routinized" either traditionally or rationally. In modern liberal democracies, any traditional routinization will most likely give way, over time, to a bureaucratic one. The irrational charisma is *per definitionem* only in individual authorities and so will either die out with the death of the individual or become institutionalized in organizations that will routinize it. Only by routine can the "everyday reality" be touched by charisma.[47]

Weber set the pattern for modern social theory in dealing with authority. This brief overview indicates how any discussion of intellectual, moral, let alone theological, virtues find no place in such theoretical analysis. Legal-bureaucracy is no antidote to authoritarianism or totalitarianism. Modern political and social theorists rejected a concern for the virtues as being "unrealistic" and too "idealistic". Yet by making the norms for authority purely procedural and extrinsic, there is no way to avoid the identification of authority with authoritarianism. Only by attending to virtue, to types of intellectual and moral and religious excellence, can one appreciate a truly just and humane exercise of authority that fosters excellence in others.

The darker, Nietzschean side of Weber grasped the sad irony of modern liberal democracies ever more reliant upon an ever expanding dominative bureaucracy.[48] At the end of *Economy and Society* he offers a somber set of reflections on the "political limitations of bureaucracy" which raise the specter of mass management of purely procedural democracies.[49] Elsewhere Weber wrote: "We are anyway involved in this development towards a world which knows only these men of order. The central question, therefore, is not how to support and accelerate this trend ever further, but rather what we have to oppose to this machinery of order to preserve a remnant of humanity from this fragmentation of the soul, from this absolute domination of the bureaucratic ideals of life."[50]

---

[46] *Economy and Society*, vol. 1: 244, emphasis mine.

[47] *Economy and Society*, vol. 1: 251.

[48] Leo Strauss recognized most profoundly this Nietzschean undertow of Weber's project, cf. the excellent study by Nasser Behnegar, *Leo Strauss, Max Weber, and the Scientific Study of Politics* (Chicago: University of Chicago Press, 2003).

[49] *Economy and Society*, vol. 2: 1403-1462.

[50] *Gesammelte Aufsätze zur Soziologie und Socialpolitik* (Tübingen: Mohr, 1924), 412 ff. Also, Karl Löwith, *Max Weber and Karl Marx* edited by Tom Bottomore & William Outhwaite (London: George Allen & Unwin, 1982).

This recalls Lonergan's comment on the unrealized promise of emancipation from the European Enlightenment and the resulting mechanization of life. In the Epilogue of *Insight,* Lonergan indicates how even fully developed empirical human sciences would need theology in order to meet adequately the issue of evil and the mystery of God's transformation of evil into good:

> In a word, empirical human science can become practical only through theology, and the relentless modern drift to social engineering and totalitarian controls is the fruit of man's effort to make human science practical though he prescinds from God and from the solution God provides for man's problem.[51]

Empirical human science becomes practical through theology. This would strike most if not all psychologists, sociologists, and other human scientists as strange, if not outright absurd. Lonergan is hardly a fundamentalist, ready to wave the Bible at any and all social problems. He goes on to state emphatically that theology can in no way substitute for the human sciences.[52] What, then, does he mean? I have begun to answer this in various studies.[53] It involves a transformation of many of the central categories of contemporary social theory within a heuristic of his analysis of the human good.[54]

In fact, the types of authority as Weber analyzes them distort the normative dialectics of authority, for they remain value-neutral and merely extrinsic. There is simply no substitute for intellectual, moral and religious excellence; there is no substitute for being attentive, intelligent, reasonable, and responsible. Liberal democracy is no guarantee against patterns of dominative authoritarianism, especially when, as Weber points out, democracy can foster an internalization of domination in individuals and groups. Indeed, the mechanization of social life gives a much wider scope to dominative patterns. As Metz and Adorno remark, is it progress when cannibals use knives and forks?

Political Theology Interrupts Modern Authoritarianism

The final section will indicate how the political theology of Johann Baptist Metz recovers pre-modern theological traditions in ways that challenge modern categories and assumptions. The way "charisma" and "institution"

---

[51] Lonergan, *Insight*, 745.
[52] *Insight*, 746.
[53] Cf. Vernon Gregson (ed.), *The Desires of the Human Heart*, 255-284; also "The Dialectics of Theory and Praxis within Paradigm Analysis," in H. Küng & D. Tracy (eds.) *Paradigm Change in Theology* (New York: Crossroad, 1989), 63-109, 453-460; and "Communicative Praxis and Theology: Beyond Modern Nihilism and Dogmatism," in D. Browning & F. Fiorenza (eds.), *Habermas, Modernity, and Public Theology* (New York: Crossroad, 1992), 92-118.
[54] Cf. Bernard Lonergan, *Method in Theology*, 27-55.

and "authority", for example, are defined in contemporary social theory, exegetes and theologians using them can easily filter out important meanings and truths contained in our theological traditions. Metz is especially interested in those notions of the past that seem to jar our modern and postmodern sensibilities. He developed his political theology not as a complete theological system, but as a critical corrective, not only to theology but also most especially to the self-assurance of the twentieth century. To modern notions of authority, Metz invokes the authority of the victims, the authority of suffering, indicating how this arises out of the "*memoria passionis, mortis et resurrectionis Jesu Christi*."[55]

Metz writes on the contemporary crisis of authority, indicating how the Enlightenment notion of equality and procedural process masks deeper alienations.[56] Thomas Hobbes, after all, came up with the first modern affirmation of universal equality as based on the fact that the weakest can kill the strongest.[57] This, Metz sees, is to reduce social relations to those of a vast exchange market. As Lonergan emphasized the importance of cooperation down the ages for the practice of genuine authority, so Metz insists, contra Weber, that a liberative exercise of authority binds it to tradition:

> Authority must not be separated from tradition. Authority is, so to speak, the import, the urgency and persistence with which tradition is remembered and argued. To the extent that tradition belongs to the constitution of critical reason, this latter has always those characteristics of the authority [of tradition], without which critical reason could not finally be liberating.[58]

The horrors of the Holocaust, the extent of contemporary cultures of death, lead me to close with some reflections on Metz's retrieval of the theological category of apocalyptic.

I should like to indicate, however briefly, how Metz's insights into apocalyptic presence break the hold of time as inexorable evolutionary continuum on modern cultures and open one to startlingly new recoveries of patristic and scholastic theologians. Metz's theses on apocalyptic, by calling into question the hegemony of history as a progressive continuum, invite us through faith and reason to be open again to the past; to realize that there

---

[55] Johann B. Metz, *Glaube in Geschichte und Gesellschaft* (Mainz: Grünewald, 1977). The first English translation of this, as with other works of Metz, is generally very poor. A new translation by J. Matthew Ashley is forthcoming from Continuum.

[56] *Glaube in Geschichte und Gesellschaft,* 36ff.

[57] Thomas Hobbes, *De Cive* Caput I, 3.

[58] *Glaube in Geschichte und Gesellschaft,* 37. My translation.

may well be achievements of the past forgotten and repressed in our contemporary cultures.[59]

American culture has deeply imbibed the Enlightenment replacements of wisdom and praxis with productivity and power. Without contemplative wisdom, along with the intellectual and moral excellence required by praxis and genuine justice, culture instrumentalizes religion, reason, and humanity itself. I recall how struck Metz was when *Time* magazine made the computer "man of the year." The United States illustrates powerfully the identification of progress with technology and industry, with mechanization. Historically, this has led to the notion of historical time as an unbroken and uninterruptible continuum. The clock keeps time. Progress marches on. Each generation is condemned to die in the waiting room of the future. We have to go forward. God help us if we go backwards. "Medieval" is a term of reproach. Analyzing this contemporary approach toward time, Metz sees it as basically a denial of any meaningful significance to the particularity of time. He calls the symptoms and system of this modern experience of time a loss of time, a loss of the "humanum" of time. It is translated as "timelessness" but might be better rendered as "time-lostness" (*Zeitlosigkeit*).[60]

What is the *Zeitlosigkeit*, this loss of time as symptom and system for Metz? It is a loss of time as real presence. Time is devalued into a mechanical process, a continuum inexorably moving from past into future. All of human history with the many histories of suffering are stuck on this endless evolutionary continuum like so many dead butterflies on an endless felt board. Metz identifies this "*Zeitlosigkeit*" with the fixation of modernity upon productivity ("*Machbarkeit*") in thesis III. Indeed, here Metz goes to the heart of the modern deformation. Modernity broke with the past. Progress would no longer be in terms of human excellence, whether intellectual, moral, or religious. Political life would no longer be defined by the praxis of virtues, as it was from Plato and Aristotle to Aquinas and Bonaventure. The moderns, from Machiavelli through Hobbes and Locke to Kant and Marx, would assimilate the political to the productive. The political way of living has become totally subordinated to the productive way of living. Praxis has been reduced to technique; doing is just another variation of making. In this, modernity has fallen into a form of idolatry.

For, as the ancients and medievals remind us, the good in the productive way of life resides not in the producers but in the things made. Skills (whether in business, crafts, or arts) can produce goods, but they do not require any virtue or excellence beyond the excellence of the skills themselves.

---

[59] *Glaube in Geschichte und Gesellschaft*, 149-158. There are XXXV theses, and I refer to their roman numerals in the text. These theses could well be for twenty-first century theology what Feuerbach's theses were to twentieth century philosophy.

[60] Cf. *Glaube in Geschichte und Gesellschaft*, 57-74, 136-148.

Murderers and thieves and generally vicious people can be very skillful. A politics built upon productive skills, with little or no attention paid to intellectual and moral virtues, is a politics of power where justice is subservient to winning and maintaining power.

Moreover, Metz has made clear that to rescue praxis from its instrumentalization into technique, it is important to recognize how genuine praxis demands theory. The system of a timeless continuum of evolutionary progress is one that can be recognized and criticized only by those who know what Metz elsewhere calls "the second order theories" determining modern cultures and societies. The priority of praxis to technique and systems of instrumental reason does not mean that intelligence, along with wisdom and science, is subordinated to immediate practical purposes. That would be an instrumentalization of theory that would be in no position to differentiate clearly praxis from technique. This is why, in my judgment, the Bielefeld project was so integral to Metz's political theology.[61] The intellectual and theoretical ways of living in universities and research institutes are vitally important to a proper transformation of culture and society. For, as Metz writes, the criterion of truth is not to be subordinated to any short term "relevance" that would cut short the universality of truth for all the dead and victims of history.[62]

Indeed, I have tried to show how precisely the prejudices which are criticized so strongly in Enlightenment and post-Enlightenment societies - racism, sexism, ageism, exploitation of the poor, of children, of the environment - are all rooted in failures to cultivate the intellectual and moral virtues.[63] Plato, Aristotle, Augustine, and Aquinas, along with others, emphasized that these virtues are needed in any just political order. Racism, as we know it, is an invention of the seventeenth century. The task of recovering wisdom traditions of the past is not a task of an archaism, a mere restoration of some past epoch. Quite the contrary, a genuine dialectic requires that the recovery of past and repressed wisdom traditions be transposed into very different contexts in order, for example, to counteract the baneful effects of their loss. The reduction of progress to technological advance is a case in point. Now that the twentieth century book of the dead has received its final chapter, the murderous use of technology is painfully evident.

The Enlightenment *philosophes* took the wrong path in their reaction to the European wars of religion. They kept the bath water and threw out the baby. They concentrated their criticisms on religion and then proceeded to

[61] The "Bielefeld Project" was a failed attempt to establish a Center for Interdisciplinary Research at the University of Bielefeld supported by the German Evangelical and Roman Catholic Churches.

[62] *Glaube in Geschichte und Gesellschaft*, 47-57

[63] Cf. Matthew Lamb, *Solidarity with Victims* (New York: Crossroads, 1982); also "The Transcultural in Bernard Lonergan's Theology" in *Method: Journal of Lonergan Studies* vol. 8, n. 1 (March 1990): 48-73; and "The Political and Social Dimensions of Lonergan's Theology."

link human nature inexorably with violence and war. Little wonder, then, that the twentieth century would witness more human beings slaughtered by their fellow humans than any other of the bloody centuries. Productivity and its skills are not enough. The openness of the past to recovery is not a romantic return to some past era, but an effort to do justice to the intellectual and moral demands of our present time. As Metz, along with some of his students such as Helmut Peukert, saw clearly, the era of modern specialization in the sciences was calling forth the need to integrate these vastly expanding special disciplines by initiating a new movement toward a wise integration in interdisciplinary collaboration. So the pre-modern quest for wisdom, with its concerns for a heuristic appreciation of wholes, can offer important contributions to the intellectual and moral integration of the sciences and other scholarly disciplines.

The Greek and Latin fathers were keenly aware of the limitations of a political order based only on productive skills. They had seen the collapse of any genuine philosophy, or love of wisdom, in the decline of the Greek and Roman empires. In the Cynics and Epicureans they had witnessed the post-imperial resignation of the intellectuals to nothing but fragmentation; indeed, as St. Augustine saw, even the Stoics were retreating into a privatized reservation of the spirit. The philosophical quest for intellectual and moral excellence or virtues retreated before the initial success and achievements of productive skills, from military prowess through business and construction to crafts and arts. Wisdom and justice gave way to power and cunning. The fathers shunned the many political theologies of empire in the first three centuries. They usually avoided "*theologia*" and preferred "*philosophia*" to designate their reflections on the Gospel, thereby linking themselves with the philosophical critiques of the many mythological theologies legitimating the political and social corruptions of empire. So, in his "new political theology," St. Augustine spelled out how the fullness of justice and peace is not a skilled achievement of the earthly cities but only comes about in the gifted friendship with the Triune God and the kingdom incarnate in Christ Jesus. In his monumental *City of God* Augustine provides a devastating criticism of Roman political theologies legitimating the disordered desire for domination ("*libido dominandi*").[64] A major theme of the work is precisely how the productive skills ("*artes*") were deformed into a demonic and idolatrous legitimation of imperial domination and injustice.[65] Only Christ can bring about full and complete justice in the city of God, because he renounces domination on the cross and redeems humankind, not by removing evil through power, but by taking into himself all the evil of the universe, all the powers

[64] Cf. *City of God*, I, 30; III, 14; XIV, 15, 28; XV, 23.
[65] Cf. *City of God*, VI-VIII.

of death. Only the Word Incarnate could suffer so profoundly and transform evil and death into justice and eternal life, rising from the dead.[66]

It is the presence of Christ in history, Truth and Justice incarnate, recognized and responded to by the theological virtues of faith, hope, and agapic love of even enemies, that breaks the cycles of domination and power. Where all the cities of men rely upon the ultimate sanction of death to enforce laws, Christ overcomes the power of death and brings about the apocalyptic realization of the eternal city of God. It is the gifted friendship with the Triune God that enables Christians to engage in the praxis of the intellectual and moral virtues, just as it had Augustine himself.

His *Confessions* spelled out how inadequate his rhetorical skills were when it came to the real questions moving his mind and heart. It was the revelation of God's covenants with us in Israel and in Christ that led Augustine to an intellectual and moral praxis or way of living surpassing that of the Greek and Roman philosophers.[67] Thus he chides even so great a genius as Plato, along with the Platonists, for failing to break with the superstitions of religious mythology and for rationalizing this anti-intellectualism with the notion of the noble lie.[68] Metz's theses on apocalyptic provide insights and categories to retrieve the work of Africa's greatest political theologian.

Indeed, Thesis VI of Metz "the shortest definition of religion: interruption" is similar to Augustine's analysis of the novelty, the newness, that comes to human history with the advent of Jesus Christ, breaking the tyranny of endless sameness in the wars and violence of sinful history.[69] Augustine is well aware of the classical meaning of "*interpellare, interpellatio*" as "to interrupt, an interruption." He uses the words in this sense in his *Soliloquies, On Music,* and *Letters*. He also uses them to designate the activity of Jesus Christ on our behalf, as in *Confessions* X, 43:

> How much you have loved us, O good Father, … for us he [Jesus Christ] was to you both victor and victim, and victor because victim. For us he was to you both priest and sacrifice, and priest because sacrifice. He turns us from slaves into your sons, by being your Son and becoming a slave. Rightly is my hope strong in him, who sits at your right hand and '*te interpellat*' for us.

This is usually translated, as in St. Jerome's Vulgate of Romans 8:34 as "intercedes with you for us" - a meaning that is widespread in Medieval Latin. But the victim who is victor *because* victim, the sacrifice who is priest *because* sacrifice - truly Christ interrupts the cycles of sacrifice and victimhood

---

[66] Cf. *City of God,* XX-XXII.
[67] *Confessions*, V-IX.
[68] *City of God*, X, XIV, and XIX.
[69] Cf. *City of God,* XII, 21.

for us before God. And is this not a crucial aspect of how Jesus as mediator intercedes for us?

The apocalyptic presence of Christ, and him crucified and raised, reveals the wisdom of God. We are redeemed, not as the empires and superpowers of history would seek to redeem, by removing evil through power and force. No, the mystery of our redemption in Christ is the mystery of God, as only God could, transforming death into life and evil into good, through suffering. Apocalyptic reveals how the Word of God transcends time and creates all time. The Jewish and Christian covenants with God do not reveal an eternal God who punishes human sin by casting down intelligent creatures into time and matter. Augustine realized how such Gnostic and Manichean myths failed to explain both the goodness of creation and the responsibility of intellectual creatures for evil. Indeed, such mythology robs time of any immanent expectation; it robs time of its presence to God. Time becomes a mythological prison for lost souls, who are inexorably chained to matter and motion. Augustine criticized such Manichean mythology that paraded as a quasi-metaphysical and rational account of things, an account that Augustine saw was at root irrational as well as opposed to genuine faith.

Metz in thesis XV criticizes the Bultmannian tendency to read eschatology and apocalyptic expectation chronologically, thereby delivering theology over to the deceptive logic of an evolutionary continuum. It was Isaac Newton who led the modern tendency to reduce eschatology and apocalyptic to a chronology of time as continuum in his commentaries on the Book of Daniel and Apocalypse.

A recovery of apocalyptic expectation, as Metz avers in thesis XXXIV, does not pit a time experienced as presence to Christ in faith against time as experienced by reason. It is here that apocalyptic expectation is one with anamnetic solidarity. Only God can bring about the resurrection of the dead. Only God can bring about a kingdom of full justice, goodness, and holiness in the eternal presence of the Triune God. The apocalyptic parables in Matthew's Gospel proclaim this truth of faith. This finds a parallel in Augustine's efforts to show how the intellectual and moral efforts of the great Greek and Roman philosophers are by no means dismissed by Christian faith, hope, and agapic love. Rather, as stated above, it is faith in the messianic mission of Christ that enables Christians to take up the cause of intelligence and justice. What Augustine narrates of his own intellectual conversions in his *Confessions* in books V-VII, and then his moral conversion made possible by his religious conversion or turning to Christ (books VIII-IX), becomes fundamental to Christian theology as constituted by both the light of reason and the light of faith. Later Thomas Aquinas would articulate this in terms of the unity of the intellectual, moral, and theological virtues.

Finally, apocalyptic faith does not set up a paradoxical opposition between eternity and time (theses XIV-XXI). God's eternity is not, as Metz correctly indicates in thesis XVI, the endless duration of Spinoza's "Deus sive natura". God's eternal presence, as Augustine saw so clearly after much struggle, creates and embraces all time. Only God is "*totum esse praesens*,"[70] each and every present moment is present because God loves it into existence. God's eternal presence in no way is a *Verblendungszusammenhang* in which all the suffering and evil of human history is forgotten. On the contrary, the Greek and Latin fathers recognize in the Word Incarnate's suffering and death Christ taking up into himself concretely all the suffering and evil of each and every human being who ever has, is, or will live and die. This can be seen in Athanasius's notion of the cosmic cross of Christ. Only a divine person incarnate could do this.

Later St. Thomas Aquinas would spell this out in his theology of the passion (*Summa Theologiae* III, 46-50). As a divine person, the Word is more intimate to each and every being than that being is to itself, for the Word as God is being. So also the Word is more intimate to each and every human being than that human being is to him or herself, for the Word as God is conscious self-presence in which each of us as created intelligent beings only participate. As God the Word with the Father and Spirit infinitely loves each and every human being. If we took all the love human beings have shown one another throughout all of history, it would only be a spark compared to the fire of divine infinite love. That is why, as Augustine remarks, marriage is a sacrament of the love of Christ for his spouse, the Church.

The more we love someone, the more we suffer in his or her sufferings. The more we love someone, the more our hearts are broken when they offend us. St. Thomas Aquinas states that Jesus Christ in his human consciousness had not the light of faith, as we do, but the light of glory, that in no way dulled his pain, suffering and sorrow. It did the opposite. The higher the created consciousness, the greater is the suffering. Knowing and loving the Triune God both divinely and humanly, only such a human nature united hypostatically to the Word could take up into his human mind and heart each and every human being with all his and her sins and sufferings. Jesus Christ as the divine Person of the Word incarnate suffered more than all the sufferings of human beings throughout history put together. As the Word Incarnate He gathers together each and every human being in all the uniqueness of each and every one of us. Every human being is present in Christ's human mind and heart, as the beloved is present in the lover, the known present in the knower. The concrete totality of all the unique and most painful histories of suffering are present in Christ's love for each and every one of us on the

[70] Cf. *Confessions*, XI, 11.

Cross. So it is that we are baptized into Christ's death. And so it is that we fill up in our own beings what is still wanting in the sufferings of Christ, for as disciples of Christ the Church carries forward the visible mission of the Word Incarnate in her sacramental rendering present Christ in his paschal mystery.

That is why, as thesis XXVI states, radical discipleship is possible only with the apocalyptic immanent expectation that cries out "Come Lord Jesus!" Only God can raise the dead and redeem the countless histories of injustice and evil present throughout all of history. The authority of Christ's passion, death, and resurrection incarnates and transforms all human suffering. Among the many sins we Christians must repent of rank all those sins of pride and hatred that betrayed the Cross of Christ for the sword of a dominative authoritarianism. Such repentance, John Paul II has remarked, is an important element in transforming into civilizations of love those cultures of death feeding on the oversights and blindness of the Enlightenment.

CAN WE TALK? GLOBALIZATION, HUMAN RIGHTS, AND POLITICAL THEOLOGY

John K. Downey

Human rights are a concrete political assertion of human dignity, an attempt to remember our mutual responsibility in political structures. Talking about human rights is talking about universals: human rights are those responsibilities we have toward every person in every situation simply because she or he is a human being. But such talk is difficult in our era of globalization. Globalization presents us with the phenomena of local cultures in relation, of irreducible differences, of adjusting identities and ambiguous borders; in addition, it infects us with postmodern worry, relativity, and pluralism. And yet we cannot surrender modernity's pleading for the dignity of the person, for the test of freedom, and for hope in our common humanity. We live confidently if ironically in a world known to be a socially constructed, contingent matrix. We have never been more aware of our differences or more committed to honoring them, and yet they have become threatened by and threatening to our conversation. Finding a way to talk about universal human rights that respects both local and global realities provides a way to resist the negative effects of globalization.

The human rights discussion attends to issues of identity, difference, and dignity within the tensions of globalization. Globalization does contain possibilities for talking about universals in terms of the emergent relations of particular contexts and language-games, but these new connections and realities can be forged without attention to the value of concrete human subjects; they can be faceless. Talking about human rights inserts human value and human responsibility into the heuristic for globalization. The fear of a hidden hegemony troubles human rights discussions as well. We need a critical and constructive common authority for grounding the international discussion of human rights in an age of globalization. I want to argue here that religion, and particularity political theology, offers us a way to speak about subjectivity and hope that is both universal and local, for its starting point is suffering, the same suffering we recognize through the discussion of human rights.

Human Rights After Globalization

Globalization razes the walls that divide us, that block our vision, and that cushion our impact on each other. The worldwide flow of connections alters the primacy of the nation state in international relations, exposes powerful economic interests, and challenges social, religious, and political differences.

Diverse cultures are moving closer in language, values, economics, and politics. We interact across borders, and our ideas cross-pollinate as people reconfigure their standpoints. Like Internet transmissions, these new connections move rapidly in many directions and cannot be regulated. While meaning does emerge in given contexts, the contexts are in flux, and they influence each other in increasingly substantive ways and in faster, more intense connections. "Culture" designates not romantically preserved specimens with precise boundaries, but dynamic networks of people, places, activities, and visions. Relations are best spoken of as flows; borders are permeable, overlapping, melding.[1] Globalization reveals other cultural grammars for self-understanding and action, and new amalgams emerge within and across established borders.

Globalization need not cancel the particular, nor does it automatically homogenize the universal. Roland Robertson describes this dialectical culture as an ongoing presence of "the two-fold process involving the universalization of particularism and the particularization of universalism."[2] This global consciousness affirms the local consciousness and retains its identity within the global. Globalization exists as a tensive interplay between the global and the local, a situation the Italians have begun to call *glocale*.

Globalization reshapes the dialogue on human rights; it does not deny it. We live in paradox, in the tension of the universal and the particular, in a space occupied at once by respect for difference and mutual alteration. Meanings in a culture naturally come into focus relative to the structures and assumptions of that culture: it is important to know the rules of the game. But while cultural relativity locates meaning in the context of local language-games, it does not demand the isolation of these games. It is a mistake to stretch the notion of cultural relativity to infer the impossibility of naming any common ground. Globalization supports both the concrete language-game being played and its poten-

[1] See Robert J. Schreiter, *The New Catholicity: Theology Between the Global and the Local* (Maryknoll, NY: Orbis Books, 1997), 4-21. For more on globalization and the theological agenda see T. Howland Sanks, Globalization and the Church's Social Mission," *Theological Studies* 60 (December 1999), 625-651.

[2] Roland Robertson, *Globalization: Social Theory and Global Culture* (London: Sage, 1992), 100. It is not a matter of *either* universal *or* particular. Globalization cannot be reduced to economic mechanics, but should be treated as a cultural, political, and religious dynamic. Robertson sketches his concept of *glocalization* and applies it to religions in "Globalization and the Future of 'Traditional Religion,'" Max L. Stackhouse with Peter Paris, eds., *God and Globalization: Religion and the Powers of the Common Life* (Harrisburg, PA: Trinity Press, 2000), 53-68.

tial transformation in interaction. And the new culture of globalization alters the political, economic, and social context for claiming human rights.

To discuss humanity and rights across cultural lines risks denying difference. Talk of universals or transcultural human identity is suspect because many so-called universals simply impose one local practice or philosophy on others. One must ask whether the discussion of human rights is merely a Trojan Horse for sneaking in the values of Western culture, economy, or religion. So, for example, there has emerged an Asian values debate which asks whether human rights talk might be a version of Western individualism and a covert assault on the equally humane but communal Confucian notions.[3] Even using the phrase "human rights" might be a trap, a cover for dominating different local traditions. At the same time, the actual international discussion of human rights has never been more universal. At the World Conference on Human Rights sponsored by the United Nations in June of 1993, 170 nations affirmed by consensus with no reservations the "universal nature" of those "fundamental freedoms" and "human rights" articulated in the 1948 Universal Declaration of Human Rights. On December 10, 1948, that same Declaration had been approved by the United Nations General Assembly forty-six to zero with eight abstentions.[4] Whatever exact rights emerge in a particular setting, there seems to be agreement that universal human responsibilities are worth talking about.

Discussing human rights after globalization requires finding universal grounds while continuing to affirm local identities and contexts. If we cannot talk across cultural, social, gendered, and political particulars - across our difference and otherness - we cannot talk about human rights. But talking across these borders has proven risks: local knowledge may masquerade as common knowledge and domination may present itself as friendly interpretation. What is needed is a common authority to serve as a critical measure for the political discussion of human rights.

The conversation over human rights must be credible, not credulous. One must be vigilant lest the conversation shift to a monologue. A global awareness that notices differences can still become a "discourse of hegemony" suppressing difference.[5] We have learned that persons, groups, and nations can use the mantle of their communal tradition to cloak pathologies of power, fear, wealth, or myopia.

---

[3] Kishore Mahbubani, *Can Asians Think?* (Singapore: Times Books International, 1998); Joanne R. Bauer and Daniel A. Bell, *The East Asian Challenge for Human Rights* (Cambridge: Cambridge University Press, 1999).

[4] José A. Alves, "The Declaration of Human Rights in Postmodernity." *Human Rights Quarterly* 22 (2000), 481-483.

[5] See Nikhil Aziz, "The Human Rights Debate in an Era of Globalization," in Peter Van Ness, *Debating Human Rights: Critical Essays from the United States and Asia* (London: Routledge, 1999), 32-55; John Ralston Saul, "The Collapse of Globalism and the Rebirth of Nationalism," *Harper's Magazine* (March 2004), 33-43.

First, global vision can be monochromatic. If enjoyment of the free market and the instant communications of computer life are typical, then globalization describes only one-third of the world. The other two-thirds experience only disruptive side effects. The poor continue to be pushed to the margins of the economy, their risky lives simply a natural part of the developed world's competitive edge. They are compelled into financial and military disasters. World media preempt the normative traditional narratives that have shaped social identity. The poor are turned into an endorsement of the narratives of the wealthy rather than being seen as a challenge to the dynamics of globalization: overpopulation is Asian or Latin American; AIDS is African; terrorism is mostly a Moslem problem in spite of American white supremacy and neo-Nazi movements; drug traffic results from Third World production rather than global demand; the poor are a drag on progress and deserve their poverty. Globalization names a web of connections, but it does not make them humane.[6]

Second, cultures are not monolithic: one can often find internal criteria of legitimacy in a particular culture to support particular human rights. Contexts may vary, but differences are not always sharp, contradictory, or essential. When, for example, China or Singapore asserts its cultural difference - its Asian values - in order to stop conversation about human rights, that recourse to cultural relativism may be a politically motivated projection or at least a failure of imagination.[7] Instead of presuming that differing cultural language-games are absolutely incommensurate, one could draw points of contact from within Chinese culture as, for example, philosopher Chenyang Li does.[8] As Joann Bauer points out, "focusing on cultural legitimation rather than cultural relativism is a surer way of meeting the many challenges to international human rights everywhere."[9] The local and the global touch, but they need not always collide.

The notion of human rights may have developed in the Western categories of Greek and later European thought, but that fact does not *a priori* mean that it

---

[6]José A. Alves, "The Declaration of Human Rights in Postmodernity,"484-486; Thomas L. Friedman, *The Lexus and the Olive Tree* (New York: Random House, 2000), 255-264.

[7] See Neil A. Englehart, "Rights and Culture in the Asian Values Argument: The Rise and Fall of Confucian Ethics in Singapore," *Human Rights Quarterly* 22 (May 2000), 548-568; Andrew J. Nathan, "Is Chinese Culture Distinctive?" *Journal of Asian Studies* 52 (November 1993), 923-936.

[8] Chenyang Li, *The Tao Encounters the West: Explorations in Comparative Philosophy* (Albany: State University of New York Press, 1999), especially 163-189. For a similar strategy within an Islamic culture see also Abdullahi Ahmed An-Na'im, "Toward a Cross-Cultural Approach to Defining International Standards of Human Rights: The Meaning of Cruel, Inhuman, or Degrading Treatment or Punishment," in Abdullahi A. An-Na'im, ed., *Human Rights in Cross-Cultural Perspectives: A Quest for Consensus* (Philadelphia: University of Pennsylvania Press, 1992), 19-43; Edward Friedman, "Asia as a Font of Universal Human Rights," in Van Ness, 56-79.

[9] Joanne R. Bauer, "The Challenges to International Human Rights," in Mahmood Monshipouri, Neil Englehart, Andrew J. Nathan, and Kavita Philip, eds., *Constructing Human Rights in the Age of Globalization* (Armonk, NY: M. E. Sharp, 2003), 253.

cannot, *mutatis mutandis*, function in other cultures.[10] Diverse sources and situations do converse. It is possible to learn global lessons, however tentative or partial, from a particular tradition, voice, or idiom. That is part of what we mean by referring to classics of literature and letters. Human rights talk injects the human person into abstract discussion of global processes. It might be possible to drill down in the Christian tradition and find *glocalized* criteria for that global human rights discussion. Specifically, attention to concrete human suffering could provide a tactic for remembering and responding to the other. This proposal comes from Christian and Western thought, but without any claim to exclusivity. Within the paradoxes of globalization, solutions will only emerge from particular stories striving for wider resonance.

The sacralization of a particular list of cultural beliefs and policies - as one sees in the politics of the right in the United States[11] - is not of service to real conversation about globalization and finding common ground for human rights. We need to go deeper, to find our mystical and political feet, to stand on our own classic but not exclusivist roots, to engage in genuine public discourse that accepts pluralism and cultural relativity. In the political theology proposed by Johann Baptist Metz we find a critical culture of questions oriented outward to the public, social, economic, structural demonstration of our hope. This theology brings compassion to the center of intellectual discourse and political justification. Such a theology may make a contribution to human rights and so to our political imagination.[12]

Awakening to the Other: Political Theology

Johann Baptist Metz, founder of the new political theology, insists that Christianity is both mystical and political. Christian memory is public. Theologians not only admit religious experience, they see that experience as intertwined with the social, political, economic agenda of all human enterprises. The new political theology insists on turning our attention to particulars and highlighting the baggage hidden in culture, science, and society. This attention calls us to remember who we human beings are by evoking past sufferings and recalling future possibilities. And this remembering requires appropriate action.

---

[10] See Jack Donnelly, "Human Rights and Asian Values: A Defense of Western Universalism," in Bauer and Bell, 60-87.

[11] See Thomas Frank, *What's the Matter with Kansas? How Conservatives Won the Heart of America* (New York: Henry Holt and Company, 2004).

[12] I do not wish to argue here that human rights entail religious justifications. For that argument see Michael J. Perry, *Human Rights: Four Inquiries* (New York: Oxford University Press, 1998), 11-41. Also see Max L. Stackhouse, "Human Rights and Public Theology: The Basic Validation of Human Rights" in Carrie Gustafson and Peter Juviler, eds., *Religion and Human Rights: Competing Claims?* (Armonk, New York: M. E. Sharpe, 1999), 12-30.

Far from providing a calming opium or a path of escape, this theology connects humankind through disruption: it names dehumanizing behaviors and structures in our ordinary world and calls upon human beings to change them. It is an antidote to the shift of religion into the private sphere in modernity. In response to Enlightenment reason, Christianity downplayed its controversial social dimension and reduced its heritage to the realm of private, intimate, apolitical decision. In this way it avoided the critical challenge to defend itself with the public and universal evidence of reason. But this move also muted the Christian biblical eschatological promises which are hardly private matters: freedom, peace, justice, reconciliation. Christian hope is a form of public responsibility. "The New Testament community knows that it has been called from the beginning to live the promise of the future in present conditions and thus to overcome the world."[13] A theology that abstracts from concrete human lives, that pretends to be situation-free, would be naïve and unfaithful.

Metz's strategy is to acknowledge "the other." This acknowledgement is a turn to the universalism of responsibility for other human beings. Attending to unreasonable human suffering, especially to others' suffering, provides direction for reasonable human praxis. The memory of suffering and the acknowledgment of the other have a practical intent. Metz uses this memory as an interruption that honors otherness. In this way the victims of structures and policies are not erased from the conversation. Metz cautions against living off a "bread of domination" that disconnects people: subjugation does not give lives their value.[14] Political theology focuses on hearing the voices of the marginal, those who have disappeared behind the projection of universal essences. Christian discipleship offers as its hope human solidarity rather than domination. All human beings are called to be subjects, that is, to be agents of human value in the world, actors who declare human value in their action.

Remembering this call to act humanly as well as remembering the suffering caused by particular actions and structures can be dangerous. This deliberate recollection warns us of traps and manipulations, it trumps the authority of political or religious structures, and it forces us to evaluate our own actions. These dangerous memories of our hope and our grief position us to build a humane future. They shape a resistance and an agenda that spring not from a theoretical naiveté but from memory and narratives of pain, suffering, and invisibility. Noticing and norming by concrete human suffering bring about an anthropological revolution. The memory of suffering makes concrete the value of the other and

---

[13] Johann Baptist Metz, "The Church's Social Function in the Light of a 'Political Theology,'" in John K. Downey, ed., *Love's Strategy: The Political Theology of Johann Baptist Metz* (Philadelphia: Trinity Press, 1999), 29-31.

[14] Johann Baptist Metz, *The Emergent Church: The Future of Christianity in a Postbourgeois World* (New York: Crossroad, 1981), 35-37.

thereby helps us to resist a homogenizing amnesia. Control and subjugation are not what makes us human - or reasonable.

This focus on suffering decenters the controlling ego: "I begin not with the question 'What happens to me when I suffer, when I die?' but rather with, 'What happens to you when you suffer, when you die?'" The classical question of theodicy, of how to justify God in the face of human suffering, should not be a question about our own sufferings. The question, "What dare I hope?" turns around to "What may I also hope for you?" As we have seen, the future in which Christians hope is innately social, a future of mutual responsibility and expectation. "To dare to hope in God's Kingdom always means entertaining this hope for others and therefore also for oneself. Only when our hope is inseparable from hope for others, in other words, only when it automatically assumes the form and motion of love and communion, does it cease to be petty and fearful, a hopeless reflection of our egotism."[15] Our hope is not a faceless metaphysical hope. The claim of the other denies the autonomous control of a disconnected ego promoted by Enlightenment notions of reason.

It is important to bring victims into the foundations of knowing and acting. The usual story must be interrupted by connecting with others in a strategic love that sides against human agony. And how one takes sides is equally important for Metz. Victims show us the edges of society and call for a response. Metz wants to interrupt the ordinary by bringing the faces of the victims to mind. Narratives about the suffering of others, including Jesus, work to highlight and disable dehumanizing structures and behaviors. "We have a duty to face these catastrophes and remember them with a practical-political intention so that they might never be repeated."[16] Thus theological investigations and constructions done before the eyes of the victims will value difference. The focus on the other, then, interrupts our projection of sameness. This interruption reorients the hope for a new life and a new world. The dignity of the other as other puts a face on "human being": the call of other can only be heard from particular persons. This limited, concrete face-to-face is the universal starting point. It is founded on a hope that the human heart will turn outward.

Jesus followed his Jewish tradition by joining the love of God and the love of neighbor. For example, the story of a man who helped a stranger who had been robbed and thrown into a ditch argues that one may not delimit who counts as a neighbor: the obligation is universal (Luke 10:30-36). It is not just remembering one's own suffering that matters but, as Metz points out, remembering the suffering of others, *even the suffering of one's enemies*. Jesus focuses not on the sin of others, but on the suffering of others. Sin is "a refusal to par-

---

[15] Johann Metz, "Communicating a Dangerous Memory," *Lonergan Workshop* 6 (1987): 40.

[16] "Communicating," 42.

ticipate in the suffering of others, a refusal to see beyond one's own history of suffering. Sin is, as Augustine put it, turning the heart inward."[17]

Human reason contains an *a priori* of suffering.[18] The European Enlightenment promoted a type of reason modeled on domination and control, of assimilation rather than of otherness. Metz proposes a new type of reason for the post-Enlightenment age: reason endowed with the power of memory. "The Enlightenment has never overcome a deeply rooted prejudice in the model of reason that it developed: the prejudice against memory. The Enlightenment promotes discourse and consensus, but - in its abstract, totalizing critique of traditions - underestimates the intelligible and critical power of memory."[19] Thinking critically is more than logical coherence, instrumental reason, or following procedures; it includes remembering others and their suffering - even the dead. This socially oriented reason focuses on not forgetting (an-amnesia) and on actions of recollection or remembrance. This epistemological mediation of human suffering is practical in that it responds in ways that prevent abstract ideas of freedom or peace from erasing the concrete history of others' suffering. Anamnestic reason recovers memory as a resource for critical thought and political life. "Remembrance allows later generations to enter into solidarity with the dead in the act of recollection that brings the suffering of the past to light today."[20] It is a reason that wants to achieve its freedom specifically as the freedom of others, as justice. This type of reason opposes models for society and cultural life which cut themselves off from the memory of suffering.

Reason endowed with the power of memory, a *memoria passionis* rooted in the memory of someone else's suffering, demands more of us than mere assent to propositions. This reason is not just a feeling, not simply compassion, but also a claim on us: it is a call to responsibility. The solidarity encouraged by our memories and hopes entails an impulse to action. After all, Christianity and Christian theology are practical at the core: "Ultimately, it is of the very essence of Christian faith to be believed in such a way that it is never just believed, but rather - in the messianic praxis of discipleship - enacted."[21] It is so simple merely to believe in compassion, but anamnestic reason asks for more: solidar-

---

[17] Metz, "In the Pluralism of Religious and Cultural Worlds: Notes Toward a Theological and Political Program," *Cross Currents* (Summer 1999), 230.

[18] See Metz, "God: Against the Myth of the Eternity of Time," in *The End of Time? The Provocation of Talking about God*, edited by Tiemo Rainer Peters and Claus Urban, trans. J. Matthew Ashley (New York: Paulist Press, 2004), 26-46; Metz, "Freedom in Solidarity: The Rescue of Reason," in Johann Baptist Metz and Jürgen Moltmann, *Faith and the Future: Essays on Theology, Solidarity, and Modernity* (Maryknoll, NY: Orbis Press, 1995), 72-78.

[19] Metz, "Monotheism and Democracy: Religion and Politics on Modernity's Ground" in *A Passion for God: The Mystical-Political Dimension of Christianity*, translated by J. Matthew Ashley (New York: Paulist Press, 1998), 142. Ashley notes that the word for remembering, or more accurately "remembrancing," used by Metz (*Eingedenken*) implies "doing in remembrance of" (181).

[20] Marsha Hewitt, "The Redemptive Power of Memory: Walter Benjamin and Elisabeth Schüssler Fiorenza," *Journal of Feminist Studies in Religion* 10 (Spring 1994), 77.

[21] Metz, "Christians and Jews after Auschwitz," in Downey, ed., *Love's Strategy*, 47.

ity and resistance that transform the world. Awareness of others' suffering provides a common ground that persists in the midst of globalization as an antidote to abstraction. Being human means remembering and responding to the strangers' suffering. And this political compassion modulates the dominating subtext that may infect global relations. Xenophobia, ethnocentrism, and religious arrogance generate human misery. Political freedom and dignity come from resisting these sources of unjust suffering in the world. Ultimately this resistance is grounded in the relationship of one person to the endangered and overlooked other.[22] This call to memory and to responsibility underlies the global pursuit of human rights.

Human Rights as Memoria Passionis

The theological category *memoria passionis* - the memory of others' suffering - jars people's amnesia and awakens them to a universal responsibility for others. This interruption necessarily reshapes the political imagination. Human rights are not only particular legal and political proposals but also a vision of the human good. When political scientists Jack Donnelly and Rhoda Howard distinguish between human rights and human dignity, they are pointing to these differing layers in the human rights discussion.[23] Chandra Muzaffar likewise notes that any list of human rights is embedded in specific cultural worldview which norms the picture of the human being, human relationships, and the good society. After excoriating the West for its deteriorating human rights standards, Muzaffar asks for some universal vision of human dignity: "Without a larger spiritual and moral framework, which endows human endeavor with meaning and purpose, with coherence and unity, wouldn't the emphasis on rights *per se* lead to moral chaos and confusion."[24]

If globalization is not homogenization, then commonalities among groups originate in a particular tradition, a local culture or - as Ludwig Wittgenstein puts it - a particular language-game. It also means we can hope to discover some universal, classic expressions within the particular and local. Globalization need not be seen as the submission of human beings and human societies to

---

[22] Metz, "Against the Myth," 38-40 and "Pluralism," 233-235.

[23] Jack Donnelly and Rhoda E. Howard, "Human Dignity, Human Rights, and Political Regimes" in Jack Donnelly, *Universal Human Rights in Theory and Practice* (Ithaca and London: Cornell University Press, 1989), 66-87. On the theological side, see political theologian Jürgen Moltmann, "Human Rights, Rights of Humanity, Rights of Nature," in Metz and Moltmann, *Faith and the Future*, 178-193.

[24] Chandra Muzaffar, "From Human Rights to Human Dignity," in Van Ness, 28-29. He believes all "people of faith" need to begin a dialogue on human life and living. Hans Küng makes the point that there will be no world peace without dialogue among the world's religions in *A Global Ethic for Global Politics and Economics* (New York: Oxford University), 114-154. See also the interdisciplinary essays in Max L. Stackhouse and Peter J. Paris, eds., *God and Globalization.*

faceless laws of economic markets, culture wars, or political evolution. Rather, the globalized world must be interwoven with the pattern of human identity and value. Globalization is a human creation and so must be fashioned as a process of humanization.

Concrete dangerous memories, memories of real suffering and hope, provide the key. They are anamnestic: they interrupt in order to awaken and reorient people. "With its creed - 'suffered under Pontius Pilate' - [Christianity] is and remains bound to concrete history, to that history in which people have cried and loved, but also hated, tortured, crucified, and massacred."[25] Political theology points to a common ground for intercultural and interreligious collaboration. This common ground is found not in a theory or policy but rather in the common human response to others' suffering. This response-ability is a human imperative confirmed, demanded, and enhanced by Christian hope. It is specific - though not exclusive - to Christian identity.[26] The attention to suffering which Metz advocates comes from the stories and traditions of Christianity, and it also highlights a basic feature of human being. It does not require acceptance of the Christian scriptures or doctrines: the authority of suffering can cross borders. For example, recognition of the suffering of Jews in the Holocaust was a major factor in generating the cautions and hopes of the "Universal Declaration of Human Rights" in the United Nations.[27]

Prior to every theory, prior to every relationship of exchange and competition should be the turn to the other. "Only by asymmetrical recognition relationships, only by one person turning to the threatened and victimized other, will the grip of the logic of the market be broken in politics."[28] The best way to effect this turn concretely is through contact with the suffering of others. (Perhaps this was one benefit of the South African Truth Commissions.) In this way the whisper of human suffering keeps the political imagination from becoming a puppet of technology and economics. The point of solidarity is not just to remember suffering but to enforce the changes needed to end it. "The catastrophes must be remembered with a practical-political intention so that this historical experience does not turn to tragedy and thus bid the history of freedom farewell. That is a great seduction: to face these catastrophes and then end up with a kind of tragic consciousness."[29]

---

[25] Metz, "The 'One World': A Challenge to Western Christianity," First Hunthausen Lecture, October 9, 1989, Saint Martin's College, Lacey, WA; unpublished typescript, 6.

[26] Keith Soko, "Human Rights and the Poor in the World Religions," *Horizons* 26 (Spring 1999): 31-53; Joseph Runzo, Nancy M. Martin, and Arvind Sharma, eds., *Human Rights and Responsibilities in the World Religions* (Oxford: One World Publicatons, 2003).

[27] Johannes Morsink, *The Universal Declaration of Human Rights: Origins, Drafting, and Intent* (Philadelphia: University of Pennsylvania Press, 1999), 36-91.

[28] Metz, "Against the Myth," 39.

[29] Metz, "Communicating," 42.

The West has, for example, the dangerous memory of Auschwitz as a warning. Its ignominy teaches that compassion without any entailed action cultivates the disconnectedness which allows Christians to go on untroubled "believing and praying with our backs to Auschwitz." Christians, as Dietrich Bonhoeffer put it, were able "to go on singing Gregorian chant during the persecution of Jews without at the same time feeling the need to cry out in their behalf."[30] The human rights discussion is not grounded finally in a consensus about definitions, laws, ethics or rights. Rather, those arguments must be anchored in something prior to any consensus: suffering. Talk about human rights functions as an interruption, prodding communities to improve human life on the planet. The conversation itself challenges personal apathy and disrupts social amnesia by keeping the faces of suffering people before our eyes and posing questions about our responsibilities toward them. Rights are ways of acting on the responsibilities elicited by the authoritative claims of others' suffering. On this we can build a constellation of values and ultimately specific policies.

This turn to suffering is not a turn to a strictly defined theoretical or metaphysical essence but rather to a contextually-normed imperative which honors particular settings. It is not a matter of finding an abstract fixed "norm." The turn to interpretation and to the social roots of human constructions has undermined the pretensions of any so-called pure, disconnected essence. Hermeneutic, social science, ethnography, and postmodernity - not to mention the horrors of the Holocaust - have raised suspicions about the assertion of any unmediated disinterested knowing of an "already-out-there-now-real." But one could speak descriptively of culturally diverse yet overlapping discussions about humane behaviors and postures. One might, with Ludwig Wittgenstein, speak not of sharply defined borders and essences but of "family resemblances" which criss-cross in our discussions.[31] Anthropologist Ann-Belinda S. Preis seems to agree when she claims that "human rights increasingly form part of a wider network of perspectives which are shared and exchanged between North and South, centers and peripheries, in multiple, creative, and sometimes conflict-ridden ways. Human rights have become 'universalized' as values subject to interpretation, negotiation, and accommodation. They have become 'culture'."[32] Such a socially described commonality can enable a global discussion of human rights

---

[30] Metz, "Christians and Jews," 48.

[31] *Philosophical Investigations* (New York: The Macmillian Company, 1966), paragraphs 66 and 67 reveal Wittgenstein asking what is common to all games. He shows that there is no invariable core to the word "game"; there are overlapping and crisscrossing similarities. He calls these similarities "family resemblances" because in a family "build, features, colour of eyes, gait, temperament, etc., etc., overlay and criss-cross in the same way - and I shall say: 'games form a family.'" No tightly patrolled concept defining an essence allows us to communicate exactly, but rather patterns of use and usage in the stream of life. "Human rights" gathers its meaning from this pattern of usage in overlapping language-games.

[32] Ann-Belinda S. Preis, "Human Rights as Cultural Practice," *Human Rights Quarterly* 18 (May 2000), 290.

and human suffering. There is an ongoing global conversation about who we wish to be.

Acknowledging a cultural location does not mean that unique persons and communities cannot converse and agree. An appeal to the authority of suffering, especially the "unreasonable" suffering of the innocent, is both universal and particular. As Michael Perry puts it, "No one believes that rape, or slicing off breasts, or ripping out wombs, or decapitating a child in front of its mother (who has just been raped), or castrating a prisoner (or forcing another prisoner to do so), or throwing a prisoner into hot oil - no one believes that such acts are or might be good for those on whom the horror is inflicted."[33] The starting point for discussion of human rights is not any sort of alternative theory or political system but a negative critique flowing from a practically oriented empathetic reaction to truncated humanity. The torturer must simultaneously know what hurts human beings and forget that the victim is a human being. As psychologist James Waller says, "The evildoing becomes justified or rationalized when its effects, however atrocious, are no longer empathically considered by the evildoer." [34] Asking about human rights helps us remember the humanity of others.[35]

Political theology voices a common human call to respond, to connect, and to imagine new political relations. It calls for an interruption that promotes the imagination of new possibilities. The human rights discussion similarly disrupts the established political order. Human rights help us remember human suffering. Human rights discourse has a protest character: the conversation itself is a strategy of protest as well as a preemptive strike aimed at changing patterns of forgetfulness. When human rights function as a call to *memoria passionis,* they interrupt that amnesia which reduces or ignores the concrete human subject in political, economic, and social calculations. Remembering not just one's own or one's people's suffering but also the suffering of others becomes a local criterion for global political dialogue. Here lie the foundations; here "our spade is turned."

---

[33] Perry, 71.

[34] See "Perpetrators of the Holocaust: Divided and Unitary Self Conceptions in Evildoing, *Holocaust and Genocide Studies* 10 (Spring 1996), 18. Waller develops this thesis and analyzes several episodes of mass violence in our time in *Becoming Evil: How Ordinary People Commit Genocide and Mass Killing* (Oxford: Oxford University Press, 2002).

[35] Forgetting human rights can lead to forgetting human suffering. In the 10 May 2004 issue of *The New Yorker* magazine Seymour M. Hersh broke the story of Americans torturing Iraqis at a prison outside of Baghdad. The Executive Order of President Bush and the legal opinion of Alberto Gonzales had stated that these prisoners were not worthy of the universal human rights demanded by the Geneva Convention. When human rights are removed from the conversation, the boundary of shame between human beings is lowered. For the official documents and reports see Mark Danner, *Torture and Truth: America Abu Ghraib, and the War on Terror* (New York: New York Review of Books, 2004); Steven Strasser, *The Abu Ghraib Investigations: The Office Reports of the Independent Panel and the Pentagon on the Schocking Prisoner Abuse in Iraq* (New York: PublicAffiairs, 2004).

This conversation calls us to act on our hope and memory by changing damaging social structures of domination. Political discourse needs a shock, an interruption that reorients: it needs to touch the authority of suffering. Putting people in contact with the suffering of others may generate new ways of acting, thinking, and living. Here is a common criterion which at the same time can be internal to particular cultures. Political scientist Richard Falk agrees that "taking suffering seriously is the Archimedes point for intermediation between the universal claim and the particular practice when it comes to resolving antagonisms between widely endorsed human rights norms and culturally ordained patterns of behavior."[36] Or in theological terms: "Articulating others' suffering is the presupposition of all universalist claims."[37]

While we must name human suffering and be in solidarity with those who suffer, these practices are not enough to change the world. We also need expectations. We need hope. A solidarity that feels the claim of the other and responds in the real world provides not just empathy or identity with the past but a chance to transform the future. When the memory of suffering is merely the memory of one's own or one's people's suffering, it can be harmful, as in the former Yugoslavia. The suffering of others must be acknowledged in political negotiations. There is no place for silence, no place for turning away from the *memoria passionis*, no place for forgetfulness of our human communion. The authority of suffering interrupts our banality, our control, and our egocentrism. It is both universal and particular: universal without falling into abstract idealism and particular without being myopically egocentric or ethnocentric.

This *memoria passionis* creates practical political results. Concrete human rights tactics give strength to the authority of the suffering. Policy and structure, law and political will - rights - project our commitments into the real world. But simply having the conversation also functions as an anamnesis: it keeps the faces of suffering people before our eyes. The dialogue on human rights challenges personal apathy and disrupts social amnesia.

Talk of human rights is talk of universals, and such talk is suspect in this era of globalization. Relativity and honoring diversity seem automatically to challenge this conversation, but Christian political theology offers us a foundation to build on: acknowledging others in their otherness and recognizing the authority of their suffering. This *memoria passionis* demands concrete social actions and structures. No conflicts on issues and cultures are peremptorily settled by this fundamental methodological commitment; rather, this commitment provides a touchstone for justifications internal to particular cultures. The non-theoretical universal starting point offered by political theology is not a particular human rights formulation but the experience of the authority of those who

---

[36] Richard Falk, "Cultural Foundations for the International Protection of Human Rights," in Abdullahi Ahmed An-Na'im, ed., *Human Rights*, 44-64.
[37] Metz, "Monotheism and Democracy," 145.

suffer. "Is there any suffering at all in the world of which we might say that it does not concern us all? Is there a single cry of suffering that is not meant for every ear?"[38]

Both political theology and human rights succeed when they remind us who we are and move us to act for justice. Asking about human rights may be asking what it means to be human, but the answer to that question remains our experience of the authority of suffering, an authority which cannot be reduced to a particular cultural agenda. There is no shortcut around compassion. It grounds a realistic hope, hope in the face of the radical denial of humanity in Auschwitz and other places of misery. It calls for a political imagination that trusts in the future, that has expectations, that transforms societal structures accordingly. "There can be no peace without hope."[39]

---

[38] Johann Baptist Metz, "The Last Universalists," in Miroslav Volf, Carmen Krieg, and Thomas Kushcarz, eds., *The Future of Theology: Essays in Honor of Jürgen Moltmann* (Grand Rapids, MI: William B. Eerdmans Publishing Company, 1996), 51.

[39] Albert Camus, *The Plague*, trans. Stuart Gilbert (New York: Modern Library, 1948), 263.

ENVIRONMENTAL CONCERN AND THE "NEW POLITICAL THEOLOGY"

J. Matthew Ashley

Introduction

It is commonly recognized that the environmental movement was galvanized in North America in the early sixties with Rachel Carson's disturbing indictment, *Silent Spring*.[1] Another frequently cited milestone for Christian environmental reflection is a brief essay from 1967 in which historian Lynn White laid the blame squarely on the Christian tradition for steering us into the environmental dead-end in which we now find ourselves. While holding up Francis of Assisi as a "patron saint for ecologists," White contended nonetheless that the regnant Christian tradition is at the heart of our present "ecologic crisis":

> Both our present science and our present technology are so tinctured with orthodox Christian arrogance toward nature that no solution for our current ecologic crisis can be expected from them alone. Since the roots of our trouble are so largely religious, the remedy must also be essentially religious, whether we call it that or not. We must rethink and refeel our nature and destiny.[2]

Few theologians would now deny that Christian faith and theology have to take some a principled stand with regard to human beings' relationship to nature, revisiting the topos of the Christian doctrines of creation and theology of nature. However, there are deep differences over how radical the re-envisionment must be.

In the same year that Carson's book appeared a young theologian named Johann Baptist Metz published an essay entitled "*Weltverständnis im Glauben: Christliche Orientierung in der Weltlichkeit der Welt heute*."[3] This essay marked the beginnings of his movement away from the transcendental Thomism of his teacher and friend, Karl Rahner, and towards what he came to call the "new political theology." By the time White's critique appeared Metz had worked out the first formulation of his new approach and was already beginning

---

[1] Rachel Carson, *Silent Spring* (Boston: Houghton Milton, 1962).
[2] Lynn White, Jr., "The Historical Roots of our Ecologic Crisis," *Science* vol. 57 (1967), 1203-1207, here 1207.
[3] *Geist und Leben* 35 (1962): 165-84. This essay was eventually published and translated into English in Metz's first collection on political theology, as "How Faith Sees the World: The Christian Orientation in the Secularity of the Contemporary World": *Theology of the World*, trans. William Glen-Doepel (New York: Herder and Herder, 1969), 13-55.

to grapple with the unsolved problems and critiques that would lead to the mature expression found in *Faith in History and Society*.[4] Despite the contemporaneity of the emergence of environmental concern and political theology, however, Metz has never taken up environmental concerns at any length. This distinguishes him from two other principal founders of this approach: Jürgen Moltmann and Dorothee Sölle.[5]

On a first reading of Metz's theology this lacuna would perhaps come as no surprise. After all, he explicitly develops his "practical fundamental theology" as a "political theology of the *subject*."[6] Environmental theologians commonly assert that the turn to the subject has been accompanied by a turn *away* from nature as a source of value and meaning, or a locus of concern.[7] They argue that theologies that start from this turn are as a consequence constitutionally incapable of perceiving the grave sinfulness inherent in our current relations with the natural world, not to mention marshaling what resources the Christian tradition might have for responding adequately. Is not, after all, Metz's principal text entitled "Faith in *history and society*," society and history being construed as human projects, in abstraction from their ground in the rest of creation? We must look elsewhere, on this reading, for the basis of a "political theology of nature."[8] It is not my purpose here to argue that Metz is an environmental theologian. It *is* my purpose, however, to argue that environmental theology is not well served by an overly hasty dismissal of Metz's analysis of the contemporary situation and his suggestions for a "practical fundamental theology" adequate to that situation. Indeed, to put my thesis as provocatively as possible, it is not in spite of but *because* Metz articulates his theology from the vantage point of the challenge of becoming and continuing to be a subject in solidarity with others, in God's presence, that his theology offers crucial resources to a contemporary environmental theology. I argue that these resources are diagnostic and substan-

---

[4] Johann Baptist Metz, *Faith in History and Society*, 2nd English edition, ed. and trans. J. Matthew Ashley (New York: Crossroad, 2004); henceforth, FHS.

[5] For Moltmann, for instance, see his Gifford Lectures from 1984-85: *God in Creation: A New Theology of Creation and the Spirit of God* (London: SCM, 1985). From Sölle one might consult the following: Dorothee Soelle with Shirley A. Cloyes *To Work and to Love: A Theology of Creation* (Minneapolis: Fortress, 1984), which stem from lectures given in 1983, or, Dorothee Sölle & Luise Schottroff, *Den Himmel erden: eine ökofeministische Annäherung an die Bibel* (München: Deutscher Taschenbuch Verlag, 1996).

[6] FHS, *passim*, but chapters 3 and 4 in particular.

[7] See, for example, Elizabeth Johnson, "Losing and Finding Creation in the Christian Tradition," in *Christianity and Ecology*, ed. Dieter T. Hessel and Rosemary Radford Ruether (Cambridge, Mass.: Harvard CSWR Press, 2000), 9-11. In his response Gordon Kaufman parallels White's analysis, placing the "anthropocentric turn" at the biblical foundations of Judaism, Christianity and Islam, with their common emphasis on modeling the divine with language and imagery of personal agency, distanced from nature as (nothing but) the object of this agency.

[8] Thus, in Stephen Scharper's comprehensive overview, which aims at a political theology of the environment, Metz does not appear: *Redeeming the Time: A Political Theology of the Environment* (New York: Continuum, 1998). The same is true of the more recent work by Peter Scott: *A Political Theology of Nature* (Cambridge: Cambridge University Press, 2003).

tive. First, Metz's assessment of our situation offers important lessons that not all environmental theologians heed. Second, the theological anthropology that Metz develops, centered on the categories of solidarity, memory, and especially (for our purposes), narrative, offers a potent conceptual framework for articulating an environmental theology that can press the case for concerted reforms of human practices vis a vis the rest of the natural world without falling into the trap of "anthropocentrism."

Metz's Assessment of our Contemporary Dilemma

The historical contours of the problem in response to which Metz set off in search of a "new political theology" bear a more than passing similarity to the situation that has sparked the quest for an adequate environmental theology. In modernity the Christian churches have been unable or unwilling to see political and economic fissures and inequalities as problems that bear directly on the coherence and credibility of Christian faith. A theological solution to these problems requires putting the substance of that faith, as articulated in its foundational narratives and dogmas, in play and at risk. At best, they have been treated outside of core Christian convictions, utilizing a set of "social teachings" that do not draw directly on or challenge the way we think about the God of Jesus and what believing in that God entails. If we look at Christian responses to our current environmental mess, a strikingly similar pattern emerges. In the Catholic Church environmental concern was virtually nonexistent until after the Second Vatican Council. Subsequently, the Catholic Church's official responses have tended to incorporate environmental concerns into existing structures of social ethics, leaving more radical revisions of our understanding and practice of the faith to proponents of deep ecology or ecofeminism.

Metz judges that much of this stems from an unreflective adoption of "the bourgeois subject" as *the* subject, both in society at large and within Christian faith and theology, where the bourgeois subject is often tacitly identified with the religious subject. Many environmental theologians are in agreement with this. However, the solution he proposes is not a wholesale dismissal of "the subject" as a locus for theological reflection, but rather a re-envisioning of that subject and its parameters that will disclose more clearly its integral social and historical intersubjectivity. Let us explore the reasons for this.

Metz begins his mature formulation of political theology with what he calls a *Situationsvergewisserung*, by which he intends a general assessment of the present situation, with a view to the possibilities of future advance.[9] Briefly

[9] The following sketch of Metz's position is taken from the first three chapters of *Faith in History and Society*, although it can be found in more recent work as well. See, among others, *The Emergent Church: The Future of Christianity in a Postbourgeois World*, trans. Peter Mann(New York: Crossroad, 1987), chapters 1,

summarized, he argues that the Enlightenment marks a critical watershed in the history of Christian faith and theology because it was then that the social conditions emerged that made it possible to see Christianity as a form of "religion," which could be isolated, analyzed and criticized as such in terms of other, purportedly more comprehensive, social dynamics and historical processes. The theoretical conceptuality and practice (variously construed and exercised) of "critique" became the object of the liberative hopes previously borne by Christian faith and practice, at least among cultural elites and the growing middle class. Religion was left with or assigned the task of compensating within the sphere of interiority (more recently, "spirituality") for the pain and disappointments arising from social and historical aspirations that are still unredeemed, and to some extent unredeemable in principle, by Enlightenment reason.

Corresponding to these developments a new understanding (both speculative and lived) of the subject emerged: the bourgeois subject. This subject was defined by the Enlightenment ideal of "majority" (*Mündigkeit*). In fact, however, "the subject" is concretized socially (1) by enlightened self-interest, exercised in and through contractual exchange with other persons authorized as subjects in society, and (2), by a technical-dominative reason that looks upon nature (including, in the limit, human nature) as raw materials to be mastered and put to the service of the market, where the aforementioned "rational" exchanges take place. Only those rights, ideals and obligations that can be deduced and justified in terms of the subject thus construed achieve social consensus and normativity (think here of classical liberal and neo-liberal "human rights"). Other rights, responsibilities and ideals, including those of "religion," have been privatized. They are normative only by the whim or taste of the individual, and beyond that are in principle unable to generate or ground any broader form of social solidarity and action.

This has far-reaching consequences both for Christianity and for modern society. On the one hand, as modern subjects (Christian subjects included) become more and more accommodated to this arrangement they become less and less inclined to find in their religious beliefs and practices any rationally grounded orientation for political action. The result is that religion either becomes increasingly abstract and impotent in broad regions of persons' lives, or it enters into the political realm in a decisionistic, spasmodic fashion. The first option describes the fate of much of liberal Christianity (what Metz calls "bourgeois Christianity"), whereas the second describes many forms of fundamentalism, Christian and non-Christian alike. Yet, it is not just Christianity that is threatened by this way of configuring human subjectivity. Modern persons have been left helplessly exposed to those threats to meaning, indeed to survival, that

5, 6, and *A Passion for God: The Mystical-Political Dimension of Christianity*, ed. and trans. J. Matthew Ashley (Mahwah, N.J.: Paulist Press), chapters 1,2, and 9.

require resources beyond the capacity of the modern bourgeois subject and the social-political praxis that can be described in relation to it. Some of these threats are perennial: the threat constituted by our finitude, by guilt, and by the individual death that ineluctably presses in on each one of us. Others, however, are particular to our age: economic, political, and environmental crises that are global problems, both in the sense that they affect the entire globe, and in the sense that any successful resolution requires that humanity as a whole take responsibility and respond. In other words, *humanity* must be recognized and held accountable as the "subject" of these historical processes. Yet, this is precisely what we can *not* do, to the extent that we have accepted the ideology associated with the bourgeois subject, according to which the only subjects we can depend on for a solution (and hold accountable for its implementation) are individual agents acting on their rational self-interest through the mediation of the market. Other than this we are left with exhortations and romantic appeals to global solidarity that are ultimately impotent, or with the dangerously seductive appeal of empire (in the United States, at any rate).

The manifest inability of these appeals to respond adequately has led to an ironic withdrawal from the very norms and ideals of the Enlightenment that underwrote the emergence of the bourgeois subject. Abandoning the long view, we think in terms of "niches" and short-term survival strategies. We are afflicted with a pervasive and usually unvoiced hopelessness and weariness with the demands of being a modern, "adult" (*mündiges*) subject. It is this that makes us more than ready to abandon these seemingly extravagant claims. "An everyday postmodernism of the heart is spreading far and wide," Metz writes, "which thrusts the poverty and misery of the so-called Third World into a greater and more anonymous distance."[10] And if this "postmodernism of the heart" can elide or mute the suffering of millions upon millions of human beings now living, how much more so the fate of those yet to be born, not to mention other biological species, to which environmental concern and environmental theology would direct our attention?

As a consequence of this analysis, Metz questions whether human beings in late modern European and North American societies are able to entertain any hopes and convictions that reach beyond their own individual survival or flourishing. If the grand and moving values that motivated the struggles for freedom and progress over the last three or four centuries no longer resonate in the postmodernism of our hearts, then why should we expect that a particular variant of them (articulated, say, in terms of "the common good" or even "the kingdom of God") will fare any better?[11] One might hope that *Christians* might still be

[10] "Teología europea y teología de la liberación," in J. Comblin, J. I. González Faus, J. Sobrino (eds.), *Cambio social y pensamiento cristiano in América Latina* (Madrid, 1993), 268.

[11] Of course, almost every postmodern thinker would contest my naive evocation of these values. Metz is quite aware of Walter Benjamin's dictum that "every great work of civilization is at the same time a work of

moved to take them seriously as an integral part of their faith, but this is where another dimension of Metz's assessment of our current situation comes into play. He argues that modern Christians have lost the conviction that the church's doctrines and theological systems are about *them* and *their* lives. In past ages this conviction was planted and nourished by a cultural milieu which formed persons into precisely this sense. This is not to appeal to a "golden age" in which Christians were all socialized into a common vision. Rather, the claim is that the social and cultural embodiment of Christianity reinforced a sense that Christianity's doctrines, memories and narratives *mattered*, that no matter how much they were contested, distorted or abused, they provided an "alphabet" with which people spelled out their life's stories, both individually and communally, in the presence of a God who became all the more real precisely for that fact. This Christian culture fragmented, beginning in the late Middle Ages. It no longer exists to do this work.[12] In response to this Metz takes over Rahner's dictum that if there are going to be Christians in the future they will have to be mystics. For Rahner, "mystics" are persons who have the deeply rooted experiential conviction that the history in which God has revealed Godself is also *their* history, a history that matters ultimately to them and makes sense of their individual spiritual itineraries.[13] Metz's only caveat, or "corrective," is that in addition to this essential intercalation of one's sense of the meaningfulness of one's own life and the doctrines and narratives of the church, there must be a similar life-giving "*circumincessio*" both of our sense of the meaning and telos of our common life together, on the one hand, and the specifics of the God of Jesus who is made present in and through the memories and narratives, construed politically and "dangerously," of the Christian tradition. This is what he means when he appeals to the "mystical-political" structure of Christian faith.

barbarism." He is quite aware that these values have often underwritten savagery and not humanization. Yet, however much they need to be "corrected" and "interrupted," even by the subversive re-reading of a Michel Foucault, can we finally do without them? On this, see Richard Bernstein, "Foucault: Critique as a Philosophical Ethos," *The New Constellation: the Ethical-Political Horizons of Modernity/Postmodernity* (Cambridge: MIT Press, 1992), 142-72. What we need is a capacity to persevere in them, in hoping in them, in spite of their failures, in spite of their frailty and vulnerability to ideologization and abuse. This is why Metz argues that emancipation projects, however articulated, will never be able to do without those resources that enable subjects to continue struggling "to become and remain subjects in solidarity with others," even in the face of their own guilty failures; see especially "Vergebung der Sünde," *Stimmen der Zeit* 195/2 (Feb., 1977), 119-128.

[12] This describes the condition of secularized Europe. In North America the situation is different. There, one could well argue that religious faith is still a formative factor in individuals' cultural milieu. The problem, however, is that the combination of pluralism and anti-intellectualism has made it impossible to build on this religiosity to generate a public conversation. As David Tracy has argued at some length, the Christian classics have lost their public character. They inform the private sphere, at best, while the public sphere is increasingly dominated either by what John Paul II has called the ideology of radical capitalism, or, since "9-11," by the ideology of empire.

[13] In this Rahner drew on the Ignatian spirituality of his Order. See Phillip Endean, *Karl Rahner and Ignatian Spirituality* (New York: Oxford University Press, 2001).

Very well then, one might respond. The Enlightenment was clearly wrong in positing "reason" as competent to replace tradition and authority for securing both an individual sense of meaning and orientation in his or her actions, and for generating social consensus necessary to manage the challenges and crises that face human beings communally. All the more reason to embrace "anti-modern" or "post-modern" conceptions of human subjectivity and agency.[14] After all, this "reason" and the subject defined by it had already fallen into crisis by the late eighteenth century, generating responses (to consider just the German speaking lands) from F.H. Jacobi, J.G. Hamann, J.W. Goethe, and J.G. Herder, flowering into the movements of German Romanticism, and, of course, the various strands of post-Kantian German Idealism.[15] To the extent that Christianity was the primary opponent of many advocates of Enlightenment, the apparent self-destruction or supercession of the Enlightenment project would seem to get Christianity off the hook. Indeed, many Christian theologies of the nineteenth and twentieth centuries appropriated understandings of the subject from German Idealism or Romanticism. These successors to the Enlightenment seemed to provide anthropologies more open to the authority of tradition and to the assertion of a "depth" dimension of human subjectivity that might correlate with divine revelation.[16] As we shall see below, some of these revisionary accounts vis a vis the Enlightenment subject have been embraced with gusto by environmental theologians as the way to get around the anthropocentrism that is taken to be at "the roots of our ecological crisis."

Metz has strong reservations about this move, particularly in Catholic theology, calling it a "hibernation strategy." This characterization paints a picture in which Catholic theology, having suspended its debates with Enlightenment intellectual culture during the nineteenth and early twentieth centuries, then "emerges," able (so it thinks) to ignore the challenges of its now vanquished former opponent. Metz is dubious of this strategy on two related grounds. First, he is clearly not persuaded that the later philosophical traditions "solved" on a conceptual level the problems raised for normative traditions, religious or otherwise, by the destabilizing impact of Enlightenment rationality. Second, he contends that the Enlightenment subject is still the regnant subject standing tacitly behind our social institutions and practices. Overcoming it "in thought" leaves it firmly lodged in practice, including its paralyzing effect on the practical potential of Christian discipleship and the "resources of meaning" on which

---

[14] Here I rely on David Tracy's categorization in "Naming the Present,"in *On Naming the Present: God, Hermeneutics and Church* (Maryknoll, N.Y.: Orbis Books, 1994).

[15] See Frederick Beiser, *The Fate of Reason: German Philosophy from Kant to Fichte* (Cambridge, Mass.: Harvard University Press, 1987).

[16] Metz groups these into three categories: transcendental theologies, with roots in Kant (of the first critique) and Hegel; existentialist theologies, with roots in Schelling; and Pannenberg's theology of universal history, with roots, again, in Hegel.

any call to action must draw, be it for greater economic justice or for environmental reforms.[17]

So-called "deep ecology," "ecofeminism," and "ecojustice" theologies concur in large measure with Metz's assessment of our situation. This is particularly true of the insight that the modern subject is a subject structured primarily by practices of self-assertion and domination. There are therefore, on this account, profound and systemic links between oppression on the basis of class, race and gender, and the devaluation and consequent exploitation of nature.[18] The corresponding prescription is often extreme. The Enlightenment project must be rejected *tout court*, and with it the project of grounding ethical claims about our actions vis a vis the rest of creation in the exercise of our subjectivity as rational, and hence responsible, human subjects. Such an approach is irredeemably suspect of "anthropocentrism," and cannot generate plans of action or structural changes that will give us anything but "more of the same" of what we have seen since Descartes and Bacon (or, for the more radical, since the time of the first millennium B.C.E. authors of the Genesis creation accounts, if not even earlier).

Recognizing that what is needed is to find some way to ground value and meaning in creation independent of the value- and meaning-creating activity of human subjectivity, various solutions are proposed.[19] If one takes meaning and value to be historical achievements, functions of some *telos* of temporal processes of development, then one might proceed by reconfiguring the subject of those processes. Rather than human individuals or human society, one could propose "Gaia," the planet understood as a living organism, as the subject of history.[20] Many have taken the Second Law of Thermodynamics and the "one-way temporality" it configures, as an invitation to see nature itself as having a history, a history than encompasses and configures human history.[21] Some then

---

[17] In the synodal document he drafted for the West German Catholic Bishops, *Unsere Hoffnung*, Metz wrote the following: "It would seem that the potential for meaning is also limited. And this is happening as the reserves dry up, and the danger persists that the great words with which we have pressed our history onward-freedom, emancipation, justice, happiness - have in the end nothing but an exhausted, dessicated meaning" (*Unsere Hoffnung*, no. 13; cited in *Passion for God*, 41).

[18] For a classic and seminal statement of this argument, see Carolyn Merchant, *The Death of Nature: Women, Ecology and the Scientific Revolution* (New York: Harper & Row, 1980).

[19] Whatever one says about Antiquity and the Middle Ages, there were ways of doing this during those historical periods, *pace* White, although they always functioned by means of an extremely fragile negotiation of any number of conceptual tensions. This "ontotheological synthesis" began to come apart in the late Middle Ages. Indeed, one can see modernity as a response to this fragmentation, with the Enlightenment as one episode in the attempt to reframe a coherent synthesis of the human, the sacred, and the cosmos. Here see Louis Dupré's magisterial narrative account: *Passage to Modernity*.

[20] For an overview of the "Gaia Hypothesis" and its appropriation by Christian environmental theologians, see Scharper, *Redeeming the Times*, 53-74.

[21] See, for example, Jürgen Moltmann, *Science and Wisdom* (Minneapolis, Minn.: Fortress Press, 2003). Leonardo Boff, *Cry of the Earth, Cry of the Poor*, trans. Phillip Berryman (Maryknoll, N.Y.: Orbis Books, 1997), 20, 32f.

make the further proposal that we see human beings as the locus of subjectivity, but only in function of their relationship to the rest of the cosmos and the vocation that this relationship brings with it. In a formulation redolent of Hegel and Schelling, human beings' role is taken to be that of "enabling the Earth and the universe entire to reflect on and to celebrate themselves, and the deep mysteries they bear within them, in a special mode of conscious self-awareness."[22]

These solutions operate by identifying a trans-human, ultimate locus of subjectivity: Gaia, nature, life, or the cosmos.[23] Just as their nineteenth century predecessors, these strategies lead into theological minefields, and often are bought at high theological price (most often paid in the area of Trinitarian theology). Moreover, it is not entirely clear that these strategies solve the legitimation crisis raised by the Enlightenment. Or, if they do so, the resolution may not be one that environmental theologians would like. Appeals to transpersonal subjectivity or to metaphors of depth need to come to terms with the "masters of suspicion," most preeminently, Nietzsche and Freud, who turned those strategies in a different direction. In them, the depth that gives rise to and comes to expression in human subjectivity is a will to power that seeks nothing other than its own self-assertion. This way of rendering the depth and subjectivity involved in human personhood generates narratives endorsed by neo-Darwinians such as Daniel Dennett and Richard Dawkins that will not underwrite environmental responsibility on any other grounds than enlightened self-interest. After history has been naturalized in *this* way, introducing notions of God's kenosis in creating, or God's suffering-with creation on the cross, strike me, at any rate as *ad hoc*, or stop-gap measures of the sort that Metz criticized in the seventies with respect to certain attempts to "add" a Christian notion of redemption on to a historical scheme that had already been determined by either a neo-liberal logic of progress, or a Marxist logic of dialectic.[24] The typically modern narrative rendering of nature-history, which is still inscribed in many, if not most, scientific interpretations of the "meaning" of evolution, needs to be confronted more directly, and at a more fundamental level.[25]

To sum up: if Metz is right, and our current situation is one of a "postmodernism of the heart," in which persons in general are increasingly numb to the suffering of others and simply tired of appeals to the costly exercises of rational and moral accountability that come with being a subject in the modern sense,

---

[22] Brian Swimme and Thomas Berry, *The Universe Story: From the Primordial Flaring Forth to the Ecozoic Era - A Celebration of the Unfolding of the Cosmos* (San Francisco: HarperSanFrancisco, 1992), 1.

[23] This is an ironic counterfigure to the strategy of evolutionary psychologists carrying on the tradition of Neo-Darwinian sociobiology, who, as John Haught has recently pointed out, locate subjectivity at the level of genes - although it is subjectivity defined in Nietzschean terms as striving. See John Haught, *Deeper than Darwin: The Prospecct for Religion in an Age of Evolution* (Boulder, Colo.: Westview Press, 2003), 111-118.

[24] FHS, chapter 7.

[25] This is, of course, the point of Metz's well-known critique of the symbol of "evolution," and his "untimely" defense of apocalyptic. I will return to this theme below.

how far will an appeal to environmental responsibility get that ignores or even negates as "anthropocentric" an understanding of human beings called to be subjects, in solidarity with one another, in God's presence? At the risk of misunderstanding, I would say that our current problem is not too much anthropocentricty, but not enough, at least in the form that arises from an understanding of the subject formed by the Christian narratives and the praxis of discipleship. To state the matter polemically: Won't persons who are already weary of the high demands placed by the Enlightenment understandings of rationality and responsibility welcome the insight that humans are not really different from the rest of nature? Why not simply let the micro- or macro-subjects of history (genes, Gaia or "nature") take on the burden of history, while human beings seek what "niches" they can find to work out their individual destinies untroubled by broader questions of meaning and suffering in our common history? If human beings bring about a destruction of the fabric of life of an order of magnitude not seen since earlier mass extinctions during the Permian or Cretaceous ages, why not take comfort from a point made by the new narratologists of the book of nature: earlier such catastrophes were followed by new outburst of creativity on the part of "nature" or the "cosmos"?[26]

It would be unfair to assert that these are necessarily the direct implications of all the "anti-anthropocentric" environmental theologies. Yet, given our contemporary situation it is difficult to see how they can avoid being *received* in this way without a more thoroughgoing confrontation with the challenges that Metz has disclosed in his new political theology. It may be that a given contemporary theology can evade the tacit infiltration of the Enlightenment subject and its understanding of sociality and historicity (both infra- and extra-human). Yet there is the further challenge that to the extent that the Enlightenment subject is still inscribed in our economic, political and techno-scientific structures, it will continue to shape our sense for what is necessary and possible and circumscribe the impact of even those theologies that successfully evade this subject theoretically. For this, Metz's political theology provides an indispensable diagnostic.

Environmental Theology as a Fundamental Practical Theology of the Subject?

I have accepted Metz's claim that many contemporary theologies do not adequately grasp the extent to which they are structured by the Enlightenment subject. Even when they reject the subject in terms of some post-Enlightenment alternative (or even the post-modern alternative of doing away with the subject altogether), they have often inadequately understood the dimensions of the

[26] A point made by Boff, *Cry of the Earth, Cry of the Poor*, 19. I will return to this issue below.

challenge that the Enlightenment set for Christian faith and theology and overestimated the capacity of these post-Enlightenment strategies to deal with those challenges. I have suggested further that contemporary environmental theologies need to take this claim seriously. In this light it seems fair to examine, if only briefly, Metz's counter-proposal. Does his proposal for an understanding of the subject that might begin to structure an adequate response to the challenges of modernity also help in revisioning our understanding of our relationship to the nonhuman natural world?

Metz's understanding of the subject is structured around three categories: solidarity, memory and narrative. The subject thus understood is essentially historical and social. It is also a subject with a painful vulnerability to suffering in history. Solidarity defines us as beings oriented by the hopes and expectations we hold for the future; more precisely, it defines us in terms of the circle of subjects *with whom* and *for whom* we hold such hopes and expectations.[27] Memory defines us in terms of the past, particularly the remembered past of those persons whose own hopes and expectations - both for themselves and their descendants - are still unredeemed. This memory can and should be a dangerous and interruptive one, because it problematizes a present that is taken to be nothing but the culminating point of a history of victors, of those who made it. As a memory of past suffering, authorized, mandated and empowered by the *memoria passionis, mortis et resurrectionis Jesu Christi*, it blocks an increasingly dehumanized form of subjectivity that can celebrate the present (and those hopes for the future that can be extrapolated from this present) only by forgetting those who died deaths marked by meaningless and unjustly afflicted suffering. Narrative, finally, is the privileged genre for expressing, communicating and even reflecting on this kind of temporally-historically articulated subjectivity. It is prior to conceptual-theoretical reflection, although the latter is indispensable to it. These three features or categories of being a subject mutually complement one another in an essential way:

> It is in … solidarity that narrating and remembering salvation wins its specific, mystical-political praxis. Memory and narrative can no more be practical categories in theology without solidarity than solidarity can give expression to the practically humanizing form of Christianity without memory and narrative. Only in concert can memory, narrative and solidarity be categories of a practical fundamental theology.[28]

---

[27] Thus, in his short definition of Christian faith, Metz associates solidarity with hope: "Christian faith … understands itself to be a solidaristic hope in the God of Jesus as the God of the living and the dead, who calls all to be subjects in God's presence."

[28] FHS, chapter 13 (first page).

Metz always uses this framework to talk about historical processes within which human beings become subjects, both as individuals, and, in a broader sense, as peoples (for the latter, the people of Israel serves as the paradigm). Subjects are agents who are actively involved in the narrative and praxic construction of their own identities, who recognize themselves in the symbols, structures, and narratively encoded memories that make up the societies within which they live and work out their individual identities, and which they play an active role in passing on to the next generation. It would appear thus far that Metz's political theology would have to be included among those theologies for which "nature" is only a neutral stage on which human history, as the exclusive locus of "salvation history," is played out, but which itself is not implicated or redeemed through salvation history. It is true that given his oft-stated suspicion about the seductive and dangerous symbolic power of the metaphor of "evolution," he will decline those strategies that move quickly to assimilate human history to natural to form one "cosmic story." Yet Metz also resists a strong separation between human history and cosmic history. In his most recent writings on time he rejects abstracting and cordoning off human biographical and historical time from cosmic time, calling it "a permanent Gnostic temptation for Christian theology."[29] Elsewhere he writes:

> Is it possible at all for us to connect our talk about God with the world's time anymore? Do we not subscribe to a secret dualism here? We cut our understanding of time completely in half, hand over the world's time to an empty, anonymous evolutionary time, and try to bring just the time of the individual's life into some relationship with God. In so doing, however, have we not - in good gnostic fashion - long ago abandoned the "creator of heaven and earth," and embraced only a redeemer God whom we think is to be found in the depths of our souls? Yet can a theology that holds to the profession of faith in creation escape once and for all the tension between the world's time and life's time?[30]

He goes on: "To state the bare minimum: It is not the individual life world, but precisely the world of *the other* as well, not just the experience of the course leading ahead to one's own death, but also the experience of the other's death that sustains apocalyptic uneasiness."[31] It is this "apocalyptic uneasiness" that opens us to hope for more from God's salvific presence in history than the current state of history and society appear to warrant to the "reasonable person"; that keeps us on the lookout for that presence in heretofore overlooked places;

[29] "Time without a Finale," in J.B. Metz and Jürgen Moltmann, *Faith and the Future: Essays on Theology, Solidarity, and Modernity* (Maryknoll, N.Y.: Orbis Books, 1995), 84.
[30] "God: Against the Myth of the Eternity of Time," in J.B. Metz, et al., *Time's End*, trans. J. Matthew Ashley (Mahwah: N.J.: Paulist Press, 2004).
[31] "God: Against the Myth of the Eternity of Time".

and finally, both encourages and challenges us to act in a correspondingly radical way.

This is, Metz avers, a minimum. It is clearly a minimum oriented once again toward human history and society. Can it be expanded to include the nonhuman natural world? Indeed, must it not be so expanded if we are to avoid "hand[ing] over the world's time to an empty, anonymous evolutionary time"? What resources are there for such an expansion and how would it proceed?

First, and negatively, we need not project full personhood on living beings or communities before they become the subjects of our regard or concern.[32] The requirement that the other be strictly equal to me before having any claim on me is precisely the kind of solidarity in exclusivity Metz criticizes as one of the hallmark features of the Enlightenment subject - whether it be solidarity among the contractually equal or the rationally equal.[33] This is to ignore the ways that society enfranchises some to be subjects, but not others. Counteracting this there is a mystical, universal solidarity that expands to include all persons, even the dead, as others worthy of our regard and concern. This mystical-universal solidarity complements the preferential, focused solidarity on behalf of specific groups who are threatened now: "A practical fundamental theology tries to hold on to solidarity in its indissoluble mystical-universal and political-particular dual structure, with the goal of protecting universalism from apathy and partial solidarity from forgetfulness and hatred. It is always foregrounding the questions: Solidarity with whom? Solidarity in what form?" This idea of a dual-structure in our future-oriented and future-orienting concern for others is a central feature of Metz's understanding of human subjectivity; it also invites the question of whether it can expand to include not just humankind, but "otherkind"-nature.

That it *could* seems to be at least a priori possible to the extent that Metz defines the mystical "pole" of this horizon of solidarity as in principle universal, not bounded by the conventions of a particular age. In this light, the better question is *how* this mystical horizon could expand, and what would keep it tied to the political-particular solidarity of action that is necessary for an environmental theology. To answer this question we must turn to the other two categories in Metz's theological anthropology: memory and narrative.

Memory weaves the fabric of both cultural and individual identity. The temptation is always to leave out of that fabric the fates of those who came before us, many of whose deaths cannot be easily made sense of and integrated into the fabric of our identities today. Many of them, after all, suffered and died unknown and unnamed, either as a result of the processes of "progress" that

---

[32] On this see Daniel Cowdin, "The Moral Status of Otherkind in Christian Ethics," in Hessel and Ruether, *Christianity and Ecology*, 261-85, esp. 262f.

[33] See FHS, chapter 13, section on "Solidarity only among the rational"? Also, "God: Against the Myth of Eternal Time".

have led to the present, or arbitrarily and utterly senselessly. Metz recalls Nietzsche's counterproposal to the difficult and apparently fruitless remembering of their fates: "Blessed are the forgetful."[34] Yet the price of such a shield of amnesia is high. It is also profoundly unbiblical, as Metz has insisted on numerous occasions. Israel's "poverty of spirit" for him is its incapacity to be consoled by the myths and conceptual idealisms that cover over or "explain" past suffering so we can forget about it.[35] The biblical narratives are full of unconsoled complaint and lamentation that even call God to account for the suffering in God's creation - most paradigmatically, the Book of Job. Yet the acuteness of Israel's memory and its painful sensitivity to suffering are in direct proportion to the strength of its hope and the capacity, so manifest in the prophetic and apocalyptic traditions, to expand the compass of that hope.

It is our capacity not to forget the suffering of the past that opens up a horizon for a more universal, mystical hope for the future, and, with our sensitivities thus sharpened, will not allow us to ignore present suffering. This fortitude is not our own, of course, but is a grace, and is underwritten by the biblical narratives - particularly texts like the Book of Job (as we have seen), or the synoptic portraits of Jesus (particularly Mark's and Matthew's, whose passion narratives end with Jesus' cry of abandonment from the cross). This brings us to narrative. Narrative forms, and, where necessary, irritates what we remember from the past and how we remember it, and gestures toward a future in which not even past suffering is left untouched. It is, moreover, particular appropriations of the biblical narratives, their re-narration and re-interpretation, that "make the connection" between the universal-mystical horizon of hope for the other and particular-political solidarity of preferential concern and political action in a particular context. The slave narratives and spirituals of U.S. history provide one instance of this phenomenon. The *Nican Mopohua*, recounting the appearances of the Virgin of Guadalupe to Juan Diego, is another.[36] Another more recent one is Ignacio Ellacuría's weaving together of the suffering servant songs of 2nd Isaiah, New Testament passion narratives, and the history of the poor in Latin America.[37] Narratives, on this account, expand (mystically-universally) but also focus (politically-preferentially) our sense for which others can and should count as worthy of concern, making a connection between the (potentially) universal mystical horizon of solidarity with all created beings, and particular, preferential commitments to solidarity here and now with specific threatened others.

---

[34] "God: Against the Myth of Eternal Time".

[35] See, inter alia, *Passion for God* 124f, 130f.

[36] See Virgil Elizondo, *Guadalupe: Mother of the New Creation* (Maryknoll, N.Y.: Orbis Books, 1997).

[37] Ignacio Ellacuría, "The Crucified People," in Ellacuría and Sobrino (eds.) *Mysterium Liberationis: Fundamental Concepts of Liberation Theology* (Maryknoll, N.Y.: Orbis Books, 1993), 580-603.

What this suggests is that new narratives that intercalate the biblical narratives with narratives that connect humans more immediately with nonhuman nature than modernity's narratives (both grand and *petit*) have done could expand the mystical horizon of solidarity to include the nonhuman natural world, and our memory of suffering to include the suffering inflicted by the rapacious human practices toward nature brought about by the juggernaut of global capitalism. The remembering of the past suffering of the whole natural world, and the greater solidarity with "otherkind" that this would elicit, could provide the kind of interconnection of humans and nature that Stephen Scharper has called for under the rubric of an "anthro-harmonic" approach to environmental theology.[38]

It has become something of a commonplace in environmental theology to insist that the human story is embedded in a more comprehensive "universe story," and to argue on this basis against an anthropocentrism that would locate all meaning in human history alone. This suggests a fruitful point of contact between Metz's new political theology and environmental concern. But, care is needed. It is very important that these narratives be *dangerous* narratives, that they not abet a tendency to forget or conceptually numb the impact of past suffering, but present it in such a way that there would be no relief if there were no God "for whom not even the past is fixed," a God who is the Lord of time and not its distant observer. It is this exigency that is behind Metz's long-standing critique of the quasi-mythical power of the symbol of evolution:

> There is an 'Ersatz'-metaphysics, a new quasi-metaphysics. Its name: the logic of evolution. In this logic the leveling out of time, which makes all time the same, has come to systematically dominate our common awareness. On its basis everything is "reconstructed" in terms of a timeless continuum: religious consciousness just as much as the dialectical consciousness that critiques religion. ... This logic of evolution is not innocent; neither is it agnostic (in the style of a methodological atheism). God - the God of the living and of the dead, the God for whom even the past and the dead are not left to rest in peace - is absolutely unthinkable within this logic. This is the real, dispassionate Godlessness - much more than all those insistent atheisms that in negating are still bound to what they negate.[39]

---

[38] Stephen Bede Scharper, *Redeeming the Time: A Political Theology of Environment* (New York, N.Y.: Continuum, 1997), 188: "An anthro-harmonic perspective acknowledges the importance of the human and makes the human fundamental but not exclusively focal." Scharper himself looks to process philosophy and theology to do this. While the approach advocated here (as Metz himself avers) relies on conceptually "weaker" categories than the "strong" ontological categories of process thought, I would judge that they are both more appropriate to the Christian tradition, and more realistic, given the formidable difficulties facing any theology that would seek a metaphysical foundation in this "post-metaphysical age."

[39] FHS, chapter 10.

Modern theologians who appropriate scientific evolutionary schemes to tell "the universe story" will, to be sure, insist that "evolution" no longer entails the sort of unilinear, ruthlessly agonistic "survival of the fittest" scheme that was appropriated by social Darwinism in the nineteenth century or by modern Neo-Darwinians such as Dennett and Dawkins in the present. But when one reads more closely, troubling doubts persist. If human history is to be understood as a part of a broader cosmogenesis, as Brian Swimme and Thomas Berry insist, then what socio-political implications follow from the basic "dialectic" of cosmogenic history described as follows:

> The cosmogenesis of Earth and universe proceeds by establishing stable regimes that are then broken apart by the activities of the parts, thus leading to new stable regimes with new members included in the new dynamics. In the best of circumstances, the succeeding regimes are characterized by an enhanced diversity, a more extensive autopoiesis, and a richer interrelatedness. But at times, given the inherent turbulence of the universe, these later regimes are ripped asunder with no further development. The unfolding of the universe proceeds with reversals and surprises, sporadically advancing in various directions and then as suddenly collapsing.[40]

This narrative scheme allows Swimme and Berry to look with some equanimity at the Permian extinction as setting the stage for an explosion of biological innovation; however, if taken as a comprehensive narrative template, it is not clear why one might not look at an ecological collapse in the coming centuries, caused by human excess, with equal equanimity. The early self-assertion of the first cells over-saturated the atmosphere with oxygen, leading to their demise; but it also forced the creative advance of a bacterium that could deal with oxygen. On this pattern, might we not look with a little more serenity at the dangerous self-assertion of modern technological society?[41] It seems to be particularly dangerous to take this view toward human history. But even with natural history, will this narrative nourish the sense of solidarity with nature that will open us to a broader hope for the future as well as a more committed solidaristic action in the present? Is this not too much like the "consoling myths" which, on Metz's reading, the Jewish people were not able to accept, an inability that marked them and their particular "poverty of spirit"?

---

[40] Swimme and Berry, 99.

[41] In fairness, Swimme and Berry insist that "In no sense do we mean to suggest that the cruelties taking place in the Earth community today will be justified by the emergence of what is to come" (60). Yet it is hard to see how this conclusion doesn't follow from the narrative scheme they adopt. It does not help (at least on inner-Christian grounds) that they attempt to escape this conundrum by a Nietzsche-like appeal to the instrumentality of suffering in the creation of new works of art, philosophy, technology, and institutional reform. "To eliminate the tension [of the bafflement produced by suffering] would be to eliminate the beauty."

What this suggests is that we should proceed with extreme caution in forming a cosmic narrative as the fundamental (some even go far as to claim fundamentally revelational) basis for elaborating a Christian consciousness of our presence in the world. First of all, we must make sure that we are reading the book of nature with the lenses provided by the book of scripture (to use John Calvin's way of putting it), and not the reverse. The fundamental paradigm should be the exodus narratives and the stories of Jesus, with particular attention to the sense of loss found in books like Lamentations and Job. Second, more "local" narratives of humans in nature would seem to be adequate (even more effective) than a "grand narrative" of the whole of cosmic history. This, after all, is what authors like Aldo Leopold, Rachel Carson, Edward Abbey and Annie Dillard have done to such effect: tell the "little stories"[42] of nature and human involvement in nature, in a way that engenders a sense of what is missed and what is missing in our modern stance toward nature, and, at times, to reach out toward a sense of hope for a future that can be different. One could take the stories surrounding Francis of Assisi as paradigmatic ways interweaving these little stories of nature with the gospel narrative. We need more of these today. We are, in other words, not yet ready to cast a new "master-myth" of the cosmos and our human place in it (if we ever will be). Attention to the "little stories" requires a Job-like humility with regard to God's desires and intentions for the cosmos, while also authorizing, indeed demanding, a Job-like lamentation and complaint before God when faced with a universe filled with so much suffering that obdurately resists even our best efforts to understand it.

This brings us finally, and appropriately, to the question of God. For Metz, theology, be it political theology, environmental theology, or a cross-fertilization of the two, is ultimately talk about God. And this talk about God must, as we have seen, have a memorative-narrative root. It must also find its paradigm in the "the language of prayer," the language in which both human wonder at the gift of creation *and* human bewilderment and pain at the suffering that crucifies it, find expression.[43]

> We cannot construct a common understanding of God based on just any image of God that we might ("postmodernly") come up with, none of which have any tolerance for negativity, for unconsoled pain. Rather, everything turns on the image of God given in the biblical traditions. Do we really take the irreducible, painful dialectic of this image of God seriously? This is what I wonder when I hear the oh so positive imagery used for God in preaching today, in which it is only the "love" of God that we hear about. Of course, I also ask myself this when I read critics say that it has only been the church that has painted a dark

[42] See Alex Garcia-Rivera, *St. Martin de Porres: The "Little Stories" and the Semiotics of Culture* (Maryknoll, N.Y.: Orbis Books, 1995), esp. 25-39.
[43] This is, on Gustavo Gutíerrez's reading, what Job learned from his struggle with suffering and with God. See *On Job: Godtalk and the Suffering of the Innocent* (Maryknoll, N.Y.: Orbis Books, 1987).

> image of God in order to terrify people and keep them down. No, it is already life itself that presents us with this dark image of God and which a mature faith must not simply paper over, but before which it has to hold its ground - even if that be with the creature's wordless sigh.[44]

As David Tracy has shown, this means recovering a way of naming God, who is the lord of history and the creator of heaven and earth, as not only incomprehensible, but *hidden*, hidden in a fearful darkness.[45] A Christian environmental theology could benefit from Metz's reflection on the mystical stance of "suffering unto God" that can stand up before the suffering of the historical (and natural world), continuing to call out to God, "How long, O Lord?" and to act out of the apocalyptically charged trust that God will answer … soon. It is this painful sensibility to suffering - which will not let itself be dulled by conceptual systems or myths that explain away the scandal of suffering - that can make those who can bear up under it open to a renewed and passionate commitment to new values and visions for our future. It is when the church's teachings, rituals and practices connect the Christian memory of the God of Jesus with the memory of suffering - both in culture and in nature - by means of appropriately modest "little stories" of our human involvement in nature, that it can become possible for believers to begin to sense again that the narratives, doctrines and symbols of Christian faith are about *them*, and that they offer an alternative way of remembering, renarrating and conceptualizing their own histories, as socially-culturally and naturally-biologically embodied persons.

Conclusion

I have argued in this essay that while Metz did not formulate his new political theology in order to respond to environmental concerns his work offers considerable advantages as a "fundamental practical theology" for a theology that would respond to these concerns. First of all, it offers a potent diagnosis of our present-day dilemma that environmental theology would do well to heed. Theologies that try to respond to our current "ecologic crisis" by offering a meta-theory or even meta-myth will, on Metz's reading, fail if they do not address the deeply rooted "postmodernism of the heart" that is endemic to our late modern situation. This weariness with being a subject is only intensified by downplaying the subjectivity of individual persons in favor of allegedly more com-

---

[44] *Time's End.*

[45] See, for example, David Tracy, "The Hidden God: The Divine Other of Liberation," in *Cross Currents* 46/1 (Spring 1996): 5-16. For historical background on the history of the tradition of the hidden God in Christianity, see Brian Gerrish, "The Hiddenness of God in . . . " and Bernard McGinn, "*Vere tu es Deus absonditus*: the hidden God in Luther and some Mystics," *Silence and the Word: Negative Theology and Incarnation*, ed. Oliver Davies and Denys Turner (Cambridge, M.A.: Cambridge University Press, 2002), 94-114.

prehensive subjects (Gaia, nature, the cosmos). I argued, in addition, that Metz's theological anthropology, with its conceptually "weak" categories of memory, narrative and solidarity can expand to encompass the natural world within the "mystical-political horizon" of human concern, although most securely so within the ambit of "little stories" of human involvement with the natural world. The larger story is, I suggest, best approached in a Job-like stance that at once recognizes the utter gratuity of all that comes from the creator God, but also practices real humility concerning our ability to conceptualize and grasp the whole scope of God's purposes for creation. As Gustavo Gutíerrez has suggested a sense of gratuitousness does not mitigate against labor for justice (extended, *mutatis mutandis*, to consider justice for nonhuman, "otherkind"), but gives it a basis that can survive the continual breakdown of our "quid pro quo" frameworks for deciding what is just and meaningful in God's plan when confronted with the very real experience of suffering.[46]

This is only the beginning of a political theology of environment, to be sure. A number of tasks would need to be completed in order to elaborate a more complete political theology of environment from this starting point. Some of these tasks are incumbent on any theology that would continue the approach worked out by Johann Baptist Metz. For example, it is necessary to continue the defense of narrative as a fundamental theological category. More specifically, however, it is important to take up and critique the "counter-narratives" that are being constructed by Neo-Darwinians and evolutionary psychologists such as Daniel Dennett and Richard Dawkins, who argue their superiority on "scientific grounds."[47] Having expressed concerns and reservations about the "meta-narratives" of the universe's story, it seems to me that more modest narratives focused on human beings' interactions with the rest of the natural world, both past and present, deserve more theological attention.[48] This will require a better framing of the relationship between nature and history than the one that Metz's political theology has used to date. As I have suggested, what needs to be avoided above all is the "naturalization of history," as opposed to a modest and piecewise "historicization of nature," at least to the extent that humans are involved in it. As the work of Jürgen Moltmann and other political and liberation theologians who have broached the topic of environmental theology suggests, this will require working out a Trinitarian theology, something conspicuously

---

[46] See Gutíerrez *On Job,*65-85.

[47] See, for example, Richard Dawkins, *River out of Eden: A Darwinian View of Life* (New York: Basic Books, 1995), and *Unweaving the Rainbow: Science, Delusion, and the Appetite for Wonder* (Boston: Houghton Mifflin Co., 1998). The religious resonances suggested by the titles are intentional.

[48] Langdon Gilkey's interweaving of some of the results of modern science and creation myths from Christian and other religions could serve as a paradigm here. See Langdon Gilkey, *Nature, Reality and the Sacred: The Nexus of Science and Religion* (Minneapolis, Minn.: Fortress Press, 1993).

absent in Metz's work.[49] It will be important to clarify what kinds of axiological and ethical conceptualities can enable us to move from the basic stance of solidarity with various groups of threatened others that I have focused on here to the subsequent, but no less important processes of ethical evaluation and discernment.

Finally, we must pay greater attention to instances of innovative praxis on the part of Christian communities that have begun to move toward an expansion of the mystical-political horizon of solidarity, hope, memory and narrative to include nature. Metz's insight that religious orders might have a crucial role to play is borne out here, especially if we consider some of the creative work being done by communities of religious women in the Catholic Church.

This is an ambitious agenda, some of which is incumbent on further development of the approach that Metz has opened up. It may be that the new political theology will not develop its own specific approach to environmental theology but will provide crucial categories and correctives to other theologians who take environmental theology and theological ethics as their specific tasks. Metz's theology should not be ignored in that work.

[49] The reason for this exigency is not difficult to see. If we follow Rahner's (and Metz's) point that the best Trinitarian theology is one that stays as close as possible to a narration of salvation history, and if we accept the need to interweave the history of non-human nature into that salvation history, at least on a modest scale, then Trinitarian theology cannot remain untouched by or unimportant to a political theology of environment.

WHAT PRICE GOD-TALK?
A Theological-Political Assessment

Johann Reikerstorfer

Religion is making a comeback. And even the "dialectical" discourse of a leveling secularization process itself full of contradictions is looking for a way to take account of this return.[1] But how does "religion" appear upon its return given that apparently there is no convincing model for the "experience of transcendence" that would make plausible the integration of all the relevant religious experiences in a symbolic-ritual complex? Is it a matter of the new shapes and forms on the religious and spiritual supply scene offering "compensation" for the damage done by modernity, for breaking through the systems constraints on a lifeworld that has become complex and confusing?[2] In this "comeback" does religion register a protest against the growing anonymity and indifference in the abstract systems of economics and technology and the culture and communications industries they foster? Can it develop forms of resistance against these new threats to human identity - perhaps simply as the quiet cry of a humanity that senses danger and seeks rescue? Could our anxiety over losing our name or being sacrificed to fate be the most profound and serious of all anxieties, our anxiety before the complete indifference of time - deadlier than death itself?[3]

It remains to be seen whether the diffuse and broad tendencies of a "re-spiritualization" are really capable of mobilizing any resistance to the immanent disappearance of humankind. In the current storm of individualization will such a movement be able to replace the sturdy solidarity formerly generated by those grand religious visions of humanity that inevitably lose their power in our "post-traditional" societies? To be sure, the identity of the human person can never be formed without others. It is *their* hopes, *their* struggles and sufferings that push the horizon of transcendence beyond limited self-referential images of the divine and human. But do the culture of life and the affirmation of life evoked in the name of spirituality simply end in a culture of survival? Or does their purely affirmative tone cultivate an art of forgetfulness which spirituality need not resist just now? Does the state-

---

[1] See interview with Johann Baptist Metz in: *KNA* (Bonn), 6/8/2004.

[2] See the report on the seminar held at the European Forum of Alpbach in 1999: Karl Gabriel/Johann Reikerstorfer, "Spirituality. Summary of the Seminar" in: *Die zerrissene Gesellschaft. Europäisches Forum Alpbach 1998* (H. Pfusterschmid-Hardtenstein), Vienna 1999, 102-108.

[3] See the appropriate analyses in Johann Baptist Metz, "Zeit ohne Finale? Zum Hintergrund der Debatte über 'Resurrektion oder Reinkarnation'," in: *Concilium* 29 (1993), H.5, 458-462 und "Ohne Finale ins Nichts. Die Herrschaft der endlosen Zeit und die Angst", in: *FAZ*, 7/13/1991.

ment, „Every philosophy that does not hold to its basis in the negative and that tries to achieve the immediate positive without it will finally die of (inevitable) spiritual depletion"[4] made by Schelling about philosophy not also apply to a shifting and hardly identifiable spirituality?

The German soccer player Jens Jeremies likes the singer Udo Jürgens. Not all his songs. Not ones like "Aber bitte mit Sahne," but the more substantial ones. Then the melody and lyrics come to him[5]:

> *Wer nie verliert, hat den Sieg nicht verdient/*
> *Wer alles will, muss viel von sich geben/*
> *Wer nichts riskiert, hat sein Glück nur gelieh'n/*
> *Wer sich nicht einsetzt, gewinnt nicht das Leben/*
> *Ich weiß noch gut, wie die Verzweiflung schmeckt/*
> *wenn selbst die Wut sich vor dem Schmerz versteckt.*[6]

At least since September 11th, the West has come to experience vulnerability to foreign cultures and religions and the problematic nature of any context-free generalization of European cultural values and humanistic ideals. The "secular project" of Europe has been asked whether or not it can publicly and structurally acknowledge the pluralism of religions and worldviews and inspire productive cooperation. An anti-pluralistic concept of secularization that automatically banishes religion from public life and privatizes it seems outdated in the light of current global developments. Post-secular societies must take into account the presence of religious communities in increasingly secular surroundings.[7]

But how could there be a pluralistic ethos of recognition without a historical remembrancing broadened to include the suffering of others too? Only in this remembrancing could there be meaningful talk today of oppression and liberation as well as protest against the new forms of injustice - against segregation, continuing impoverishment, and a grinding poverty. In these times of globalization, a Christianity that renewed its *cultic* memory and cultivated solidarity with those who suffer in opposition to the worldwide oppression of humankind could prove itself to be an effective gadfly in

---

[4] Friedrich Wilhelm Joseph Schelling, *Sämtliche Werke*, edited by K.F.A. Schellung, Stuttgart, 1856-61, X 176.

[5] Quotation taken from an interview in: *SZ*, 6/12&13/2004.

[6] "He who never loses does not earn the victory. He who wants everything has to give away much of himself. He who does not take risks has only borrowed his luck. He who does not compete does not win life. I still remember what despair tastes like, when even rage hides from the pain."

[7] Jürgen Habermas, „Glauben und Wissen. Friedenspreisrede 2001," in: Habermas, *Zeitdiagnosen. Zwölf Essays 1980-2001*, Frankfurt am Main 2003, 251 f.

the encounter with other cultures and religions.[8] Such an ethos would be extremely valuable not only for ecumenism among Christians but also for an "ecumenism" of world religions in shared responsibility for meaning. It is in this profound "this-worldliness" in which the death and resurrection of Jesus is present[9] that responsibility for others becomes the occasion for the communicative disruption of all of our usual images of God, images that look suspiciously like projections.

Theological Orientation

This spirituality of remembrancing[10] requires the formulation of some theological observations:

First: Christianity rests on the conviction that God - who wants to be our brother and so would like to meet us in an open human encounter - always stands before us in the faces of others: our relationship to others concretely determines our relationship to God. Faith needs "the other" in order to be able to experience and articulate who God is. When we recognize the other, the illusive mystery of God becomes present in the world, or put the other way around, the sinful "No" to God is evident in our concrete lives as the denial of this recognition. The eschatological images of the Kingdom of God are all about a universal promise that goes beyond the individual and connects us with others at the deepest level. These images can be seen as contextualized illustrations of God's will for communion in the perfected human society as it is expressed in His covenant. Especially in a religion where the love of God and neighbour are identified, the orientation towards others must not be seen as simply a moral consequence of believing, but rather as a condition for encountering God.

Second: For a long time theology has interpreted this unity of the love of God and love of neighbor using an interpersonal encounter paradigm that also served as a model for understanding God. Today, however, this same unity insists on taking its political form. The others who connect us to God are not only those others whom we directly encounter, but also those people around the world who are *threatened*, the systematically disadvantaged and marginalized others. Therefore, love has to take the form of resistance in these relationships, for only if it remains responsible for social structures can

---

[8] This is the thesis stated by Johann Baptist Metz, in: Günther Virt, ed., *Facetten einer Dynamik aus ethischer und theologischer Perspektive*. Freiburg/Schweiz-Freiburg/Br.-Wien 2000, 130-141.

[9] Dietrich Bonhoeffer, *Widerstand und Ergebung, Briefe und Aufzeichnungen aus der Haft*, Neuausgabe München 1970, 401. See also Nicoletta Capozza, *Im Namen der Treue zur Erde. Versuch eines Vergleichs zwischen Bonhoeffers und Nietzsches Denken*, Münster 2002.

[10] See the contribution referred to in footnote 2. This category from Walter Benjamin is used here in its interpretation by Johann Baptist Metz and will be integrated into our line of argumentation.

it remain related to the world. Love cannot be undialectically affirmative if it wants to effectively maintain itself as the negation of negation among conflicting perspectives. A Christianity that discovers the definitive self-communication of God in the Crucified One - a Christianity that grasps the transcendence in this "descent" - must not rise above the fates of others and, untouched by them, attempt to rescue its identity in a socially and politically neutral inwardness. How narcissistic must a faith be that would not permit itself to be disturbed by looking at the world - even for the sake of its own memory of God?

Third: This God we encounter in others remains always incognito, the shadowy, surprising God. God's incarnation has not made God clearer, more understandable, more intelligible and easier to bear. God's advent in the "form of a servant" only sharpens the subversive attention to stories of broken lives, lives of dashed hopes and disappointments that have no time for easy and cheap consolations. Through this memory, stories of suffering are snatched from the jaws of a completely indifferent fate and - in the light of revelation - become stories of "suffering unto God" in which in the pain of transcendence the unapproachable comes near. This painful nearness, suffered by the Son in his cry of abandonment from the cross, has been indelibly inscribed in our history as a trace of God.

Expressed in terms of a theology of creation, the covenant, as the inner ground of the love of God and humankind is the foundation for creation and has a real history of self-realization within creation. In other words, it is the law of nature within grace, the recognition of the dignity of the created and in it the mediated form of this covenant itself. All the same, the recognition of human dignity *in* its woundedness - that is, in this negative experience of the *mysterium passionis* - shatters any ontological or identity-philosophical interpretation of the transparency of creation: creation is only conceivable as something outside of God (*Aus-Stand*). God is not out of time and otherworldly, but rather is the nearby outsider, the presence of the not-yet, the *expected one* who is coming.

Such a notion of time prevents us from continuing to separate and hypostasize the memory of God and the memory of human suffering apart from each other out of a desire to bring them together later. As demonstrated by the history of how atheism was fuelled by the question of suffering, such an attempt must fail due to the dilemma of the omnipotence and goodness of God. The path of a gnostic internalization of suffering in God also is blocked as an other-worldly expectation that flees the world. Biblically, the name of God remains indelibly encrypted in the passion of humankind. God cannot be established "beyond" or "above" human suffering; on the contrary, this suffering is the cost of affirming God. Only in this dialectic can human dignity in suffering be respected and God eschatologically proclaimed as the one God of all reality. This dialectic stands in opposition to the "post-humanism" of a mythical history of being (*Seinsgeschichte*), a history without humankind and so also without God.

The pressing question today is why evil, why the senseless, isolating and destructive suffering of innocent people. This powerful and dramatic "why-question" can no longer be bent into the much more satisfying "what-for question." Only *as* questioning God can this why-question resist obscuring and covering over the horrors of history. What would be the alternative? A forgetfulness without compassion that is unable to escape from its own de-humanizing consequences.

In this brokenness, our memory of God says more than any metaphysical God encoded in an ahistorical doctrine of salvation. Put differently: The memory of the resurrection is not the suspiciously ideological wish for an other-worldly history, but the beginning of another history in the midst our history, a counter-history in which the nearness of God becomes palpable in the disguised and suppressed passion of humanity.[11] In this "folly," God remains the name for an outrageous hope against all hope. Only those who taste the nihilism lurking in suffering can experience God as an antidote, as a liberating word of hope.

This also means that God broke any sense or meaning in history (including those of the religious imagination) on the cross and negated every attempt to look beyond the world for a successful outcome. In this way God compels us to a remembrance of the many crosses in our world and remains historically close to us as the God of promise and interruption. On this path of God, like Jesus, Christianity hears God's call out of our contemporary world with a new historical urgency. It cannot avoid the question whether today it is able and willing to find a new possibility for its future in the endangered lives of human beings. Then the memory of suffering would be the sort of hope *pro aliis* which would let in the world of the other and bind itself to their concrete historical experience. Only such an orientation prevents Christianity from appearing to be a religion of complaint and victimization turned in on itself and evoking violence against others.[12]

Christology has to face the question of whether its terminology has helped to turn God's saving act into an abstract principle that conceals its temporality rather than making it effective. If Jesus Christ were a "problem-solving strategy," the answer to the theodicy-question, he would be sepa-

---

[11] On this thought about a revelation "in contradiction," see Kurt Appel, *Entsprechung im Wider-Spruch. Eine Auseinandersetzung mit dem Offenbarungsbegriff der politischen Theologie des jungen Hegel*, Münster 2003.

[12] In so far as Mel Gibson's Jesus-movie ("The passion of the Christ"), for example, intensifies the history of suffering into the one horrible scene of the suffering of Jesus, it is almost a perversion of the Christian way of dealing with suffering in the world. See Jürgen Manemann, *Rettende Erinnerung an die Zukunft. Essay über die christliche Verschärfung*, Mainz 2005.

rated from history and, thereby, history would lose its dynamic movement toward God. The only way Christian hope is more than (and can clearly be differentiated from) mere utopianism is if it does not spare itself the world of the theodicy-question but rekindles the blaze of that question time and again. Isn't this basically where the substantive meaning of religion becomes apparent?

How must one view the world in order to want to speak of God only with a purely affirmative, undisrupted, undialectical imagination? The purely affirmative believer does not recognize that God can only be experienced as the God of controversy and struggle. The God of comfort who encourages us in situations of despair, the God worthy of belief and worship, is a God whose survival is always under threat. A person who has never tasted despair, never faced the abyss of profound futility and senselessness, can never find support and rescue. This negativity - which can never be stilled, not even by religion - is part of the *memoria Dei*. This alone guarantees in its "uncomfortable God" [*unpassenden Gott*] (Johann Baptist Metz) a universal promise to humankind which has its ground and measure precisely in God.

What would really be the alternative to this negative theology? A kind of theology which no longer misses anything, which cultivates the "happiness of immediacy" [*Glück der Unmittelbarkeit*] (S. Kierkegaard), and abandons the transcending power of these sorrowful interruptions? Such a theology would lose not only humankind, but with it, God as well, because - as we have been trying to show - only suffering unto God preserves the dignity of humankind in the face of the "objective" oblivion of an indifferent and levelling time. Such theological commentary would be superfluous and promise nothing. For this reason, the future of God and humanity depends at its heart on this inner dialectic of the affirmation of God. This historical remembering of God and humanity is in its tension between memory and forgetting prior to any "concept," and thereby remains the basis for any theological talk about God and human beings.

Second Courage

The *historical consciousness* that was once brought about by the belief in the biblical promises seems to be losing its provocative importance and depth in our time of psychology, aesthetics and religious transfiguration. With this loss comes the abandonment of those "others" who, full of hope, might be able to expand the small and shrinking horizon of our own search for identity. But allowing history to come to the fore in its awkward non-identity, to give it room to do so, requires a *second courage*, a courage that could unmask how God has long been sought out and passed on in an undialecticaffirmative manner that makes it easy to remove God to the height of a world-denying consolation for an inconsolable world.

This courage to face non-identity does not want to spare itself the "pain of negativity" (Hegel) in God as it confronts devious harmonisations (even in religious imagination).[13] It says "Yes" in remembrancing as a form of resistance which refuses to stop asking whether there is justice for the innocent who suffer unjustly. As Kierkegaard says: "The immediate relation to God is paganism: one can only speak of a true relation to God after the break has taken place."[14]

Why is it today that our talk of God often seems so empty, so used up and unconsoling? Is it because we too rarely allow others to interrupt our view of the world? Is it because we create a God in our own image who does not promise anything? When we retreat so quickly from the danger zones of history and attempt to avoid the sight of others, we become deaf and insensitive to the consolation of our great hope, a hope which remembers and hears all. God holds, supports, and consoles only when we make it possible to suffer unto God as the God also of the other.

The new political theology is well-known for wrestling with the plausibility of the biblical *memoria passionis* within the current debate over reason.[15] This remembrancing requires and establishes a rationality with an *a priori* of suffering ["*Leidensapriori*"]. By acknowledging this unalterable claim within the concept of reason itself, this *memoria* might become an organon not only for universal talk about God but for understanding between cultures and religions as well.[16] This remembrancing is not meant to be sentimental, but political - an active, productive, and effective remembrancing with a critical and liberating intention. Faith is ignited in *compassion*: a passion for God [*Gottesleidenschaft*] is the passion for engagement. In this version of the union of the love of God and the love of neighbor, faith stings and sharpens the "human conscience" in a world threatened by the decline of humanity. So we must ask ourselves whether the loss of the moral and political authority of Christianity is due to an almost pagan propensity to affirmation, which does not allow for any suffering unto God, does not know about any suffering unto God and so suppresses any kind of eschatological unrest.

---

[13] See the essays in: Johann Reikerstorfer (ed.), *Vom Wagnis der Nichtidentität. Johann Baptist Metz zu Ehren*, Münster 1998.

[14] Sören Kierkegaard, *Die Leidenschaft des Religiösen. Eine Auswahl aus Schriften und Tagebüchern*, Stuttgart 1968, 19.

[15] See Johann Baptist Metz, "Athen versus Jerusalem? Was das Christentum dem europäischen Geist schuldig geblieben ist," in *Orientierung* 60 (3/15/1996), 9-25.

[16] Johann Baptist Metz, „Im Eingedenken fremden Leids. Zu einer Basiskategorie christlicher Gottesrede," in Metz, Johann Baptist/Reikerstorfer, Johann/ Werbick, Jürgen: *Gottesrede*, 2.aktualisierte Auflage, Münster 2001, 3-20, and ibid., „Memoria passionis. Zu einer Grundkategorie interkultureller und interreligiöser Begegnung," in Hans-Peter Müller, *Das Evangelium und die Weltreligionen*, Stuttgart 1997, 109-118.

On the Nearness of the Missing God

Does our worrying about God belie an unsatisfied yearning? Is God perhaps announced in this yearning historically in a new way, so that if we describe it only as a longing for God, we have not fully understood it? Everything depends on grasping God in the longing itself as his nearness in our responsibility for others. At the same time, we must reject the over-used question and answer schema as an inadequate interpretive model. "Nearness" means "the incomparability of the incomprisable that moves us without sublating us; it is longing, that is precisely a thought that always thinks more than it thinks."[17]

This longing is not focused on an otherwise known or familiar God, it rather aims at the distant God, the missing God, who turns our concern into curiosity about God. Only a God with whom everything stands and falls is the kind of God who in the freedom of purposeless can be affirmed and gratefully celebrated for God's own sake.

Why is it that we are unable to accept injustice happening to others without losing our own selves? Is there a bond of solidarity by which their pain and vulnerability disturb us and affect our identity? What gives us the courage to resist the triumph of an indifferent fate which devours everything? Why is a sense of time that devours everything deadlier than death? Why do we feel close to the dead even though they are no longer useful to anyone? Do we perhaps hear in their memory a quiet protest against the death-dealing relations we ourselves produce through the language of the market which infuses our every pore and squeezes human relationships into the corset of a "self-referential orientation to personal preferences?"[18] By interrupting the world of the objectifying marketplace and the scornful degrading power of "exchange," do they not make possible the intimation of the "bond" of a profound and compelling humanity and in this also something of the unconditional love of God? A spirituality nurtured by this longing does not relativize the Christian promise potential, does not turn it into a general disposition, but renews the concrete practical context in which the enormity of a hope "against all hope" can begin to be expressed and passed on. How much mysticism of Christ does one need, how powerful must his or her real sympathy be, in order to bring the broken, suffering, and futureless victims to public attention in our daily lives?

Whoever longs for God in others and for others cannot be content with a "reduced transcendence" (Niklas Luhmann). They are moving toward the "ever greater" transcendence of an uncompensated future for the world - without guarantees and without confusing God with the concept of God. In

[17] Emmanuel Lévinas, „Menschwerdung Gottes?," in: ibid., *Zwischen uns. Versuche über das Denken an die Anderen*, München/Wien 1995, 79.
[18] Habermas, *Zeitdiagnosen*, 257.

this negative but communicative way God and the world remain temporally related to each other. And only in such a context can over-used and suspect words such as love and reconciliation have (that is, regain) any substantive meaning.

A spirituality with this feeling for the vulnerability of humankind can connect to and communicate the life-stories of human beings and cultures. This would make it an acceptable basis for mutual understanding and of decided importance for intercultural and interreligious dialogue.

The Boundless Language of Prayer

God is not made more god-like when we think of God as "purer," less threatening, or utterly timeless. Only the God who is also constantly assailed, disputed, and denied is truly worthy of worship. Don't we also devalue prayer when we isolate it from the crises of assent we each experience in our lives, crises that should not be left out of our prayers but brought directly into our affirmation of God?[19] The great traditions of prayer in the Old Testament Psalms and Prophets do not suffer from any sort of excessive affirmation. Even the praise of God is sparked by abysmal experiences of crisis and failure - by the horizon of danger. Pure affirmation might not be so much an expression of confidence as a sign of our lack of courage and our inability to take on doubts, anxieties, and threats as we struggle for God.

The language of prayer does not lend itself to lessening anxiety or finding compensation. And it is never the language of humiliating surrender. It is much more the language of rebellion in which those who pray connect with their God within the "profound this-worldliness" of profane life and finds thereby a name, a face, and a dignity. Is prayer, then, more common among humankind than is generally acknowledged?[20] What's going on when people are affected by the fate of others around them, suffering themselves because of the suffering of others? What's going on, when people won't accept the terrible scenarios of suffering throughout our world – even if their protest often ends in a powerless and stifled "sigh"? Isn't it in the "respect" given to the other that God, the God beyond God, the "uncomfortable God," touches our lives in a rare way? Indeed, it is in this rebellious language of prayer that God remains both the one we are calling for and the one bound up with the history of humankind. And this avoids the old cliché that only those who

---

[19] See also Johann Reikerstorfer, „Über die ‚Klage' in der Christologie," in *Klage. Jahrbuch für biblische Theologie*, Bd.16 (2001); Ebner, Martin (Ed.): Neukirchen-Vlyn 2001, 269-287.

[20] See also the related interview with Johann Baptist Metz: „Sis mihi Deus!", in *Das Prisma. Beiträge zu Pastoral, Katechese & Theologie,* Hagemann, Wilfried (ed.): 15.Jg. (2003) H.2, 20-28.

believe are able to pray. Karl Rahner is said to have remarked: I do not pray because I believe; I believe because I pray.

Can the breaking of idols in practice become the occasion for a new experience of God? Does the destruction of the standard images of God make possible respect for the life-stories of others riddled with suffering and allow us to feel an expectant nearness – quietly and not forcibly, to be sure – even in pain? "You shall not make yourselves any image of God or any likeness of anything in heaven above, on the earth beneath or that is in the waters under the earth." (Exodus 20:4)

Translated by Katharina Hedding, John K. Downey and Steven T. Ostovich

Appendix

POLITICAL THEOLOGY: HISTORY OF A CONCEPT*

Bernd Wacker and Jürgen Manemann

"Political theology" might generally be defined as "the reflection on those contexts in which theology and religion become political (if they are not already), that is, in which they have ideological and practical political consequences" (Mauer in Taubes 1983, 117). Such a definition is merely descriptive and leaves out of consideration the normative-operative aspect of political theology. In addition it does justice neither to the historical contexts of the concept nor to what is done today under this rubric.

I. The Philosophical Stigma

Origins of the Term

The expression "political theology" goes back to various schools of Hellenistic philosophy that made a three-fold distinction in theology: *theologia mythike (theologia fabularis), physike (naturalis), politike (civilis)* (Lieberg 1973). If the first refers to poetic speech about the divine in terms of sagas of gods and heroes, the second refers to philosophers' claims regarding the true essence of the divine. The third expresses the widespread ancient relationship between cult and politics in which the conduct of the former effects the health of the latter. It serves representation and establishment in traditional religion insofar as its knowledge is indispensable for the correct execution of public praise of the gods and thereby for the wellbeing of the state. This tripartite division of theology assumed canonical status in Rome through Q. M. Scaevola (d. 82 BCE) and M. T. Varro (116-27 BCE), wherein *theologia civilis* assumed the priority formerly accorded *theologia naturalis* (Cancik in Taubes 1983, 136-139).

Although mentioned by Tertullian (*Ad Nationes* II 1, 8-15) and referred to critically by Eusebius (*Praep. Evang.* IV, 1), familiarity with this "tripartite theology" in Christian thinking remained limited to the excerpts handed down by Augustine in *De Civitate Dei* (locus classicus: VI, 5) until the end of the eighteenth century.

---

* See: Bernd Wacker/ Jürgen Manemann, Artikel „Politische Theologie", in: *Neues Handbuch Theologischer Grundbegriffe*. Bd. 3, München 2005, 388-398.

Augustine's criticism of Varro

As part of his response to the claim in Roman political theology that the cause of the fall of Rome (plundered 410 CE) could be traced back to Christian rejection of the old gods, Augustine closely examined Varro's *Antiquitates Rerum Divinarum* (among other works), a work held in high esteem by contemporary representatives of the old Roman religion (see *City of God*, Book VI). In this work, ostensibly supportive of the state theology, Varro so described the actual praxis of public worship that its intimate relationship to moral monstrosities and metaphysical absurdities could not be ignored (although he also criticized sharply the mythical theology of fable and theater). Furthermore, behind the literal level of the text, one could recognize the spirit of contempt in which Varro held political theology and his unacknowledged preference for natural theology. And most relevant for Augustine's apologetic, insofar as Varro taught that political theology should be understood as part of mythical theology (as the latter had long been transcribed philosophically - compare, for example, *City of God* II, 4), the contemporary heathen ideology of Roman restoration already had proved unsustainable even on the ground of its own logic. That Varro did not risk openly rejecting political theology made the *Antiquitates* documentary evidence of the demonic alliance between spirit and power, an alliance which in its maintenance of the status quo did not refrain from intentionally deceiving the people even in religious matters (*City of God* IV, 27.32, et al).

What Augustine found in Varro was a mode of grounding politics in the arbitrariness of interests rather than in truth that therefore could not be philosophically defended. But Augustine failed to capitalize on the critically negative concept of political theology in his own criticism of Christian imperial ideology as a way to sharpen this criticism theologically. And this failure may have been the decisive factor contributing to the insignificance of "political" theology until the 20th century.

Citing Augustine

The concept was hardly mentioned in the Middle Ages, although it was known from the *City of God*. But one finds it more often (and again in the context of Augustine's reference to the Roman tri-partite division of theology) from the 16th-17th centuries onward. Even then, however, it is in the form of a historical reminiscence. In light of the devastation caused by the religious-political civil wars of this era and in increasing opposition to the attempt to establish peace on the "*cuius regio, eius religio*" principle in which confessional-state absolutism early on found a formula, it was believed that the humanistically inspired recourse to the Augustinian citation of Varro's ancient *theologia naturalis* could serve as a supra-confessional "natural theology." This offered a potential "third way" between obsessive confessional-dogmatic quarrels and authoritarian dictated public religion. Indirectly, however, this not only called into question the (religio-) political praxis of the new territorial national states and the theologians who legitimized them (classic example: J. Bossuet, *La politique tirée des propres paroles de l'Ecriture*, 1679-1709), but pointed out the depravity of secular theories of the state and sovereignty insofar as these made the preservation of the state their absolute norm and treated religion solely from the functional perspective that emphasized its importance for the inner stability and capacity for outward expansion of the state. Like Machiavelli (*Discorsi* I, 11), Hobbes (*Leviathan,* chapter XII), and Rousseau (*Contrat social* II, 7; IV, 8) these theologians did not conceal their pagan Roman ancestry.

Conceptual Struggle with Atheism

Already at the beginning of the 18th century, however, one can find among the defenders of *theolgia naturalis* comments regarding unnamed atheists for whom theology in general is simply an invention of political authority (Feil 1969, 120f.). This atheistic ideological criticism with its reproach of any form of religious or metaphysical discourse as mythological repeats Augustine's confrontation of Varro under the intensified conditions of the radical Enlightenment. In this connection the expression "political theology" becomes in the 19th century an important term of denunciation (albeit without reference to its historical place in the ancient theological schematic). Whether as used by Marx against Hegel's justification of constitutional monarchy (see Schrader in Taubes 1983, 220), or by M. Bakunin against the "*Dio e popolo*" democratic theory of G. Mazzinni (Lehning 1961, 19-77), or by H. Albert against the "critical theory" of the Frankfurt School (Albert 1971, esp. 101-105), the predicate "political theology" is used to disqualify the opposed theory as undercutting the prevailing ideological criticism of Christianity and its secular derivatives whose political doctrine of salvation cannot be considered rational.

State Theory of the Counter-Revolution

Edmund Burke, in professing this Christianity, identified some of his compatriots as "political theologians and theological politicians" in his *Observations on the French Revolution.* These were the people who tried to give theological and ethical justification to the events of 1789, but whom Burke had identified already in his 1790 work as representing a not insignificant danger for the English constitution and crown.

Despite Burke's sustained influence on the European conservatism of the first half of the 19th century, the concept "political theology" is not explicitly found in the work of the Catholic state theorists of the Restoration (even though many of these theorists are now considered political theologians). It makes no difference whether they were in France (J. de Maistre, L. G. D. de Bonald, the earlier, F. R. de Lammenais), Spain (J. Donoso Cortés), or Germany (A. Müller and J. von Görres, among others). (This applies also to Protestants.) With their common claim that the political order of a society was to be understood as a function of its religious confessions, they set themselves a double task: to make clear that the revolutionary crisis overwhelming political and social constitutions was a consequence of the rejection of Catholic dogma by the Reformation and its denial in Enlightenment philosophy; and to provide proof of the truth of this dogma as necessary for establishing public security, peace, and order (for example, Donoso Cortés; A. Maier 1950, 159-174). In this context the phrase "political theology" must have appeared essentially unusable: as a critically negative category, too general to express the heretical roots of the revolutionary present; while Burke's specification of it as revolutionary theological propaganda precluded using it to characterize their own programs for reproducing the monarchic-corporate confessional state. It was not by chance that K. L. von Haller chose as the title of his biblical doctrine of the state "Political Religion" (Winterthur 1811).

II. Theological End?

Carl Schmitt's Political Theology

The proverbial exception to the rule was the French journalist Louis Veuillot. He used this term, neglected since Augustine, in a positive way with reference to the Spanish diplomat and lay theologian Donoso Cortés (Tejado 1854, 356). In reaction to the inner-ecclesial criticism of the political thinking of his subject's basic traditionalism, he felt obliged to differentiate the clarity and decisiveness of the theological analogies made by Donoso Cortés in his "political or practical theology" from a "Scholasticism" that while indeed dogmatically unassailable, was clueless with regard to the political implications of dogma.

In what has become a famous treatise of the constitutional theorist Carl Schmitt (his doctrine of sovereignty published under the title *Political The-*

ology in 1922 in which this term first achieved critical notice), Veuillot's distinction appears again in the context of an appreciation of the work of Donoso Cortés (Schmitt 1934, 73). Schmitt defends the traditionalist (and counter-dogmatic) radicalization of the doctrine of original sin with reference to its political-polemic rather than dogmatic intention: the political consequences of the atheistic and anarchistic axiom of humanity's natural goodness require that a defender of order who writes of "a religious and political decision of the greatest current relevance" must formulate a counter-proposition in theological and anthropological terms. This counter-proposition is to be assessed in terms of the foundational political act, that is, the distinction between friend and enemy, and not according to its dogmatic authenticity. Although this recovery of honor would have been fatal for the Spanish ultramontanist himself, it is characteristic of Schmitt. What goes by the name of "political theology" in the work of this anti-democratic Weimar theorist takes its orientation from the avowed political necessity of safeguarding the plausibility and effectiveness of the sovereign decision of the strong state, that is, its concrete determination of the political enemy within as well as without. In Schmitt's diagnosis of the present as an epoch that had lost the capacity for God and whose desires and wishes reflect the mass as addicted to the myth (Schmitt 1950, 11), the legitimizing myths of political praxis remain isolated from any theological demands made by the gospel. The truth of these myths is assessed solely in terms of their social acceptance and with regard to how well they serve political decisionism. "Political theology" here is not simply academic shorthand for a research program into certain analytically meaningful and historically explainable structural analogies between central theological concepts on the one hand and central legal concepts on the other. In the last analysis, "political theology" means here rather the motivating force for concrete political praxis that draws on the rich ideological arsenal providing for political legitimacy equivalent to Varro's pantheon of gods.

The "Peterson Thesis"

Accordingly theology raised an (admittedly theological) objection to this political mythology. Thus Erik Peterson in a published 1933 remark aimed at Schmitt (who himself had advanced in the meantime to become "crown jurist" of National Socialism): "Political theology is not really an element of theology but rather of political thought," and is in truth a political theory of a "particularly heretical nature" (Peterson in Taubes 1983, 174). It was not just a modern phenomenon but could be found already in early Christianity in

Origen and Orosius and above all in the work of Emperor Constantine's court theologian, the "politician" Eusebius of Caesarea.

The historical analysis and interpretation undertaken by this political theology legitimized the Roman Empire by proclaiming the monarchy to be based on the model of singular power evident in monotheism. Further, it identified the promised eschatological peace with the Augustan/Constantinian Pax Romana. Peterson skewered this political theology in the now famous last sentence of his tract *Monotheism as a Political Problem* (a work dedicated to " Sancto Augustino"): "... the doctrine of divine monarchy necessarily failed in light of Trinitarian dogma, and the interpretation of the Pax Romana in light of Christian eschatology. Thereby ... a fundamental break is made with any 'political theology' that misuses Christian proclamation to justify a political situation ... and the mystery of the triune God remains in God, not in the creature. So also the peace which the Christian seeks cannot be kept by any emperor but remains a gift that passes all understanding" (Peterson 1951, 104f.)."

Later examinations (see, for example, Schmitt 1970; Schindler 1978) have shown that what is systematically the main point of Peterson's claim overburdens the evidentiary value of the historical material he offers and that his interpretation of this material itself cannot be maintained. Moreover, it remains possible to show the incongruity between Peterson's claim to "break with *any* 'political theology'" and his analysis of political-theological thinking since Origen. Finally, the issue is not what Peterson imprecisely formulates as the *misuse* of *Christian* proclamation to legitimize a political situation, but the politically motivated and prejudiced historical deformation of that proclamation in political Arianism. What Peterson was really after, what according to him was shattered by the Trinitarian confession and which he was attempting to break again in its historically encoded form, is the religious absolutism resurrected in the theological-ecclesial accommodation to National Socialism (Fellechner in Schindler 1978, 111-118) that made church dogma compliant to the political maintained as the total (Schmitt 1934).

Peterson claims, despite the material specificity of a political theology of the "heretical type," to have "broken with *any* political theology," and therefore sees Christian proclamation misused wherever it serves to justify a political arrangement even if this arrangement is a legitimate criticism of the political implications of heresy. Further, this claim rests on his observation that even formally orthodox theology *in politicis* tends toward a selective and therefore heretical engagement with the Christian message (exemplary though brief is Cat. Rom. III 5 q 8; for further examples see Koslowski in Taubes 1983, 32-41). More important may be Peterson's conviction, repudiating Augustine's eschatological dualism of both *civitates* (*City of God* XI-

XXII), that the one, indivisible truth of Jesus Christ, as it confronts a political order which manifest itself as untrue over against this judgment and crucifixion, bears testimony not in terms of earthly power and wisdom, but only through the existence of the one who suffers, a witness to truth who is confident in Christ, of a Christian martyr. This is the ever new marker that "the gospel in this world will be preached to lambs before wolves…now as then" (Peterson 1951, 165-224, 176). It is precisely this radical eschatological downgrading of the world that conceivably makes Peterson unsuitable as the prime witness in the trial for or against a new political theology (Scholz in Schindler 1978, 170-201).

Political Theology/Political Religion

The concept "political religion" in its current and predominantly negative meaning goes back to Eric Voegelin (Voegelin 1938). Unlike Schmitt or Peterson, Voegelin does not examine the use or misuse of Christian literary symbols and cultic forms "to justify a political situation." He aims instead at a secular critical uncovering of a inner-worldly ("innerweltlich") but none the less objective religious phenomenon. The specific characteristic of this phenomenon - paradigmatically evident in National Socialism - is "the conviction of a reality as absolute recognized in faith (theory) and demanding total commitment (praxis and action program) that serves as a final ground of meaning, is bound to a political community of this type, and that religion cannot exist without the kind of political ground that is itself at least partially identified with the absolute" (Behrens in H. Maier/Schäfer 1997, 257). In relation to historical "spiritual religions," political religions would be interpreted as "Ersatz"- or false religion.

In contemporary academic and public discourse, "political theology" and "political religion" are not always clearly differentiated. While talk of "political theology" in a descriptive sense is widely understood (even in the social scientific study of religion), "political religion" in Voegelin's sense remains restricted to theological or more normative concepts of political theory building (Moltmann 1984; H. Maier/Schäfer 1997). When one encounters it in research in the history of religion, the theologically inspired distinction between "innerworldly" and "supernatural" religions no longer plays a role in most cases.

III. Contours of a Fundamental Theological Concept

The "New Political Theology"

The current positive *theological* use of political theology has to be understood as a reinvention of the term. After the Second World War, political theology was almost forgotten and even repressed in theology and the church, but it came back as part of the reform symbolized by the year 1968. And so when Johann Baptist Metz set forth his theological program under this heading (Metz 1968, 99-116), it resonated well with a politically sensitized theological and church public. (Protestant counterparts include Jürgen Moltmann and Dorothee Sölle.) He had to turn directly, however, to the historical baggage carried by the term (H. Maier 1970). Sölle acquiesced when faced with these reservations regarding the term's conceptual history and presented her work as an exercise in "liberation theology" (Sölle 1995, 188f.). Metz, however, stuck to strict theological standards for his concepts and began to speak of a "new political theology" (Metz 1997) in order to set off his work from the "traditional or classical political theology" criticized by Peterson. The most important organs for this thinking are the *Jahrbuch Politische Theologie* and the *Ahauser Forum Politische Theologie*.

Six Markers of the "New Political Theology"

a) Political theology, as a result of sustained hermeneutical reflection, admits to the awareness that as a matter of fact theological theories unavoidably have political implications. Accordingly, in order to avoid falling back into the traditional form of political theology, it aims to ensure the critical influence of the whole spectrum of Christian convictions on political life with the intensity of religious symbols, values, and norms of political or re-politicized religions. At the same time it sets itself positively over against the common belief that the Enlightenment and modernity necessarily lead to the strict privatization of God-talk and religious matters generally. Rooted in the prophetic-apocalyptic social criticism of biblical monotheism, it sees itself as duty-bound by its subject to be involved in the public realm, or, more precisely, to "develop an 'interrupted' counter-public" (K. Gabriel). It aims at confronting Christian belief with the public problems dealt with (or concealed) in politics as well as confronting politics and the public realm with the challenges of religion in order to get modern societies to engage and reconstruct their normative foundations in a critical and honest manner.
b) The new political theology relies on its place within the church to escape the danger of becoming merely a religious legitimation of political interests,

initiatives, and ideologies that are fundamentally foreign to religion and arise without reference to it. Political theology without the church amounts to theory without praxis. But this also makes indispensable a critically differentiated ecclesiology and therewith the historically-politically mediated and concretely applied criticisms of the church. So far, these have been missing from this theology.

c) The new political theology has taken as its task formulating theology as a theory of history and society. Its leading concepts are "subject" and "praxis." This subject in its religious and theologically relevant meaning is not the liberal individual. This is why this new political theology calls for a deprivatization of theology and understands itself as doing theological criticism of "bourgeois religion." Methodologically, it is based on the theory-praxis dialectic under the primacy of praxis (showing its roots in the priority assigned practical reason by Kant and, in a different manner, by Marx). It starts with the intelligibility immanent to praxis and grasps the Logos of Christian theology in its practical constitution. Christian praxis here is no longer seen only the application of a truth previously revealed but as the moment of its verification and site of its concrete definition in the present situation. It proves its liberating meaning in the innovative praxis it makes possible, while it also takes on the role of a heuristic principle in criticism of praxis accommodated to existing conditions.

d) The basic categories of such a "postidealist" project are memory, narrative, and solidarity (Metz 1992). The *memoria passionis*, as a "dangerous memory," is foundational to biblical thinking. It comprises the conviction that there is no suffering in the world that does not concern us. In its consequent commitment to realizing the capacity of all humans to become subjects, it is challenged by four crises: the crisis of modernity, the catastrophe represented by the name "Auschwitz," the fading credibility of a church that understands itself in Euro- and Rome-centered terms, and the problem of what is called globalization.

e) Without doubt, the catastrophe of Auschwitz is the decisive rupture of experience for political theology (even though political theologians were relatively late in turning to an examination of this topic - around the middle of the 1970s). The singularity of the Shoah led to the conviction that theology could only conceive of itself as "after Auschwitz." Theodicy returned as the central theological question with a challenge to resist any kind of system-thinking. Theology is to be understood not as solving problems but as intensifying them in a manner that appeals to traditions of negative-theological thinking: the proscription of idolatry (*JPTh* 2), analogy (Rottländer 1993), and the study of the arcane (Peters 1998). For this reason the new political theology works on developing the anamnestic reason (Taubald 2001) that makes possible standing firm in the experience of non-identity.

f) Political theology emphasizes the productive non-contemporaneity of Christian religion. Thereby it turns itself with apocalyptic intensity against contemporary myths of time as evolutionary that result in indifference to suffering. "Apocalyptic" is the critical concept with which it underlines the limit character of time and gives prominence to this motif as foundational to biblical talk of God.

Prospects

More than a few of the keywords, motifs, and problem statements of political theology have been picked up and used in the past decades. Still, one can hardly speak of a widespread and sustained acceptance of the new political theology in the Catholic world or in Protestant theology. And while there is a qualified way in which political theology can be linked to the dialectical theological tradition in Protestant theology (as in the reform of the doctrine of the Kingship/Lordship of Christ inaugurated by the Barmen Confession of 1934), there is no model in Catholic scholastic theology for the kind of radical criticism of reason set forth here (along the lines of Horkheimer and Adorno). Objections to the postidealist understanding of reason at the heart of political theology come from contemporary representatives of a transcendental philosophical foundational paradigm who press for greater precision in political theological thinking (Th. Pröpper, H. Verweyen, Langthaler 2000). Moreover, the relationships among political theology church and university social teachings, biblical hermeneutics, and liturgy remain unclear.

Despite these issues, the impetus Metz has given to the development of a theology "after Auschwitz" has continued to be of great significance. He not only has had a decided influence on other theological disciplines (not least exegesis), but has contributed to developing a lasting sensitivity within the ecclesial public to the dangers of anti-Judaism/anti-Semitism.

WORKS CITED

Albert, H. *Plädoyer für kritischen Rationalismus*. 4th edition, München 1971.

Assmann, J. *Herrschaft und Heil. Politische Theologie in Altägypten, Israel und Europa*. München-Wien 2000.

Böckenförde, E.-W. "Staat - Gesellschaft - Kirche." *ChGimG* 15, 5-120.

Brockmann, D. and Eicher, P., eds. *Die politische Theologie Friedrich von Spees*. München 1991.

Faber, R. *Die Verkündigung Vergils. Zur Kritik der „Politischen Theologie."*

Hildesheim/New York 1975.
________, ed. *Politische Religion - religiöse Politik.* Würzburg 1997.
Feil, E. *Von der "politischen Theologie" zur „Theologie der Revolution."*
________, and Weth, R., eds. *Diskussion zur „Theologie der Revolution."* München/Mainz 1969, 110-132.
Fiorenza, F. "Religion und Politik." *ChGimG* 27, 59-101.
Große Kracht, H.-J. *Kirche in ziviler Gesellschaft. Studien zur Konfliktgeschichte von katholischerKirche und demokratische Öffentlichkeit.* Paderborn/München/Wien/Zürich 1997.
Kantorowicz, E. H. *Die zwei Körper des Königs. Eine Studie zur politischen Theologie des Mittelalters (1957).* München 1991.
Kraus, H. Ch. "Eric Voegelin redivivus. Politische Wissenschaft als politische Theologie." *Der Nationalsozialismus als politische Religion.* Ed. by Michael Ley and Julius H. Schoeps. Bodenheim 1997, 74-88.
Kroh, W. *Kirche im gesellschaftlichen Widerspruch. Zur Verständigung zwischen katholischer Soziallehre und politischer Theologie.* München 1982.
Langthaler, R. *Gottvermissen. Eine theologische Kritik der reinen Vernunft? Die neue Politische Theologie (J. B. Metz) im Spiegel der kantischen Religionsphilosophie.* Regensburg 2000.
Lehning, A., ed. *M. Bakounine et l'Italie 1871-1872,* part 1. Leiden 1961.
Lieberg, G., "Die ‚theologia tripertita'" *in Forschung und Bezeugung: Aufstieg und Niedergang der römischen Welt*, I, 4. Berlin/New York 1973, 63-115.
Maier, A. *Donoso Cortés.* Köln 1950.
Maier, H. *Kritik der politischen Theologie.* Einsiedeln 1970.
________, and Schäfer, M., eds. *Totalitarismus und Politische Religion. Konzepte des Diktaturvergleichs*, vol. II. Paderborn, et. al., 1997.
Manemann, J., ed. "Demokratiefähigkeit." *Jahrbuch Politische Theologie 1.* Münster 1996.
________, ed. „Bilderverbot." *Jahrbuch Politische Theologie 2.* Münster 1997.
________, ed. „Befristete Zeit." *Jahrbuch Politische Theologie 3.* Münster 1999.
________. *Carl Schmitt und die Politische Theologie. Politischer Anti-Monotheismus.* Münster 2002.
________, ed. "Monotheismus." *Jahrbuch Politische Theologie 4.* Münster 2002.
Metz, J. B. *Zur Theologie der Welt.* Mainz 1968.
________, *Glaube in Geschichte und Gesellschaft.* 5th ed. Mainz 1992.
________, *Jenseits bürgerliche Religion.* München/Mainz 1980.

________, ed. *"Landschaft aus Schreien." Zur Dramatik der Theodizeefrage*. Mainz 1995.
________, *Zum Begriff der neuen Politischen Theologie: 1967-1997*. Mainz 1997.
Moltmann, J. *Der gekreuzigte Gott*. München 1972.
________, *Trinität und Reich Gottes. Zur Gotteslehre*. München 1980.
________, *Politische Theologie - Politische Ethik*. München/Mainz 1984.
Morrill, B. T. *Anamnesis as Dangerous Memory. Political and Liturgical Theology in Dialogue*. Minnesota 2000.
Peters, T. R. *Mystik, Mythos, Metaphysik. Auf der Spur des vermissten Gottes*. Mainz/München 1992.
________, *Johann Baptist Metz. Theologie des vermissten Gottes*. Mainz 1998.
Peterson, E. *Theologische Traktate*. München 1951.
Peukert, H., ed. *Diskussion zur „Politischen Theologie."* Mainz/München 1969.
Rottländer, P. „Ethik in der politischen Theologie." *Orientierung* 57 (1993), 152-158.
Schindler, A., ed. *Monotheismus als politisches Problem? Erik Peterson und die Kritik der politischen Theologie*. Gütersloh 1978.
Schmitt, Carl. *Donoso Cortés in gesamteuropäischer Interpretation*. Köln 1950.
________, *Politische Theologie. Vier Kapitel zur Lehre von der Souveränität*. 2nd ed. München/Leipzig 1934.
________, *Politische Theologie II. Die Legende von der Erledigung jeder Politischen Theologie*. Berlin 1970.
Sölle, D. *Politische Theologie*. Stuttgart 1971.
________, *Gegenwind. Erinnerungen*. Hamburg 1995.
Taubald, B. *Anamnetische Vernunft*. Münster 2001.
Taubes, J., ed. *Der Fürst dieser Welt. Carl Schmitt und die Folgen*. München et. al. 1983.
Tejado, G., ed. *Obras de Don Juan Donoso Cortés*, vol. 4. Madrid 1854.
Voegelin, Eric. *Die politischen Religionen (1938)*. Stockholm 1939.
Wacker, B. *Revolution und Offenbarung. Das Spätwerk von Joseph Görres (1824-1848) - eine politische Theologie*.
________, ed. *"Die eigentlich katholische Verschärfung..." Konfession, Theologie und Politik im Werk Carl Schmitts*. München 1994.
Wiedenhofer, S. *Politische Theologie*. Stuttgart et. al. 1976.

Translated by John K. Downey and Steven T. Ostovich

LIST OF CONTRIBUTORS

J. Matthew Ashley is Associate Professor of Systematic Theology and Director of Graduate Studies at the University of Notre Dame (USA). His current work focuses on the relationship between Ignatian spirituality and the theologies of Karl Rahner, Ignacio Ellacuría and John Courtney Murray.

M. Shawn Copeland is Associate Professor of Systematic Theology at Boston College, Chestnut Hill, Massachusetts (USA). She also serves as Associate Director for the Th. M. Program at the Institute for Black Catholic Studies, Xavier University of Louisiana (USA).

John K. Downey is Professor of Religious Studies at Gonzaga University in Spokane, Washington (USA). A former Director of the Coolidge Research Colloquium, he publishes in the areas of political theology, language and method, human rights, and higher education.

Matthew L. Lamb recently published several articles on Aquinas and has a forthcoming book, *Eternity, Time, and the Life of Wisdom*. He serves as Professor of Theology and Chair of the Theology Department at Ave Maria University in Naples, Florida (USA).

Jürgen Manemann is Professor of Christliche Weltanschauung, Religions- und Kulturtheorie at the University of Erfurt. He was an assistant to Johann Baptist Metz and is the editor of *Jahrbuch Politische Theologie* as well as the founder and organizer of the *Ahauser Forum Politische Theologie*.

Johann Baptist Metz, founder of the new political theology, is Ordinary Professor of Fundamental Theology, Emeritus, at Westphalian Wilhelms University in Münster (Germany).

Bruce T. Morrill is Associate Professor in the Theology Department at Boston College (USA). His *Divine Worship and Human Healing* is forthcoming.

Steven T. Ostovich is Professor of Philosophy at the College of St. Scholastica in Duluth, Minnesota (USA). He publishes in the areas of German Studies, critical theory, and higher education reform.

Tiemo Rainer Peters is Professor of Theology, Emeritus, at Westphalian Wilhelms University of Münster (Germany). He wrote his doctoral thesis on Dietrich Bonhoeffer with Johann Baptist Metz and has been his colleague for many years. Among his recent publications is an important introduction to Johann Baptist Metz: *Johann Baptist Metz. Theologie des vermißten Gottes*.

Johann Reikerstorfer is Professor of Fundamental Theology at the University of Vienna. He is author of numerous articles on political theology.

Johann M. Vento is Assistant Professor in the Department of Religious Studies and Theology at Georgian Court University in Lakewood, New Jersey (USA). She publishes on trauma, suffering, forgiveness and theologies of the body in relation to violence against women.

Bernd Wacker is co-editor of the *Jahrbuch Politische Theologie*, an Organizer of the *Ahauser Forum Politische Theologie* and author of many books about political-theological issues.

Religion – Geschichte – Gesellschaft

Fundamentaltheologische Studien

hrsg. von Johann Baptist Metz (Münster / Wien), Johann Reikerstorfer (Wien) und Jürgen Werbick (Münster)

K. Hannah Holtschneider

German Protestants Remember the Holocaust

Theology and the Construction of Collective Memory

Bd. 24, 2001, 232 S., 25,90 €, br., ISBN 3-8258-5539-2

Ulrich Willers (Hg.)

Theodizee im Zeichen des Dionysos

Nietzsches Fragen jenseits von Moral und Religion

Ist Nietzsche der Anfang vom Ende des Christentums? Seine Invektiven haben eine argumentative Kraft und Suggestivität, der man sich, wenn man einmal sich auf sie eingelassen hat, fast nur durch Flucht entziehen kann. Jedenfalls ist das die Haltung vieler Christen. Bemerkenswert ist dabei: Nietzsche gewinnt nicht nur dann an Gewicht, wenn man sich seinen Anfragen stellt, sondern auf eigentümliche Weise auch dann, wenn man ihm ausweicht. Im vorliegenden Band, der kompetente und renommierte philosophische und theologische Nietzsche-Kenner zu einem vielstimmigen Gespräch über Moral, Religion und Christentum versammelt (u. a. Ch. Türcke, J. Simon, J. Salaquarda, J. Figl, W. Stegmaier) geht es um eine kritische und kontroverse Konfrontation mit Nietzsches aus dionysischen Antrieben gespeister Analyse der platonisch-moralischen und christlichen Weltdeutung.

Bd. 25, 2003, 248 S., 20,90 €, br., ISBN 3-8258-5561-9

Ansgar Koschel (Hg.)

Katholische Kirche und Judentum im 20. Jahrhundert

Mit Beiträgen von Herbert Bettelheim, Ernst-Ludwig Ehrlich, Gabriel Padon, Gerhard Riegner, Herbert Smolinsky und Erich Zenger

Das Verhältnis zwischen Kirche und Judentum ist belastet von Anfang an. Im 20. Jahrhundert jedoch führten Einstellungen und Verhaltensweisen von Kirchen und Christen zu einem Tiefpunkt. Christlicherseits ist er nur durch Umkehr, jüdischerseits durch die Annahme aufrichtiger Umkehr heute lebender Christen zu überwinden. Gleichgültigkeit und Schweigen sind Kennzeichen des Verhältnisses von Kirche und Christen zu den Juden, namentlich angsichts der geplanten wie ins Werk gesetzten Vernichtung durch das nationalsozialistische Regime in Deutschland. Nach der Schoa werden zunächst nur vereinzelt Handlungen sichtbar und Stimmen vernehmbar, die in den Juden Geschwister des Glaubens erkennen.

Bd. 26, 2002, 176 S., 17,90 €, br., ISBN 3-8258-5507-4

Lydia Bendel-Maidl

Tradition und Innovation

Zur Dialektik von historischer und systematischer Perspektive in der Theologie. Am Beispiel von Transformationen in der Rezeption des Thomas von Aquin im 20. Jahrhundert

Fragen wir in der Gegenwart, wie eine zeitsensible Theologie aussehen könnte, so ist eine wichtige Spur die selbstkritische Vergewisserung des Weges katholischer Theologie im 20. Jahrhundert. Zentrales Feld der Transformationen, dem sich die vorliegende Studie widmet, war die lehramtlich vorgeschriebene Rezeption der Philosophie und Theologie des Thomas von Aquin. Als kardinale Aufgabe im Horizont der Moderne stellte sich die Wahrnehmung der eigenen geschichtlichen Relativität. Sie wurde eingelöst, plakativ formuliert, im Umbruch von einer neuscholastischen Theologie mit einer gegenweltlichen Mentalität zu einer Theologie der „Zeichen der Zeit", die in dialogischer Zeitgenossenschaft steht. Die Reflexionen zum Verhältnis von Historiographie und Systematik in der Theologie sind ein Beitrag zur virulenten Frage nach der Einheit der theologischen Disziplinen.

Bd. 27, 2004, 608 S., 45,90 €, br., ISBN 3-8258-5589-9

Christian Heller

John Hicks Projekt einer religiösen Interpretation der Religionen

Darstellung und Analyse – Diskussion – Rezeption

Die "Theologie der Religionen" hat sich in den letzten Jahren zu einem theologischen Brennpunkt entwickelt, der weit über die Fachwelt hinaus auf großes Interesse stößt. Im Mittelpunkt der Diskussion steht die Position des englischen Religionsphilosophen und -theologen John Hick, die im vorliegenden Buch von seinen epistemologischen Ansätzen bis zu seiner pluralistischen Theologie der Religionen nachgezeichnet und analysiert wird. Die Entwicklung, die sich in Hicks Denken aufzeigen lässt, kann als ein Prozess der fortwährenden Anwendung grundlegender theologischer Optionen auf neu ins Bewusstsein getretene Erfahrungen und Erkenntnisse verstanden werden. Seine pluralistische Religionstheologie sieht sich schwerer Kritik ausgesetzt. Neben einer ausführlichen Analyse der vorgebrachten kritischen Einwände beschäftigt sich die Arbeit mit zwei neueren Ansätzen von Jacques Dupuis und Roger Haight, die Hicks Anliegen – die Anerkennung der Werthaftigkeit von Plurali-

tät auch im religiösen Bereich – im Rahmen einer christlichen Theologie gerecht werden wollen.
Bd. 28, 2001, 528 S., 40,90 €, br., ISBN 3-8258-5528-7

Peter Zeillinger
Nachträgliches Denken
Skizze eines philosophisch-theologischen Aufbruchs im Ausgang von Jacques Derrida. Mit einer genealogischen Bibliographie der Werke von Jacques Derrida
Dieses Buch versucht das Denken des franz. Philosophen Jacques Derrida (*1930) für die Theologie nicht nur wahr-, sondern auch ernst zu nehmen. In Reaktion auf eine global gewordene „Grundlagenkrise" (von J. B. Metz theologisch als „Gotteskrise" diagnostiziert) wird die spezifische Wahrnehmung des Verlusts unhinterfragbarer Gewissheiten im Werk selbst nachgezeichnet. Derridas konsequent „performatives Schreiben" lässt die Dekonstruktion dabei, entgegen weit verbreiteter Meinung, als einen praxisfundierenden, das Wagnis konkreten Engagements kriteriologisch eröffnenden Diskurs erkennen, der sogar die notwendige Möglichkeit von Theologie philosophisch artikuliert. Prägende „Begriffe" wie *différance*, Spur und Schrift, das *donc*, die Erfahrung des Unmöglichen, sowie das notwendige Sprechen im Modus des *Vielleicht*, werden in einer genealogisch-chronologischen Lektüre aus den Texten Derridas selbst herausgearbeitet.
Bd. 29, 2002, 296 S., 35,90 €, gb., ISBN 3-8258-6144-9

Kurt Appel
Entsprechung im Wider-Spruch
Eine Auseinandersetzung mit der politischen Theologie des jungen Hegel
Ziel der vorliegenden Arbeit ist es, die Offenbarung Gottes in der Weltwirklichkeit und deren Brüchen herauszuarbeiten. Ausgangspunkt sind dabei die Jugendschriften Hegels, deren gesellschafts- und erkenntniskritisches Potential freigelegt und für das Offenbarungsthema fruchtbar gemacht werden soll. Dabei wird ein „positives" Herrschaftsdenken kritisiert, welches der Anerkennung der Anderen in einer freien Gesellschaft, an deren Gestaltung das Subjekt nicht nur formal partizipiert, entgegensteht.
Bd. 31, 2003, 208 S., 29,90 €, br., ISBN 3-8258-6605-x

Bertil Langenohl;
Christian Große-Rüschkamp (Hg.)
Wozu Theologie?
Anstiftungen aus der praktischen Fundamentaltheologie von Tiemo Rainer Peters. Mit Beiträgen von U. Engel, J. Manemann, J. B. Metz, O. H. Pesch, H. Steinkamp u. a.
Theologie hat mindestens zwei Subjekte: Gott und ein Ich, das „Gott sagt". Was meine ich aber, wenn ich Gott sage? Warum rede ich überhaupt von Gott? Wozu Theologie? Diese Frage kommt so einfach daher. Sie ist aber die schwerste, eine „kinderschwere Frage" (J.B. Metz), weil sie das Ganze der eigenen Glaubensexistenz und des eigenen Denkens betrifft und weil sie dort, wo es um das Ganze geht, zur Klarheit zwingt. Zu Ehren des 2004 emeritierten Münsteraner Fundamentaltheologen Tiemo Rainer Peters (OP) stellen sich einige seiner Lehrer, Kollegen, Freunde, Schülerinnen und Schüler in teils sehr persönlichen Beiträgen dieser Frage.
Bd. 32, 2005, 328 S., 24,90 €, br., ISBN 3-8258-8119-9

Nicoletta Capozza
Im Namen der Treue zur Erde
Versuch eines Vergleichs zwischen Bonhoeffers und Nietzsches Denken
Am Leitfaden der „Treue zur Erde" werden die Arbeiten Bonhoeffers und Nietzsches einer eingehenden Interpretation unterzogen. Dabei zeigt sich, dass Bonhoeffer in intensiver Rezeption von Nietzsches Denken dessen Appell „Bleibt der Erde treu!" aufgenommen hat. Allerdings vermag er durch seine der Alterität verpflichtete Christologie und die aus ihr entspringenden ethischen Kategorien, die Geschichtlichkeit und Transzendenz verbinden, der nihilistischen Paradoxie des Philosophen zu entrinnen.
Bd. 33, 2003, 336 S., 29,90 €, br., ISBN 3-8258-6667-x

Peter Hardt
Genealogie der Gnade
Eine theologische Untersuchung zur Methode Michel Foucaults
20 Jahre nach dem Tod Karl Rahners ist dessen Theologie bleibend aktuell. Die Methode der *Genealogie* des Philosophen Michel Foucault eröffnet eine neuartige Perspektive auf Rahners Gnadenlehre, die ihre befreiende Rolle in den Machtprozessen und Diskursen des katholischen Milieus beleuchtet. Diese „Genealogie der Gnade" ist das Ergebnis einer kritischen Diskussion der Methode Foucaults, die der Verfasser mit Hilfe des Denkens von Michel de Certeau SJ führt. Sie ist die Grundlage für eine anregende Skizze, wie die Gnadenlehre Rahners durch eine „Theologie des Begehrens" zu ergänzen sei.
Bd. 34, 2005, 408 S., 34,90 €, br., ISBN 3-8258-8484-8

Ernst-Wolfgang Böckenförde
Kirche und christlicher Glaube in den Herausforderungen der Zeit
Beiträge zur politisch-theologischen Verfassungsgeschichte 1957 – 2002
Bd. 36, 2004, 456 S., 39,90 €, gb., ISBN 3-8258-7554-7

Michaela Willeke
Lev Šestov: Vom Nichts durch das Sein zur Fülle
Eine russisch-jüdische Perspektive auf Glauben und Wissen
Die Frage nach dem philosophie- und kulturkritischen Potential von Religion bestimmt das Werk des russisch-jüdischen Religionsphilosophen Lev Šestov (1866-1938). In der ersten deutschsprachigen Monographie zu Šestov stellt M. Willeke dessen Leben und Werk eingehend vor. Unter Berücksichtigung der zeit- und geistesgeschichtlichen, interkulturellen und interdisziplinären Hintergründe zeichnet sie die Koordinaten seines Denkens nach, wobei insbesondere Šestovs Verhältnisbestimmung von griechisch-christlicher Tradition (*Athen*) und jüdischem Denken (*Jerusalem*) erschlossen wird. Vor diesem Hintergrund erscheint sodann die Frage nach Gott als geistig-kulturelle Kardinalfrage nach der Zukunft des Menschen.
Bd. 37, 2006, 352 S., 29,90 €, br., ISBN 3-8258-9012-0

Stephan van Erp; André Lascaris (Eds.)
Who is Afraid of Postmodernism?
Challenging Theology for a Society in Search of Identity. With a Preface by Robert Schreiter
To the authors of this book, today's world is "postmodern". They see a fragmented world. It seems to have become implausible to find a common point of view, a unity in purpose or truth. Postmodernity challenges Christian faith, because it appears to go against the very grain of a sense of tradition, communion, and commitment. On the eve of his election pope Benedict XVI warned against the "dictatorship of relativism". Would it still be possible to find genuine Christian ways to live in postmodern times? This collection of essays by a group of Dutch theologians will stimulate the imagination of anyone who reads them.
Bd. 38, 2006, 120 S., 19,90 €, br., ISBN 3-8258-8781-2

Andreas Hellgermann
Vom Design zur Sache
Eine fundamentaltheologische Untersuchung zum Umgang mit den Dingen
Design ist einer der schillerndsten Begriffe des ausgehenden 20. und des beginnenden 21. Jahrhunderts. Alles ist Design und das Design selbst ist zur Sprache der Globalisierung geworden. Eine eingehende Analyse dieses Phänomens bringt die „andere Seite" von Design und damit auch eine politisch-theologische Dimension in den Blick: Das Gestalten, das nicht in die Enge übergestülpter Formen führt, sondern einen an der Sache und ihrem Gebrauch orientierten Umgang mit den Dingen ermöglicht. In Abgrenzung zu ästhetisierenden Ansätzen kann das unscheinbare Verb „gestalten", durch die politisch-ökonomischen Rahmenbedingungen in der Postmoderne in höchstem Maße bedroht, entscheidend dafür sein, dass die Dinge, die wir machen, auch zu Dingen für andere werden können.
Bd. 39, 2006, 272 S., 24,90 €, br., ISBN 3-8258-9321-9

Jürgen Werbick
Von Gott sprechen an der Grenze zum Verstummen
Schweigen oder Sprechen? Als Glaubender wie als Theologe hat man nicht die Freiheit, das Eine zu tun und das Andere zu lassen. Einerseits: „Wovon man nicht sprechen kann, darüber muss man schweigen" (Wittgenstein). Aber andererseits: Das Zeugnis darf nicht verschweigen, wovon es hervorgerufen ist: Erfahrungen mit dem Elend der Menschen, die Herausforderung, Gottes Ruf ins Leben zu folgen. Dieses Buch will Rechenschaft geben über die Bedeutung der Grundworte, die die Theologie dabei in den Mund nehmen muss: Wahrheit, der Eine, Leben, Menschwerdung, Erlösung, Geist, Geschenk, Handeln Gottes, Ewiges Leben.
Bd. 40, 2004, 368 S., 29,90 €, gb., ISBN 3-8258-7946-1

Martin Rohner
Glück und Erlösung
Konstellationen einer modernen Selbstverständigung
Die Philosophie hat die Frage nach dem Glück wiederentdeckt. Doch eine Herausforderung hat sie dabei vernachlässigt: „Es schwingt in der Vorstellung des Glücks unveräußerlich die der Erlösung mit" (W. Benjamin). Ist die Sehnsucht nach Erlösung für ein gutes Leben in der (Nach-)Moderne noch (philosophisch) relevant? Der Verfasser skizziert abgewogen die ethischen, kulturtheoretischen und religionsphilosophischen Facetten einer komplexen Problemlage. Dabei nimmt er neben philosophischen Positionen – vor allem Charles Taylors Theorie der Moderne – auch theologische Perspektiven auf. Damit zeigt das Buch exemplarisch, wie sich Philosophie unter Bedingungen moderner Selbstverständigung auf den spannungsreichen Dialog mit der Theologie einlassen kann.
Bd. 41, 2004, 288 S., 24,90 €, br., ISBN 3-8258-7991-7

LIT Verlag Münster – Berlin – Hamburg – London – Wien
Fresnostr. 2 48159 Münster
Tel.: 0251 – 62 032 22 – Fax: 0251 – 23 19 72
e-Mail: vertrieb@lit-verlag.de – http://www.lit-verlag.de